AMERICAN MOVIES: THE FIRST THIRTY YEARS

THE SILENT COMEDIANS

Richard Dyer MacCann

Charlie Chaplin in *The Gold Rush*

AMERICAN MOVIES: THE FIRST THIRTY YEARS

THE SILENT COMEDIANS

Richard Dyer MacCann

THE SCARECROW PRESS, INC.
Metuchen, New Jersey & London

in association with

IMAGE & IDEA, INC.
Iowa City, Iowa

1993

Printed in the United States of America.

Other Books by Richard Dyer MacCann:

Hollywood in Transition (1962)
Film and Society (1964)
Film: A Montage of Theories (1966)
The People's Films (1973)
The New Film Index (1975)
    (with Edward S. Perry)
Cinema Examined (1982)
    (with Jack C. Ellis)
The First Tycoons (1987)
The First Film Makers (1989)
The Stars Appear (1992)

In Preparation:

Films of the 1920s
The Eye Is Not Satisfied

Film/Video Works:

Degas: Master of Motion (1960)
How to Build a Freeway (1965)
How to Look at Freeways (1965)
Murder at Best (1981)
The Quiet Channel series (1983)
American Movies: The First 30 Years (1984)
A New York Boy Comes to Iowa (1988)

British Library Cataloguing-in-Publication data available

Library of Congress Cataloging-in-Publication Data

MacCann, Richard Dyer.
    The silent comedians / Richard Dyer MacCann.
        p.   cm. — (American movies)
    Includes bibliographical references and index.
    ISBN 0-8108-2725-5; — ISBN 0-8108-2730-1(pbk.) (alk. paper)
    1. Comedy films — United States — History and criticism. 2. Silent
        films — United States — History and criticism. 3. Comedians —
        United States — Biography. 4. Motion picture actors and actresses —
        United States — Biography. I. Title. II. Series.
        PN1995.9.C55M23   1993
        791.43'617—dc20   93-11399

Contents

Acknowledgments

For their willingness to read and respond to my introductory essay (and certain essays on individual comedy figures) I owe special thanks to Charles Maland (University of Tennessee), Donald McCaffrey (University of North Dakota), Henry Jenkins (Massachusetts Institute of Technology), and Ira Jaffe (University of New Mexico). They are not responsible for what now appears here, but their letters gave me important advice, pleasure, encouragement, and a sense of the value of the project.

It was Henry Jenkins who alerted me to the existence of Sennett's piece on the "psychology" of film comedy. And I was first aware of Chaplin's article on laughter through McCaffrey's *Focus on Chaplin* (1971).

Acknowledgment is made of the following permissions to use material from copyrighted works:

Extracts from "Comedy's Greatest Era," by James Agee, appearing in *Life Magazine* September 3, 1949, and in *Agee on Film* (McDowell Obolensky 1958). Reprinted by permission of the James Agee Trust, Mary Newman trustee.

"Mabel Normand" from *Classics of the Silent Screen*, by Joe Franklin. Copyright © by Joe Franklin. Published by arrangement with Carol Publishing Group. A Citadel Press Book.

Extracts from *My Autobiography*, by Charles Chaplin, with permission of the Estate of the author, represented by the Random Century Group, and by the British publisher, The Bodley Head. Published in the U.S. in 1964 by Simon & Schuster.

"The Gold Rush," "Sherlock Jr.," and "The Kid Brother," reprinted from *Magill's Survey of Cinema: Silent Films*. By permission of the publisher, Salem Press, Inc. Copyright © 1982, by Frank N. Magill.

Preface

Convinced that the silent era had been inadequately served by writers and critics — if compared to the mountain of books on sound films — I chose in 1976 to begin a search through published works for lively materials that might make a series of topical anthologies, first for classroom use, later as books.

Beginning with *The First Tycoons* (1987), the series of books has continued with *The First Film Makers* (1989), *The Stars Appear* (1992), and this fourth volume, *The Silent Comedians* (1993).

Since Scarecrow Press follows the trade book practice of selling through bookstores and promoting sales through newspaper or magazine reviews in a limited way, the printings have been relatively small and the books will be found mainly in libraries. The reader of these lines is therefore holding what amounts to a rare book.

It was an act of considerable faith and courage for Scarecrow to take on such a series of volumes at all, even with the burden of editorial work shared by a co-publisher. A quite different series by Scribners at about the same time — a chronology of the early movie business based on trade paper reports — was underwritten in part by a granting agency.

The series title, "American Movies: The First Thirty Years," refers to the years 1896 to 1926. "Movies" is a comfortable colloquial word, representative of the time, suggesting also that pictures were popular and that they moved. Such an umbrella term may deserve rehabilitation in these days of technical hassles over what is film and what is video.

And wasn't it Pauline Kael who claimed that "cinema is what we study, film is what we make, and movies are what we go to"?

As various "hundredth" anniversaries of the birth of the motion pictures are celebrated, the silent era will gain more attention.

Film study educators may also find themselves reexamining the substantial value — for the humanities and for students — of history focusing on creative personalities.

Assuming, as I do, that the art of the film is not the result of unseen impersonal forces, but is related in some way to the artists who do the work, I have felt it important to show how each of five personalities struggled in early years to find themselves, rise above limited circumstances, and make their entries into production at a time when Hollywood was the new frontier of the twentieth century.

For each of the five, it has been possible to present some kind of statement by the artist himself as to comic goals and methods (although Keaton was as reluctant to do this as he was to smile).

For Chaplin and Keaton, there are reviews or summaries of early short subjects and two or more of the features, together with the best short critical studies of the artist's work I could find. I have been fortunate in being able to bring together the unique and stimulating views of Chaplin by Maland, Petrie, and Roemer and the varied Keaton pieces by Houston, Lebel, and Moews.

I have tried to balance out in my various introductory pages whatever is lacking, either in biography or criticism.

History seen through an anthology should be experienced as life itself is experienced — a rather disconcerting panorama of multiple viewpoints. This reminds us of the difficulty of attempting to write history at all.

Essentially a secondary work, the present project also uses many original sources and can be useful for reference. I hope it is a representative selection of events, achievements, and artists, so that the interested reader might in the end feel comfortably well-informed, not deluged with professional data. There will be in the future, I suspect, studies of Charlie Chase, Larry Semon, and Ben Turpin, comparisons of Mack Sennett, Hal Roach, and Al Christie as producers, and examinations of the influence on Chaplin of Max Linder and Rene Clair. This book is simply a modest guide to the lives and works of the most important silent comedy movie-makers in America.

Introduction

Is Comedy Inferior?

*Comedy is an imitation of characters of a lower
type.* — Aristotle.[1]

*People as a whole get satisfaction from seeing
the rich get the worst of things.*
— Charlie Chaplin.[2]

Why do we take it for granted that comedy is an inferior
form of drama? Why do we so often ignore comedies when
awards are handed out? Why do we find it confusing to
evaluate performers who make us laugh and difficult to com-
pare them with "serious" actors?

One of the more famous pronouncements about comedy is
that it concerns inferior beings. Even this label is in the nature
of a throwaway, for Aristotle was mainly getting ready to talk
about tragedy when he said it. He never got around to taking
up comedy as a subject of equal importance — or if he did,

---

1 One place to find the relevant parts of the *Poetics* is in Paul Lauter,
Theories of Comedy, (1964). It is interesting that Lauter's career has
included work not only in literature and comedy but in peace
research and education.

2 Chaplin's assertion is found in his *American* magazine article, "What
People Laugh At" (November 1918).

those comments are lost to us. In the *Poetics*, comedy is referred to only in passing, as dealing with "characters of a lower type," to prepare for the more lofty observation that tragedy deals with actions of "a certain magnitude," with people of some importance.[3]

So we have, like a ball and chain on the dragging feet of the critical constabulary, this double Aristotelian weight: comedy is distinctly low-grade in comparison to tragedy, and its proper subjectmatter is low-life people, or people made to look that way.

Knowing this, we can hardly be surprised that the common run of critics, especially the academic variety, are a pretty gloomy lot. Many of them are actually convinced that comedy is praiseworthy only when its mask hides an underlying mood of pathos or hopeless fate. Ball and chain in hand, these observers limp to the strains of the tragic muse even when they deal with comedy.

Film study is hardly old enough to challenge this tradition. The subsection of theory called genre study has now been pretty well articulated, and some observers are prepared to include comedies among its categories, along with westerns, musicals, melodramas, and horror stories. But the broader notion of a comic mode vs. a tragic mode has not gained much attention. Gerald Mast's *The Comic Mind*, unlike most books devoted to film theory, is filled with lively descriptions of actual movies, and is therefore a valuable introduction, as its subtitle suggests, to "comedy in the movies." Much of the

---

3   In regard to Aristotle's non-analysis of comedy, the reader might like to look at a remarkable book by Lane Cooper, then professor of English at Cornell University, called *An Aristotelian Theory of Comedy* (1922). Embellished with many exquisite turns of scholarship (such as an examination of later commentators who may have read an essay by Aristotle no longer available to us) his search is in the end only sufficient unto itself, for no firm evidence of such a document exists.

One observation of special interest (p. 181) is his expansion of Aristotle's famous claim that pity and fear are "purged" by our exposure to these feelings in the performance of tragedies. He asks if it is not true that comedy also provides a kind of catharsis in that it displays for us a high degree of disproportion and therefore "frees us" through laughter from the burdens of disproportion in life.

time, however, the viewpoint of his book seems to be that the best comedies have an underlying tone of sadness and despair, and are to be judged by the values of tragedy.[4]

Must film makers and critics be shackled to such a dismal point of view? Dorothy Parker, successful screenwriter and erstwhile member of the Algonquin circle of wits in New York City, was supposed to have laid down the law on this to one of the tycoons of the sound era. Confronted with his preference for a happy ending, she declared, "There have been billions of men and women on this planet and not one of their stories ever ended happily."

This is a very sharp remark, and a good debating point under the circumstances. But it is exceedingly remote from the philosophy most people live by. Within any life there may be a hundred short stories, many of them with happy endings. Those are the kind most people enjoy retelling, the kind they like on the screen.[5]

There is no accounting for taste, however, and critical arbiters are not much interested in the common life. They are fascinated by the worst of things, the exceptional downturns, the lives Thoreau claimed were mostly lived in "quiet desperation." Tragedy seems to be the queen of literature, and determinism, not comedy, is the king. Pessimism is the true and honest sign of excellence in both plot and characters, with irony the only allowable delight along the way.

The cumulative arrivals on the world scene of Darwin, Freud, Marx, and the atomic bomb have cheered the pessimists and made them more certain of their gloom. The upshot is that the jolly fat clowns of comedy must more than ever be critically stretched to conform with lanky and lugubrious Hamlets in order to be worthy of praise. The celebration of the sad clown is a triumph of philosophy over art.

4   Mast, *The Comic Mind* (1973). Mast's early death was a serious loss for the field of film study. He was the author of several editions of *A Short History of the Movies*.

5   In regard to the question of happy endings, Zvi Jagendorf has given us an absorbing volume called *The Happy End of Comedy* (1984) in which he describes one of the familiar elements as riot, chaos, and (quoting Lorenzo da Ponte, Mozart's librettist) "uproar." Mack Sennett would have been pleased to know about such precedents.

The clowns themselves have been convinced, from time to time, that they must become serious if they are to go down in history. Charlie Chaplin was attracted by the traditional moral dilemmas of the comedy of manners when he decided to direct (but not star in) *A Woman of Paris* in 1923 — a solemn picture with few jokes in it. Woody Allen's *Interiors* (1978) displayed hot and cold conflicting emotions in a high-fashion family — a homage to Ingmar Bergman, the Swedish director he admires who has been so lavishly praised by critics of a literary bent. Thus these directors demonstrated they could do something grand and formidable. But the films will be included in film history only because they were made by geniuses of comedy.

Fortunately not every critic bows to the tragic muse and applies the grid of Oedipus to jesters. Gilbert Seldes was a rare case — a critic alert enough to respond to film as a popular art. Instead of trying to apply to a new experience Aristotle's ancient terminology, Seldes chose to use his own wits and do what Aristotle did. He looked around him and dealt directly with the actual works he found at hand.

His rambunctious rallying cry, "The Keystone the Builders Rejected," in *The Seven Lively Arts* (1924), insisted on the cinematic rightness of Mack Sennett's slapstick and speed, neither of which had figured at all in Aristotle's *Poetics*. The delicious terrors of fast-moving automobiles, trains, and streetcars were notably American, and pretty much unlike anything encountered by literary critics before.

Seldes discovered he was fond of the vulgarity, the "animal frankness," of the Keystone movies, with their menagerie of beasts, beauties, cops, and crazies. He hailed "the madness which is a monstrous sanity in the movie comedy" and decried the "stupid newspaper critics" who would not give Mack Sennett the "encouragement and criticism" he deserved.

He offered a description of *A Night Out*, for example, with Ben Turpin and Charlie Chaplin, as "two men on a drinking party . . . mutually assisting and hindering each other in a serious effort to do something they cannot define, but which they feel to be of cosmic importance."

This gets us close to a working understanding of the hilarious elements of a drunk scene. It does not quite tell us why we laugh at such a scene. Very likely, for that, we must return to the superior attitude of the Aristotelian view.

Seldes himself was somewhat snobbish in his stubborn preference for the Keystone exhibitions of irrationality and vulgarity. This may have been partly because he saw in it some social significance — a blunt edge of burlesque that carried, as it did in the time of Aristophanes, satirical clout.

It does seem that almost all the main characters in early silent comedies are low-life and less than brilliant — characters we can look down upon: Mack Sennett's Keystone Kops, Charlie Chaplin's tramp, Harry Langdon's sad adolescent, Stan Laurel and Oliver Hardy, Buster Keaton. They are also, in varying degrees, childlike.

With Keaton the "low-life" rule starts breaking down. Sometimes he is poor and downtrodden, sweeping out the theater or in trouble with the law. But he very often has a clearly defined job. In *The Navigator* and in *Battling Butler*, Keaton is a rich playboy, and the jokes are partly directed at his wealth, partly at some ineptitude which is gradually overcome. Harold Lloyd, too, is frequently well-off and welldressed, comic just the same because of surprising conditions and contrasting characters he encounters.

American silent film comedies are often class conscious, but by that very token can be expected to make fun of rich as well as poor. Aristotle is not to be taken too seriously as a guide for our time.

Charlie Chaplin in fact called Aristotle in question when he took the position (in an article in the *American* magazine of November 1918) that people "get satisfaction from seeing the rich get the worst of things." After all, "nine tenths of the people in the world are poor and resent the wealth" of the others.

Of course we could say that Aristotle means that whoever is the target of comedy — whether rich or poor — seems to us a character of a lower class. But isn't that changing the meaning of his words so as to preserve his definition? There is a clear edge of superiority in his brief dictum which fits well with his seven-year post as tutor to Alexander, one of the most powerful monarchs in history.

Chaplin claimed in his autobiography that he could not be comfortable in the role of a prince. His 1957 performance in *A King in New York* certainly bears him out. A child of the London streets, he was willing to direct all sorts of jokes and pratfalls at himself as the little tramp. His own character was of low degree, but it was the symbol of the downtrodden and carried the protection of pathos, the call on us to wish for his better luck or self-improvement. His other targets in the story were often high class and highfalutin'.

He knew he was serving a more or less democratic audience, in America and abroad. They responded happily when he dropped ice cream down the back of a rich dowager. They knew they were supposed to reject the erratic millionaire in *City Lights* (1931). Chaplin's dramatic representation of the dispossessed found its timely counter-response in plebeians who brought their millions of nickels to the boxoffice.

But if there is class consciousness in American silent comedies — whether the barbs are launched from above or below, whether the fun is at the expense of the downtrodden or the dignified — such content analysis is not sufficient to explain the sustained popularity of the one- and two-reelers which dominated the screen from about 1913 to 1925. If we are to get anywhere with critical explanations we are probably going to have to make unsatisfactory short lists of recurring situations, mechanisms, structures, and actions which were united harmoniously with these themes. After that, each observer can draw on such theories of philosophy, psychology, and metaphysics as may seem sufficient to explain audience response.

What makes people laugh? Old Hollywood hands, when queried on this, often back off and claim not to know. Or else they mention, almost invariably, "contrast" or "surprise." Professionals are all too aware that successful comedy invention is a precious gift and has a high value on the market. The old schemes must always seem new.[6]

One favorite explanation centers around something called "the trapdoor triple." In this mechanism, combining sadism and surprise and used often in very different forms in farce comedies, there will be three actions covering the same ground. At first the comic comes along and suddenly falls through an unseen trap door — a surprise for the character

6   See Richard Dyer MacCann, *Hollywood in Transition*, (1962), for interviews reprinted from the *Christian Science Monitor* with Judy Holliday (1956), Alec Guinness (1956), and Cary Grant (1957).

and for us. Then someone else comes by. We wait now for what we know will happen, and we laugh at the fall this time because we expect it. Then the comic comes back and walks right across the trapdoor (unaccountably closed) and nothing happens. We're surprised again — maybe even relieved. That's the trapdoor triple, a specific slapstick mechanism.

The slapstick tradition, with its obvious physical punishments, is sadistic in its satisfactions. Its appearance and reappearance down through the centuries testifies to a more or less universal eagerness to watch pain. Some observers, leaning confidently on both Aristotle and Freud, would identify our responses to comedy with a sense of superiority mingled always with sadism.

In Mack Sennett's very first comedy exercise for D.W. Griffith in 1909, *The Curtain Pole,* that lengthy gadget sticking out of either side of a careening vehicle knocked down a lot of people and resulted in riots in the streets. In the late 1920s and early 30s, Laurel and Hardy were ready at any time for the piece-by-piece destruction of a house or a car. They also pounded on each other and on various bystanders, innocent or otherwise.

Kicking, punching, whacking, slipping, falling, and all sorts of multiple abrasions and embarrassments caused by encounters with custard pies, banana skins, bricks, or two-by-fours make up a lot of the footage of early comedy in the silent era. That silence gives distance (and therefore less pain) we may agree; silent comedies are like a cartoon world because of this distance from us, the observers. Yet we should not avoid or discount, consciously or unconsciously, the cruel aspect of our desire to laugh at the plight of others. Are we willing to laugh as much at ourselves? This may be more civilized and praiseworthy. It is also more uncommon. Most people probably laugh quicker and harder when they know the target is someone else.

What about the perilous play on our nerves that danger represents, especially in the Harold Lloyd comedies, and even in the athletic entertainments of his predecessor, Douglas Fairbanks? In *Never Weaken* (1921), his last short subject, and in his most famous feature film, *Safety Last* (1923), which also has him dangling from a high building, Lloyd exploited this special thrill for audiences in search of laughter. He became known as "the king of daredevil comedy." Danger pleases viewers because they know it is not happening to them — and they think they are too smart to let it happen to them. Even in the film, they know it won't happen disastrously for the hero.

Buster Keaton has given us a whole catalogue of disasters and dangers, so expertly delivered that we are not adequately aware of what he has been through. In *Our Hospitality* (1923) he has to do a rescue at the top of a roaring waterfall. In *The Navigator* (1924) he must cope with an ocean liner. In *Sherlock Jr.* (1924) he undertakes one of the wildest rides ever attempted on a motorcycle: part of the time he is seated on the handlebars with no one behind him in charge. In *The General* (1927) he is a railroad engineer behind enemy lines in the U.S. Civil War and in *Steamboat Bill Jr.* (1928) he fumbles with a riverboat, finds himself inside a tornado, and has the front of a house fall on him, his head emerging safely through a window.

But are we willing to say that all comedies appeal to superiority and/or sadism or danger? If we try to perform, like Aristotle, the feat of examining dispassionately actual dramatic arrangements flourishing in the silent era, we surely see a need for a wider range of explanations.

Seldes held to his preference for the "custard-pie school of fun," rejecting what seemed to him the enervating gentility of the early films of Mr. and Mrs. Sidney Drew — episodes of courtship and marriage which forecast a long American tradition of situation comedy. This consistent stand tended to close off his enjoyment of a rich and valid branch of fun-making that flourished especially during and after the 1930s, from *It Happened One Night* to *My Man Godfrey* in the movies and *I Love Lucy, All in the Family, Happy Days, Barney Miller* and a hundred other series on television.

The stratagems of love, for many critics, are central to the traditions of dramatic comedy — of acted-out comedy, as opposed to stand-up monologues or Sennett's episodic thrillers and parodies. Whether making fun of romance or exploiting misogyny — whether rushing toward or escaping from a member of the opposite sex — the scenes and characters of thousands of comedies are bound up with the hazards of human relations. Sennett himself spent far more time on the dreary joke of the wandering double-standard husband than critics like Seldes and James Agee have remembered.

Certainly the Chaplin and Keaton features are seldom without a girl as a focus for desire and achievement, although Keaton's women seem less desirable than Chaplin's. Laurel and Hardy are often confronted with a hopelessly disagreeable wife, just as John Bunny was in the beginning years of film. Lord Byron summed up this tradition by saying that tragedies end in death, comedies in marriage.

Contrast and surprise are of course subdominant and contributing mechanisms of all these categories — of class consciousness, of sadism and danger, of romance and misogyny. They are also instrumental elements in other, less widely accepted, approaches to the explanation of comedy's appeal.

Henri Bergson, for example, suggests that laughter will greet any situation in which conformity-minded human beings act like machines. Presumably the moral is that oppressive custom cramps the creative *élan vital*, and we laugh at the exaggeration that points the moral. Sennett of course deployed the Keystone cops in absurd mechanical patterns all the time. Keaton's work comes closest to this notion in *The Navigator*, in which he must adapt himself to the huge pots and utensils available to him in the ship's mess. Chaplin offers a rather self-conscious application in *Modern Times* (1936), when he gets the twitches after working under the harsh demands of a production line, then is caught in what appears to be a giant printing press.[7]

A corollary to this theory, less satirical in tone and more affirmative, is the proposition that audiences (especially in America) respond with special pleasure to mechanical contrivances used in an ingenious way, helping a character gain the upper hand. This is often true of Keaton. A notable example is Chaplin, in *Easy Street* (1917), manipulating the gas jet in a street light to subdue his giant enemy.

More broadly, as J.P. Lebel and Daniel Moews say of Keaton, the whole notion of triumph over odds — the adolescent surpassing himself, the childlike character succeeding where adults may fail — is perhaps attractive to Americans. In the country in which individualism as a theory of life is most at

---

7   A good source for Henri Bergson's *Laughter* (1900) is *Comedy* (1956), which includes essays by George Meredith (1887) and the editor, Wylie Sypher.

home, such situations naturally make for happy viewing in movie houses.[8]

There should be no real objection to such stories even by the most doom-struck critics reared in the tragic mode. The record of American life includes many examples of individual self-help and success through hard work and ingenuity. Such plots are frequent for Fairbanks, Keaton, and Lloyd. Chaplin, the European immigrant, is more likely to get by with sudden luck or with a bit of cheating. But these too were a part of recognizable reality for movie-goers expecting happy endings.

There can be no question that Keaton had some sly fun with the sudden improvement in his capacities to cope, once a woman's favor was at stake. Lloyd, too, was quite open in his exaggeration of the chances of success and satisfaction in the world of the twenties, although he didn't make satire the main point, as Fairbanks did. Since all these comedy players became very rich and very famous by working in the American movie industry, there was nothing hypocritical or falsified in putting success stories into their films. In fact it was the most natural thing in the world.

Outsiders often claim that one of the characteristic aspects of Americans is readiness to laugh, and especially at themselves. Political leaders like Lincoln, both Roosevelts, and Kennedy have often found identification with the electorate through humor. There are a variety of humorists in our literary tradition: the crackerbarrel philosopher who makes sharp comments on politics and personalities in the manner of Finley Peter Dunne and Mark Twain, the master of wordplay like Ogden Nash, the relaxed satire of James Thurber and Robert Benchley, so akin to the blank-face performance of Buster Keaton. Benchley himself, in a series of short subjects in the early sound era, took the part of a sad-eyed lecturer making droll observations on peculiar aspects of American life.

Laughter means a lot to Americans. Probably there are more comics per square thousand of population than in any other land on earth, and many of them have turned up on

---

8 J.P. Lebel's *Buster Keaton* was published in 1967, Daniel Moews, *Keaton: The Silent Features Close-Up* in 1977.

Saturday Night Live and its successors on cable television. Musical comedy may be our most characteristic theatrical art, whereas the grimness of grand opera has never really found popularity in this country. Early sound movies generally disposed of the subject in a brief scene showing the head of the family being dragged to the opera against his will, a role often played by a rotund perspiring Eugene Pallette.

We may remember all those annual liars' contests in 19th-century towns, reporting on elaborate superhuman deeds. We may even be tempted to attribute to humor and creative nonsense some aid to human survival, whether as a kind of shout against the freezing winds of the plains or a weapon against the vast overbearing continent itself.[9]

Humor is not only spontaneous and natural for Americans. They also work at it. It is a vital part of that dedication to self-improvement which honestly obsesses Americans as citizens of a democratic society. For there is an extra burden of learning which somehow clings to the spirit of comedy, at least in those contrivances above the level of the Three Stooges. Contemplative comedy does not merely leave us where it found us. Its characters find things out about themselves. In tragedy this may also happen, but generally it is too late. In comedy, protagonists tend to remain alive and revelations occur in time to do something about them. This may happen even in a sequel, or a next episode on television.

Such familiar continuity of life and learning is reserved for the comedy mode or the soap opera. We do not have a TV genre called "situation tragedy." By an effort of will, we might try to put that label on crime shows. But the characters who could be expected to benefit from their experiences are not the continuing characters, the detectives and the cops. They are

---

9 Max Eastman spent many hours in conversation with Chaplin, and despite the seriousness of his commitment to Marxism, he later came to think that we neglect the possibility of laughter resulting from sheer high spirits, from simple play. He gives the example of taking a ball away from a very young child, who gives the loss no ego-significance but laughs and accepts it as part of a game. Eastman expands our sense of comedy when he offers us this extra dimension, which connects up with the dance and the carnival. Eastman, *The Sense of Humor* (1921), *Enjoyment of Laughter* (1936).

the ones who do not survive. As for the audience, they only learn methods of killing and tracking killers.

Tragedies are likely to be single works. And it is not so hard to create one. Anybody with a fair amount of talent who is also equipped with a suitable attitude of gloom and doubt can write a tragedy. It is simply necessary to cause terrible things to happen, either without a reason at all, or because of an irrevocable and fatal flaw of character planted by the author. After the violence and dying are completed, the members of the audience are supposedly purged (according to Aristotle) of pity and fear. Perhaps for that reason they will not be tempted to act like the murderous characters on the stage. But it has never been clear under the terms of the catharsis theory whether that matters or not. The notion of audience learning is supposed to belong to social science, not to dramatic theory.

Writing comedy is more difficult because there need to be so many necessary connections with ordinary reality in order to work out its development. Its standards for believable dialogue and structure call for skill in presenting slightly differing personality traits and then achieving lighthearted conflict with both naturalness and surprise. Beyond these skills, there is the expectation that the best comedies demand our attention to issues of our common humanity: they tell us things can be better if we will only confess our foolishness to each other. They can even suggest faith in the miniscule possibilities for social change such learning may provide.

Tragedy is careless of detail as it seeks the ultimate heights and depths of human behavior. It is grand and portentous, its gestures broad, its best scenes so intense that we tend to award acting honors only to performers in this mode. Its themes are overwhelming and often discouraging. After tragedy we may learn, but mostly we regret. We are left wasted, drained — purged perhaps but unprepared for action.

Comedy offers ranges of behavior and adjustments of thought which are within the possibility of human expression by ordinary people. It is close to diplomacy and persuasion, as tragedy is close to war. Its best performers give us subtleties and pleasures that deserve awards of the highest degree. Yet Cary Grant never received an Academy Award for a performance.

The twists and turns of ideas in a comedy, during which home truths are revealed and vanities chastened, are admirably adapted for presentation on the screen. The mental adjustment implied by a single close-up of a downcast eye can be more powerful than a witty Shavian declamation. We come away laughing and at the same time sobered, our sense of dislocation tickled — perhaps purged — and in the mood to attach the screen experience to our own in some profitable way.

The silent comedians, like the other silent stars, were young, as their country was still young. The exhilaration in their lives did not come from conquering the landscape but from winning an audience. Yet in the consciously frontier atmosphere of early Hollywood there were fortunes to be made, often simply by calling attention to the process of success.

Charlie Chaplin came from the depths of despair and privation to win year by year, by sly charm and inventiveness, incomparable wealth and fame. His central figure was a little tramp, aspiring to better himself and sometimes succeeding.

Buster Keaton, having gained through years of family enterprise a modest fame in vaudeville, risked all by starting over in the movies at $40 a week. His central figure was an earnest, unpromising adolescent who finds self-realization and wins the girl, in spite of dangers and challenges, through inspired adjustment and hard work.

Harold Lloyd, after working conscientiously at various jobs in Nebraska and as a theater actor and bit player in southern California, finally found a partner in Hal Roach who helped him reach spectacular financial success. His central figure was an eager young man, committed to optimism and self-help, who overcomes himself and all opposition and wins the girl.

Is it a coincidence that Chaplin's most notable and most unified feature comedy was called *The Gold Rush*? In the closing scenes, the little tramp hears his benefactor say, "I'll make you a millionaire in less than a month." He promises Georgia, "I got your note and I'm going to make good!" In *Safety Last*, Harold Lloyd, like Keaton, must win the girl by getting a job and getting ahead.

Thus early comedy in America can be connected in criticism with the confident forward drive of individuals seeking the American dream. Of course that dream was mostly equated with material success and only rarely with learning how to live together.

Since 1930 depression and war have profoundly and rightly shaken the confidence of Americans in their frontier tradition of optimism and individualism. Tragedy and irony are increasingly woven into the web of culture as expressed in fiction, drama, and cinema. The crisis of identity today is profound, as genial John Wayne traditionalism encounters Native American history and multiculturalism.

Comedy can help us to examine our attitudes and actions, most of all in the adjustable areas of conflict between personalities and between society and the individual. But it can hardly be expected to help us on the large, intractable subjects — racism, religion, overpopulation, pain, death, and war.[10]

When comedy tries to cope with such questions, it is likely to cross the line, sooner or later, into that tragic area of doubt which says that humanity cannot change, that our sins and cruelties are inborn, that certain problems are fixed by their nature and by our own. The American theme and dream has always been that nurture, not nature, guides our course — that nothing is inevitable and no one should say "I can't help it." The tragic mode, inherited from Europe, has not been allowed to dominate our hopes. By small increments and gradual solutions, we have expected to make progress all along the line.

Our faith in education and experience is supposed to give us the right to laugh at ourselves, shift our plans and try new methods. It would be unfortunate for all of us if a guilt-charged America, confronting its history and its hoped-for goals, were to change in such a way as to deny and downgrade both optimism and effort. If so, the atmosphere will be cheerless and comedy will become more and more bitter, depressing, vulgar, sad, and cold.

---

10 The cheerful confusions of Keaton's *The General* (1926) and the brilliant bitterness of Stanley Kubrick's *Dr. Strangelove* (1964) have not enlightened us much about war. Neither Keaton nor Lloyd appear to have had any clear consciousness of African-Americans as anything much beyond convenient objects of ridicule.

Chapter 1

Sennett and Others

*Pie-throwing ... became in time
a learned routine like the pratfall,
the double-take, the slow burn,
and the frantic leap, all stock
equipment of competent comedians.*
— *Mack Sennett*[1]

Mack Sennett: producer, actor, director, editor, the first and most prolific American impresario of film comedy. From March 1913 to August 1915 he delivered to Mutual Film Corporation, his distributor, an average of two one-reelers every week. His trademark in those early pictures was "pandemonium and chaos," but in the studio, he was a model of dictatorial control and creative authorship.

An Irish immigrant from Quebec, six-foot-one and 210 pounds, Michael Sinnott called himself a boilermaker. As a youth, he worked in Connecticut and Massachusetts ironworks. His father first was a manager of small hotels, then a carpenter and contractor. His mother ran a boarding house.

Meanwhile Mike insisted on dreaming of a career as an opera singer. He was a basso and frequently inflicted "Asleep in the Deep" on the general neighborhood, exercising his hefty voice under the tutelage of one of his mother's boarders.

---

1   Mack Sennett, *King of Comedy* (1954), p. 137.

According to an autobiography called *King of Comedy*, elaborated by Cameron Shipp in 1954, Michael's mother finally agreed that her son could use some stage training. She turned to a local Northampton lawyer named Calvin Coolidge, who wrote a terse note to Marie Dressler, then performing in town. Marie (who would later star in a Sennett feature, *Tillie's Punctured Romance*) tried to dissuade the young man, explaining that showbusiness is always uncertain and is very hard work.

"Have you ever," he asked her, "driven hot rivets all day long?"

She gave him another note, this time to David Belasco in New York. The famous stage producer advised him to learn first of all the basics — in burlesque. Before long the oversize boilermaker from Canada was striving to be the hind end of a horse. He gave up the idea of opera when he learned about the pay-scale of such singers. Soon he found his way to 11 East 14th Street, where a certain D.W. Griffith was hiring actors (as they used to say) "to pose for pictures."

At Biograph from 1908 through 1911 he worked steadily as an actor, wrote scripts (including one for Mary Pickford), and during the last year became a director. He claimed he often walked home with Griffith from 14th to 37th Street, drawing him out, listening to his experiences and ideas as a director.

Griffith apparently refused to agree that policemen could or should be funny on the screen, but Sennett knew better. The sublime incompetence of Keystone Kops would begin to astonish the screen in *The Bangville Police* on April 24, 1913, to the satisfaction of audiences throughout the land. It was a land already well supplied with new comedies — upwards of 30 a week in 1912, according to a recent study by Henry Jenkins.[2]

When Charles Bauman and Adam Kessel agreed to finance Sennett in a new production company, he moved to Hollywood in 1912 with Fred Mace, Mabel Normand, and Ford

2   See Henry Jenkins III, *What Made Pistachio Nuts?* Early Sound
    Comedy and the Vaudeville Aesthetic (1992) p. 39, and his
    unpublished seminar paper, University of Wisconsin, 1985, "Film
    Comedy Before Mack Sennett." Jenkins spot-checked production
    schedules in *Moving Picture World* 1907-1912. For *Bangville* date and
    others, see Kalton Lahue, *Mack Sennett's Keystone: The Man, the Myth,
    and the Comedies,* (1971), p. 195.

Sterling. These actors were later joined by others who gained fame: Fatty Arbuckle, Mack Swain, Louise Fazenda, Charlie Murray, Chester Conklin, Al St. John, Minta Durfee, Alice Davenport — and Charlie Chaplin. (Buster Keaton never worked at Keystone; he did make a short sound film with Sennett in the 1930s.)

Various legends have been set in motion by this practiced story teller about his own life and labors. One was the notion that Mabel Normand, the darling of the studio, was the first performer to throw a pie — whether berry-and-cream or custard — and that it was directed at the cross-eyed comedian, Ben Turpin. Kalton Lahue informs us that pies appeared in comedies before Keystone. Also that Turpin "did not join the company until late 1916 and the earliest known Keystone pie on record struck Roscoe Arbuckle in *A Noise From the Deep*, a release of July 17, 1913."[3]

The steady productivity of the Keystone studio in the early teens was of course a response to the demands of nickelodeons and larger movie houses which were building the public's movie-going habit. But the supply to meet the demand was conceived, put into action, recorded on film, and edited under the supervision of a single person.

The boss of Keystone was not a myth. Certainly he depended day by day and more and more on the talents of directors and actors who caught the frenzy of his bumptious temperament and enjoyed the excitements of the scratched-down scripts and inexplicable gags and intolerable dangers he blithely prescribed.

Yet the final product had to please Mack Sennett, as he rode back and forth in his rocking chair in the projection room. (A fast ride meant he was satisfied.) And the premises and predicaments planned for the next day's shooting had to tickle him on the day before, as he soaked in a hot tub on the top floor of the tower he built in the middle of the lot — a tower which enabled him to look down on everyone and keep them moving.

Before the sauna had ever been exported from Scandinavia to California, Sennett determined that his body needed to be boiled a little before his head knew what he wanted. Through

3   Lahue, p. 218.

that head filtered all kinds of remembered gags from French short subjects plus the ideas proposed by his own writers and gag men. Then his Irish ruminations assembled action piled on action that needed no logic of plot to please Americans.

Lewis Jacobs, who was usually preoccupied with social problems in his landmark history book, *The Rise of the American Film* (1939), fell into a regular fit of enthusiasm in trying to describe his memories of Keystone's "world of absurdity" in which there was so much wonderful camera trickery:[4]

> Cops chase their victim at a mile-a-minute pace; fat men leap hundreds of feet in the air; the hero dashes through walls or over a speeding train with the greatest of ease; explosions send characters sailing serenely through treetops; motorcycles swoop down waterfalls; the lowly two-seater Ford ejects literally hundreds of policemen, and after the last cop is finally out, bursts into fragments . . . . The incongruous was exploited: beautiful girls languishing for the love of pot-bellied, bald, ridiculously fat men; or the poor, innocent, lonely damsel in distress embracing her rescuer and at the same time stealing his watch. . .

We must expand the Jacobs record by adding emphasis on one constantly repeated theme — so common in all eras from Greek to Restoration times — the inconstancies of women and the infidelities of men. These apparently were sure-fire for hilarity in American audiences during the second decade of the 20th century.

Over and over again, Puck's lament, "What fools these mortals be!" was the underlying theme, as loutish characters fought over a woman or tried to escape from one. Absurdity coupled with cynical views of human nature persuaded viewers that no banker, politician, preacher, or policeman could be rational or have a happy home life.

This appeal to lower-class consciousness was of course unwelcome in most middle-class circles. Comedies put out by the former boilermaker were given less than fulsome responses even by the reviewers of the film trade papers. Epes Winthrop Sargent, in his *Moving Picture World* columns from 1910-1917, gave voice to the notion of "refined" comedy, praising the works of John Bunny and of Sidney Drew, whose polite plays before the camera made comments on human foibles but never exploded them with the vulgar passion of Key-

---

4   Lewis Jacobs, *The Rise of the American Film* (1939), p. 211.

stone. Drew himself wrote articles explicating his views on "sentimental human comedy."

Sargent professed to find in Sennett a spark of originality going beyond the "water throwing and senseless chases" of his even less genteel competitors. But he claimed to look forward to an evolution of comedy which would in time improve audience tastes and stimulate serious thought.[5]

Certainly the acceptance of feature length by Lloyd, Keaton, and Chaplin in the 1920s tended to require plot and character development at the expense of gags and slapstick. Thus the genteel tradition of the stage more and more gained the upper hand over the vaudeville influence, in theory and in practice.

Meanwhile Sennett was recognized as America's leading producer of comedy shorts when he was invited by Harry Aitken to form one point of his Triangle Productions, along with the other two most famous producer-directors in the world, Thomas Ince and D.W. Griffith. Each producer was to supervise and deliver one film a week. This noble experiment lasted only from late 1915 to early 1917. More or less simultaneously, the three artistic partners found the arrangement financially unstable. Sennett formed his own company, releasing first through Paramount, and in the 1920s through First National and Pathe.

It was during the Triangle period that the concept of the "Bathing Beauties" developed as a regular attraction. Mack's business manager, George W. Stout, brought a proposal to him for one of the first self-contained studio publicity offices containing a photo studio and darkroom. The ravishing single and group portraits that resulted, especially those featuring bathing gear, met conveniently the hunger of the *Los Angeles Times* for just such material. The Bathing Beauties, while seldom important to the plot, were often in the background, and Sennett discovered that their publicity stills prospered his pictures.

Mack Sennett's private life embraced more chaos than it needed to. If he had exercised as much control over his own cynical view of the necessities of male libido as he did over the films which expressed that attitude, he might have man-

5 Jenkins, pp. 54 and 49 and footnotes passim pp. 294-295.

aged to marry Mabel Normand — an outcome insiders were constantly expecting. He was always playing the field, and on one particular day Mabel discovered him in action with her friend Mae Busch, whereupon she began a long fadeout (assisted by a tragic drug habit) that took her away from the macho basso and from his movies. She had directed thirteen films for him and played in nearly two hundred.[6]

Mack had set up for Mabel a film company under her own name and produced with her a feature-length comedy, *Mickey*, in 1916. But it was not released to theaters for nearly two years, either because Sennett doubted its possibilities or because distributors objected to the lack of slapstick in it. It was a surprising success, and she made several other features, two for Sennett.

Frank Capra, who worked for him in 1925, had some unhappy memories of Sennett's ego and methods of working. As one of several staff gag men who were always circulating around the boss, Capra offered an idea about a loose wheel on a buggy (with lovers inside) on the edge of a cliff. Sennett denied it was funny and denied Capra the right to suggest it to anyone. When it turned up in one of the films coming through the editing rooms, Sennett blew up and ordered Capra off the lot. The angry future director listened to the advice of old-timers and agreed to "walk the gate" — that is, to stand outside the studio until Sennett might invite him back. He was picked up in Mack's car the third day. Capra never forgot the boss's bullying tactics and used them himself on occasion in later years.[7]

His personal qualities may have limited his achievements. Yet Sennett was certainly the boss, and artistic arbiter as well. In November 1918, which was quite a long time after his 1913 beginnings, Sennett allowed himself some reminiscence and analysis in a piece printed in *Motion Picture Classic*.[8] He declared there were two main reasons for laughter: mistaken identity and injured dignity. This prescription was much too limiting for a film maker who put a lot of effort into parodies

---

6   Adela Rogers St. Johns was a witness. See her *Love, Laughter and Tears: My Hollywood Story* (1978).

7   Frank Capra, *The Name Above the Title* (1971), pp. 53-56.

8   Mack Sennett, "The Psychology of Film Comedy," November 1918.

of familiar aspects of human society, on the one hand, and the slapstick excess of danger on the other.

Sennett did share, however, a revealing professional skill in his article. He had been puzzled by a scene of crashing chinaware, which he was sure was funny but didn't get a laugh. He examined the preceding material and discovered it was too full of tension and excitement and was not followed by a necessary lull to get ready for the "noisy" smashing scene. He stretched out the connecting material in the editing room and got the audience reaction he wanted.

The films were his, and he checked every foot. The Sennett archives of scripts and films and letters are mostly at the Academy of Motion Picture Arts and Sciences, and before 1975 there were certain competing claims that raised legal problems about making them freely available. As scholars take up the task of evaluating what he gave the Academy, more may be learned about his own role in production. But looking at the present state of the record, limited as it is, it becomes apparent that Sennett was one of the true authors of the cinema.

In terms of productivity and longevity alone — the number of performers he kept at work, the hundreds of titles he produced, the number of companies he worked for· — he can hardly be put down as some kind of mechanical man, responding to universal comedy rituals. His appeal to the audience was achieved by his constant consciousness of the changing desires of that audience, expressed in responses to particular mechanisms in particular films. But he was a worker who cared deeply about the medium of which he was one of the founders. His eye and hand brought forth week after week the kind of mirth that not only rocked his rocking chair but rang the bell for the audiences of his time.

JAMES AGEE
Comedy's Greatest Era

If there is such a thing as a gallery of folklore in criticism, this essay might well be enshrined there. It stirred immediate and widespread response among the readers of Life magazine when it appeared September 3, 1949. As a word-picture of the feelings induced by silent comedies in a devoted fan, Agee's nostalgic piece has probably not been equalled. Its tone of mourning for the absence of slapstick from the screen is just as valid today and enables us to feel nostalgic deprivation for movies we haven't even seen.

In the article he gave us first a round of applause for the dizzy clowns and vulgar parodies of Mack Sennett — very much an echo of Gilbert Seldes' critical response to Keystone comedies. Then he took up in turn the look and style of Chaplin, Lloyd, Langdon, and Keaton. Although this leaves out a great many performers whose personalities no doubt deserve remembrance, his advocacy has been an important factor in elevating these four to the status of the "greatest" figures of the era.

We have chosen, in order to avoid repetition in later selections (and also some minor outdated material) to limit our selection to the first five pages of the reprint in the first volume of Agee on Film (N.Y., McDowell, Obolensky, 1958).

In the language of screen comedians four of the main grades of laugh are the titter, the yowl, the bellylaugh and the boffo. The titter is just a titter. The yowl is a runaway titter. Anyone who has ever had the pleasure knows all about a bellylaugh. The boffo is the laugh that kills. An ideally good gag, perfectly constructed and played, would bring the victim up this ladder of laughs by cruelly controlled degrees to the top rung, and would then proceed to wobble, shake, wave and brandish the ladder until he groaned for mercy. Then, after the shortest possible time out for recuperation, he would feel the first wicked tickling of the comedian's whip once more and start up a new ladder.

The reader can get a fair enough idea of the current state of screen comedy by asking himself how long it has been since he has had that treatment. The best of comedies these days hand out plenty of titters and once in a while it is possible to achieve a yowl without overstraining. Even those who have never seen anything better must occasionally have the feeling, as they watch the current run or, rather, trickle of screen comedy, that they are having to make a little cause for laughter go an awfully long way. And anyone who has watched screen comedy over the past ten or fifteen years is bound to realize that it has quietly but steadily deteriorated. As for those happy atavists who remember silent comedy in its heyday and the bellylaughs and boffos that went with it, they have something close to an absolute standard by which to measure the deterioration.

When a modern comedian gets hit on the head, for example, the most he is apt to do is look sleepy. When a silent comedian got hit on the head he seldom let it go so flatly. He realized a broad license, and a ruthless discipline within that license. It was his business to be as funny as possible physically, without the help or hindrance of words. So he gave us a figure of speech, or rather of vision, for loss of consciousness. In other words he gave us a poem, a kind of poem, moreover, that everybody understands. The least he might do was to straighten up stiff as a plank and fall over backward with such skill that his whole length seemed to slap the floor at the same instant. Or he might make a cadenza of it — look vague, smile like an angel, roll up his eyes, lace his fingers, thrust his hands palms downward as far as they would go, hunch his shoulders, rise on tiptoe, prance ecstatically in narrowing circles until, with tallow knees, he sank down the vortex of his dizziness to the floor, and there signified nirvana by kicking his heels twice, like a swimming frog.

Startled by a cop, this same comedian might grab his hatbrim with both hands and yank it down over his ears, jump high in the air, come to earth in a split violent enough to telescope his spine, spring thence into a coattail-flattening sprint and dwindle at rocket speed to the size of a gnat along the grand, forlorn perspective of some lazy back boulevard.

Those are fine clichés from the language of silent comedy in its infancy. The man who could handle them properly combined several of the more difficult accomplishments of the acrobat, the dancer, the clown and the mime. Some very gifted comedians, unforgettably Ben Turpin, had an immense vocabulary of these clichés and were in part so lovable because they were deep conservative classicists and never tried to break away from them. The still more gifted men, of course, simplified and invented, finding out new and much deeper uses for the idiom. They learned to show emotion through it, and comic psychology, and more eloquently than most language has ever managed to, and they discovered beauties of comic motion which are hopelessly beyond reach of words.

It is hard to find a theater these days where a comedy is playing; in the days of the silents it was equally hard to find a theater which was not showing one. The laughs today are pitifully few, far between, shallow, quiet and short. They almost never build, as they used to, into something combining the jabbering frequency of a machine gun with the delirious momentum of a roller coaster. Saddest of all, there are few comedians now below middle age and there are none who seem to learn much from picture to picture, or to try anything new.

To put it unkindly, the only thing wrong with screen comedy today is that it takes place on a screen which talks. Because it talks, the only comedians who ever mastered the screen cannot work, for they cannot combine their comic style with talk. Because there is a screen, talking comedians are trapped into a continual exhibition of their inadequacy as screen comedians on a surface as big as the side of a barn. . . .

Mack Sennett made two kinds of comedy: parody laced with slapstick, and plain slapstick. The parodies were the unceremonious burial of a century of hamming, including the new hamming in serious movies, and nobody who has missed Ben Turpin in *A Small Town Idol*, or kidding Erich von Stroheim in *Three Foolish Weeks* or as *The Shriek of Araby*, can imagine how rough parody can get and still remain subtle and roaringly funny. The plain slapstick, at its best, was even better: a profusion of hearty young women in disconcerting bathing suits, frisking around with a gaggle of insanely incompetent policemen and of equally certifiable male civilians sporting museum-piece mustaches. All these people zipped and caromed about the pristine world of the screen as jazzily as a convention of water bugs. Words can hardly suggest how energetically they collided and bounced apart, meeting in full gallop around the corner of a house; how hard and how often they fell on their backsides; or with what fantastically adroit clumsiness they got themselves fouled up in folding ladders, garden hoses, tethered animals and each other's headlong cross-purposes. The gestures were ferociously emphatic; not a line or motion of the body was wasted or inarticulate. The reader may remember how splendidly upright wandlike old Ben Turpin could stand for a Renunciation Scene, with his lampshade mustache twittering and his sparrowy chest stuck out and his head flung back like Paderewski assaulting a climax and the long babyish back hair trying to look lionlike, while his Adam's apple, an orange in a Christmas stocking, pumped with noble emotion. Or huge Mack Swain, who looked like a hairy mushroom, rolling his eyes in a manner patented by French Romantics and gasping in some dubious ecstasy. Or Louise Fazenda, the perennial farmer's daughter and the perfect low-comedy housemaid, primping her spit curl; and how her hair tightened a good-looking face into the incarnation of rampant gullibility. Or snouty James Finlayson, gleefully foreclosing a mortgage, with his look of eternally tasting a spoiled pickle. Or Chester Conklin, a myopic and inebriated little walrus stumbling around in outsize pants. Or Fatty Arbuckle, with his cold eye and his loose, serene smile, his silky manipulation of his bulk and his satanic marksmanship with pies (he was ambidextrous and could simultaneously blind two people in opposite directions).

The intimate tastes and secret hopes of these poor ineligible dunces were ruthlessly exposed whenever a hot stove, an electric fan or a bulldog took a dislike to their outer garments: agonizingly elaborate drawers, worked up on some lonely evening out of some Godforsaken lace curtain; or men's underpants with big round black spots on them. The Sennett sets — delirious wallpaper, megalomaniacally scrolled iron beds, Grand Rapids *in extremis* — outdid even the underwear. It was their business, after all, to kid the squalid braggadocio which infested the domestic interiors of the period, and that was almost beyond parody. The comedies told their stories to the unaided eye, and by every means possible they screamed to it. That is one reason for the India-ink silhouettes of the cops, and for convicts and prison bars and their shadows in hard sunlight, and for barefooted husbands, in tigerish pajamas, reacting like dervishes to stepped-on tacks.

The early silent comedians never strove for or consciously thought of anything which could be called artistic "form," but they achieved it. For Sennett's rival, Hal Roach, Leo McCarey once devoted almost the whole of a Laurel and Hardy two-reeler to pie-throwing. The first pies were thrown thoughtfully, almost philosophically. Then innocent bystanders began to get caught into the vortex. At full pitch it was Armageddon. But everything was calculated so nicely that until late in the picture, when havoc took over, every pie made its special kind of point and piled on its special kind of laugh.

Sennett's comedies were just a shade faster and fizzier than life. According to legend (and according to Sennett) he discovered the speed tempo proper to screen comedy when a green cameraman, trying to save money, cranked too slow.* Realizing the tremendous drumlike power of mere motion to exhilarate, he gave inanimate objects a mischievous life of their own, broke every law of nature the tricked camera would serve him for and made the screen dance like a witches' Sabbath. The thing one is surest of all to remember is how toward the end of nearly every Sennett comedy, a chase (usually called the "rally") built up such a majestic trajectory of pure anarchic motion that bathing girls, cops, comics, dogs, cats, babies, automobiles, locomotives, innocent bystanders, sometimes what seemed like a whole city, an entire civilization, were hauled along head over heels in the wake of that energy like dry leaves following an express train.

*Silent comedy was shot at 12 to 16 frames per second and was speeded up by being shown at 16 frames per second, the usual rate of theater projectors at that time. Theater projectors today run at 24, which makes modern film taken at the same speed seem smooth and natural. But it makes silent movies fast and jerky.

SAMUEL GILL
John Bunny

Three years before Fatty Arbuckle joined Keystone, another equally sizable fellow offered his services to Vitagraph, and his five-year career forecast the kind of sudden fame that could come to a movie personality. John Bunny made an effort to establish himself as an individualized clown, but he usually worked in the kind of plotted domestic situation comedy that has survived over the years in film and television.

The chapter on John Bunny in Clown Princes and Court Jesters, *by Kalton C. Lahue and Samuel Gill, was written during or shortly after the young co-author's student days at the University of Kansas. Gill later became archivist for the Academy of Motion Picture Arts and Sciences in Beverly Hills. His chapter (which includes a number of pictures) was on pages 58-67 of the book published in 1970 by A.S. Barnes & Co., Cranbury, N.J.*

In 1910, the man destined to become America's first motion picture comedy star left a promising stage career to enter the infant industry. While most of his generation viewed the "flickers" as a novelty that could not seriously threaten the legitimate theater, John Bunny was perceptive enough to realize the potential importance of movies and abandoned a twenty-five-year career, which had carried him along from minstrel troupes to Shakespearian roles. Almost alone among his contemporaries in feeling that moving pictures had made serious inroads into the theatrical business, Bunny foresaw the beginning of a great amusement enterprise and the emergence of an aesthetically legitimate art form.

And so the summer of 1910 found the genial, rotund actor applying for work at the primitive studios in the New York area, but with little success. None of the fledgling producers felt they could afford this enthusiastic applicant. Exasperated, he finally offered to work in one picture for no salary just to prove his point. Albert E. Smith and J. Stuart Blackton of the Vitagraph Company agreed to use Bunny in one film but insisted on paying him the regular wage of $5.00 a day.

When Smith and Blackton saw the rushes of Bunny's trial film, they were convinced that the portly stranger knew a great deal about acting. Inquiring about his background, the producers were amazed to discover that the man so eager to break into movies that he would work for nothing was actually an experienced and successful stage comedian. While this first picture was being completed, they offered John a part in another picture. Bunny agreed and started production on the second film. As Bunny himself recounted the incident years later, Smith and Blackton "plainly indicated that they were pleased with my work, but when I broached a permanent engagement, they advised me that it could not be considered." The Vitagraph officials knew they could not come close to approaching Bunny's salary on the stage. "I insisted that they make me their best offer and after they apologized for doing so, they offered me $40.00, about one-fifth of what I had been receiving in the theater. To their great surprise, I readily accepted."

Bunny's films were an immediate hit with exhibitors, fans and critics alike. In fact, the *New York Dramatic Mirror* of January 18, 1911, pointed out the emergence of John Bunny as a new screen talent in their review of Bunny's comedy, *Doctor Cupid*, saying, "The character work of the cranky old father of the girl is a bit of acting worthy of the warmest praise. The old man could take no prize at a beauty show, but he has ability in picture expression of the highest order." Although it was not the accepted practice at this time to list players' names, the clever Bunny capitalized on his unusual name, managing to work it first into the subtitles and then the titles of his comedies, effectively creating a one-man star system long before Vitagraph and the industry generally accepted the idea.

While Vitagraph continued to raise his salary, Bunny knew he was worth far more than he was being paid, considering the huge financial success of his comedies, and unsatisfied with his progress, John took a shrewd step to correct this iniquity. Albert E. Smith recorded this incident in his memoirs shortly before his death in 1958, published here for the first time with the kind permission of his widow, Lucille B. Smith:

One day, when I was at an important business conference in New York, Bunny called me on the telephone and said that he must see me for a few moments, on very important matters. . . . I finally agreed to go down to the entrance of the building at three o'clock — he, faithfully, promising to be there.

This building overlooked Longacre Square. Precisely, at three o'clock I excused myself and went down to the entrance of the building. There was no John Bunny there! I looked around and then saw him walking across the Square, toward me. When he arrived, he apologized for being a little late and commenced to talk about nothing at all. I was annoyed at his getting me to break away from the meeting and finally I said, "What is it you wanted to see me about, John?"

Meanwhile, although I didn't notice it at the moment, he had manipulated me around so that my back was to the street, and his back to the building. Then I commenced to hear a murmuring noise behind me, and looking around, there was the whole of the Square jammed with people who had gathered to see John Bunny! When I turned back to him, he said, "That was all I wanted you to see, Governor." After which, he pushed his way through the crowd to a car he had waiting and drove off. While I knew how popular some of the stars had become, it was the first time I had seen such a crowd gather to look at one.

Eventually, this strategic action paid off for the determined Mr. Bunny.

Engaging in what he regarded as a new art form, John Bunny believed the ultimate value of film would be centered in adaptation of the world's greatest dramas and stories, available to everyone in the simplified form of the moving picture. By May 1912, Vitagraph was apparently convinced enough to send Bunny to England to film Charles Dickens's *Pickwick Papers* on location. Mobbed by admirers wherever he went abroad, Bunny now realized the extent of enormous admiration and affection moviegoers held for his work in comedy. The most immediate benefit was a large salary increase — the result of English producers bidding for his services. Vitagraph did not want to lose their star comedian, so Bunny's $250 a week became $30,000 a year. A salary increase was not the only result of his extraordinary reception in England; along with Carl Laemmle's public advertising of his new star, Florence Lawrence, and Vitagraph's new attention to Maurice Costello, Florence Turner, Arthur Johnson and Jean ("The Vitagraph Dog"), John Bunny heralded the birth of the star system in motion pictures with a special position reserved for Bunny himself as the first comedy "star" in the American film.

John Bunny's mastery of screen comedy was the mastery of intricate facial expression and body movement. The Bunny comedies reflected John's concern for a natural acting performance and he attacked each one with a believable approach, exercising but a slight touch of exaggeration, and then only for comic effect. The memorable moments of *A Cure For Pokeritis* (1912) were not the clever quirks of plot or comic action but an almost indefinable overall impression — the smiles and handshakes among old cronies, the unspoken request for enough money to get home from an old friend "spoken" only by glances out of the corners of his eyes and down to his empty pockets, the cautious and hesitant control of his bulk when mounting the squeaky steps at 2:00 a.m., and those infectious smiles of almost inexpressible self-pleasure as he tricked his wife in some childishly simple deception. . . .

In many of his comedies, John Bunny was paired with Flora Finch, that marvelous character actress who looked and acted much like an emotional needle — the perfect opposite to Bunny in size and temperament: to his immensity, she was fragile and flighty; to his controlled emotion, she was one long emotional outburst; to his childlike playfulness, she was the school teacher disciplinarian. When attired in laces, ankle-length dresses and flowery hats, Flora looked much like those old spinster types so superbly described years later by W.C. Fields as "well-kept graveyards."

When Bunny arrived at Vitagraph, Flora Finch was already a recognized talent in eccentric comedy and character roles. Her teaming with Bunny was not a conscious decision, rather their work together seemed to make such a combination inevitable. The "Bunnyfinches," as their films were referred to by fans, were enormously popular, and by 1913 the team stood at the pinnacle of their profession.

Evidence of Bunny's popularity was no more apparent than on the studio lot itself. Apparently as well-liked off-screen as on, Bunny was father confessor to half the Vitagraph company and old and young alike greeted him as Uncle John. Bunny also performed all but the most dangerous stunts himself despite his unusual size and weight. "He was also very patient and kind in instructing anyone unfamiliar with the making of movies," recalls Bunny's son, John Francis Bunny, "and when any new person had been hired by Vitagraph, my father's company was the training ground where they learned the movie business. He demanded only one thing — eagerness to learn."

John Bunny's screen career was brought to a close by his death in 1915. On leave of absence from Vitagraph to return to the stage in *Bunny in Funnyland* the comedian found the overwhelming crowds, honorary banquets and formal welcoming celebrations physically exhausting. The result of this tour was a general breakdown of Bunny's health, with the gradual development of heart and kidney complications, and finally Bright's Disease. Throughout April 1915, newspapers around the world carried reports of Bunny's progress in his struggle with death until the 26th, when the beloved comic succumbed...

WILLIAM ADDISON LATHROP
The House Next Door

This calm and pithy little story is included here primarily to indicate that not all of the humor in early American films derived from those graduates of vaudeville and the English music halls who announced themselves as comedy stars and whose names come down to us in the history books as masters of slapstick and mayhem. Here there is a lively sense of romance and a humorous situation based on character development provided by a professional script writer.

The story also illustrates the very kind of elaborate prose description of personal traits and internal responses which could never be translatable in screen terms. Nevertheless, Lathrop couldn't help writing like this, and it may be that his extra care and elegance won him attention as a "literary" writer.

Britton Publishing Company brought out a number of his Little Stories From the Screen *in 1917. This one (on pages 123 to 128) was produced by Vitagraph under the title of* The Professor's Romance, *directed by its featured player, Sidney Drew.*

For more than ten years, the housekeeper had opened the library door at exactly thirty minutes past six, and announced that supper was ready. And the Professor would close the volume — Humboldt's *Cosmos* or Kant's *Critique of Pure Reason* — put the book carefully back in its place, pocket his glasses, and follow her into the little dining room for his toast and tea and canned peaches. The serenity of his bachelor household and its clock-like regularity had been undisturbed for years. About his only callers were the male members of The Society for Ethical Research, who

came to sit at the feet of this Gamaliel, and drink in the words
that fell from his lips.

The Professor was "gun-shy" when it came to the ladies. No
romance had ever rippled the calm of his methodical life; there
was nothing about dimples or star-eyes or ringlets in any of the
text-books he had either written or read, and a picture of a heart
looked to him like a conic plane, attenuated at the apex, and with
a curvilinear indented base. His interest in Venus was confined
to the theories in regard to the missing arms of the Milo variety,
and the way to differentiate the Fourth Avenue antiques from
the ones Schliemann dug up at the Campanile or the Acropolis
— or somewhere. He could translate the hieroglyphs on the sar-
cophagus of Cleopatra, and tell you how she was mummified
differently from Ptolemy II, and that let him out about the lady.
All of which is pertinent to this story.

The house next door had a new tenant. Louise had taken it for
the summer, and had arrived with Bill, and Elizabeth, and a dog
and a nurse; and forthwith the serenity of the Professor departed.
A low fence separated the two cottages; but no fence was ever
built that would keep out Bill and Elizabeth when they had once
made up their minds to get on the other side. They soon had a
picket pried loose, and went in and out as they listed.

Any dignified man who wears an out-of-date silk hat and a
very long frock coat is a natural mark and a perpetual temptation
to children like that pair. They broke his windows and dispersed
the meetings for the furtherance of Ethical Research. They ran
the gamut of annoyance, until his deductions became faulty and
his conclusions illogical — it is difficult to reason accurately
when in fear of a half-brick or the water from a garden hose. He
had to listen to the piano as played by Louise, and it drove him
to shut the windows and put on ear-muffs.

And as he walked one day in the cool of the afternoon, beneath his own vine and fig tree, reading something light in the
original Sanskrit, by way of recreation, a deluge of water from
the hose overwhelmed him. As soon as he could gather his dripping senses and his glasses, he grabbed the pair and hustled
them to their mother; and — fie upon her — when she saw him
she laughed!

Now, when Louise laughed, anybody else laughed too, and
that is exactly what the Professor did. Louise took him into the
drawing room and spread a mackintosh over a chair and sat him
on it, and made him drink some whiskey, after he had made a
forcible but ineffectual protest. She spoke sadly of the children,

and making little dabs at her eyes with a lace handkerchief, told him that they needed the firm hand of a father.

The Professor thought so too, but said it was a mere nothing and didn't matter in the least. And that evening, as he sat with his feet in a mustard bath, with a blanket wrapped around the rest of him, the telephone rang — it was Louise inquiring if he had taken cold — and he told her, catarrhally, "Do, dot a bit. I have dot suffered ady idcodvediedce" — and went back and put his feet in the mustard bath, and smiled!

And a few evenings later, after he had arranged his hair for the eleventh time, he went out and talked to Louise over the fence for a few moments. When she went in, he saw that the moon was beautiful. He had always thought of it before as a cold satellite of the earth, without atmosphere, and the radius of whose orbit was 240,000 miles.

He sat in the library, and the music from the piano came tinkling through the window; old Mary, the housekeeper, brought the ear-muffs and shut the windows. But he discarded the ear-muffs as soon as she had gone, and softly opened all the windows, and sat with clasped hands, beating time with his foot.

As he glanced through the window the next day, he saw a man, dressed in the height of fashion, enter Louise's gate and ring her bell. For the first time in many years, he realized that his clothes were not exactly in style. A visit to the tailor and the hatter and the haberdasher and the boot-maker soon fixed that, and arrayed like Sullivan in all his glory, he emerged from the chrysalis of his sombre vesture, and almost scared old Mary to death when she saw him.

He called on Louise, and the kids "didn't do a thing to him." And Louise told him that they needed the firm hand of a father. He offered to assist her in any way that he could — and Louise sighed, wistfully. He bought an authority on the bringing up and control of children, by Miss S.P. Inster; and when "mother's angels" did something particularly outrageous, he consulted the book — and always found that "Children should never be spanked."

But after they had stolen his outing flannels and Mary's best dress from the line for a dress parade, and had pulled the plug out of the boat in which he took Louise boating, compelling them to wade ashore, and had done other ingeniously devilish things, he told Louise that "he was inclined to doubt the accuracy of the dogma as laid down in Miss S.P. Inster's book." And Louise said, "They need the firm hand of a father." He placidly admitted that that was so, and again Louise sighed.

But even the most bashful of men comes to taw at last. He sat with Louise on the sofa in her drawing room, and had laid his hand on his heart, and had swallowed hard several times, when the awful knowledge was borne in upon him that somebody was under the sofa — and he dragged out Elizabeth and Bill. He started to consult the book — but closed it, and taking Bill across his knee, spanked him with it heartily. Bill finally wriggled out of his grasp, and he and Elizabeth were sent to bed. Louise told him that "The children needed the firm hand of a father" — and after thinking a moment, he held up his good right hand and asked her if she thought it would do. She fell on his neck — being taken so by surprise!

Together they went later, to the nursery. There lay Elizabeth and Bill, tucked safe in their little beds, their sweet, gentle, child-faces dewy with the beauty sleep. Tenderly Louise kissed them, and the Professor, smiling, followed suit. He put his arm around Louise, and they softly went out. Then Bill and Elizabeth sat up in bed and winked at each other.

KALTON C. LAHUE
Sennett Stories

Lahue described his frustration with the state of Keystone scholarship in the introduction to his book, Mack Sennett's Keystone: The Man, the Myth, and the Comedies *(A.S. Barnes, 1971). The "Sennett collection" was for a long time kept under wraps after it was given to the Academy of Motion Picture Arts and Sciences because of certain "legal problems" raised by other claimants. Since about 1975, however, the Academy has seen to it that the collection is well organized and available for scholars to examine. Lahue meanwhile did his best to interview survivors and seek out the films available up to 1971, also sharing with us a large assortment of still frame enlargements.*

From the final chapter in Lahue's book, we have chosen paragraphs which give us descriptions of a few stories. (Pages 265, 267, 275, 277, 279, 281, 286.) Lahue claims these suggest some kind of change toward tighter planning and complex story development during the 1910s. Donald McCaffrey doubts that this went very far, especially not in the 1920s, giving the advantage rather to Sennett's competitor, Hal Roach, in adjusting plots and characters to more dramatic standards.

It took no special genius or education to view and enjoy the Keystones, and unlike much of their competition, these comedies were conceptualized entirely on Sennett's lot; he never purchased a story from any outside source. Producers were becoming accustomed to charges by would-be screen writers that their material was being used without payment or credit (a fair share of it was) and this was a headache Sennett chose to avoid. In addition, Mack had once written a script for Biograph based on an O. Henry story, only to discover much to his chagrin that the adaptation was much too close to the original to suit Biograph executives. . . .

It was nearly impossible for any writer to develop a Keystone in shooting-script form, as Ince did for his films. The Keystone of 1912 and early 1913 depended too greatly upon comic improvisation to be planned in any great detail that well in advance; about all that could be put into writing was a skeleton outline of the major action. When analyzing some of these earliest Keystones today, it becomes apparent that even a sketch of the story thread is difficult to capture on paper. These comedies were long on gags and short on both logic and story line, bearing out Sennett's contention in later years that in spite of his strong belief that comedy had to be logical to be successful, he had paid little attention to plot and continuity at the time by the simple expedient of piling one gag on top of another so fast that audiences weren't able to look for a linear story line to follow.

This sort of non-structure was characteristic of the majority of the split-reel Keystone releases. *Peeping Pete* (released June 26, 1913, and directed by Mack) opened by establishing Sennett as the culprit watching Sterling's wife through a knothole in the fence. When Sterling steps around the fence to catch Mack in the act, a chase begins and continues in and out of buildings on a western set (probably Ince's). When this form of hide and seek is exhausted of its comic potential, the two bump into each other around a corner during a momentary lull in the action and the sequence takes off with another chase. The wrap-up comes in a cut-away shot to Nick Cogley and the rest of the cast dashing around a corner where they find the two adversaries seated calmly at a table toasting each other, apparently the best of friends. Other than as the result of the opening confrontation between the two comics, there was no logic to the chase between the opening and closing scenes, and no explanation for the sudden friendship that brought it all to a close. . . .

One of the most memorable Kop pictures centered around *A Muddy Romance*, 1913, filmed when Echo Park lake was drained.

Ford eyes Mabel across the yard and she responds. Thinking she's his, our hero rushes across the way with flowers, only to receive a drenching from her boyfriend inside. Picking up a pie from the barrel, Ford lets Mabel have it by mistake. The two lovers rush off to the park and hire a boat. Right behind them, Sterling has a bright idea and opens the drain. Officer Sennett calls for help and Rube Miller leads the Kops to the scene of the dastardly deed where the blundering idiots get stuck in the mud as the water level disappears. Park attendant Mack Swain puts in an appearance which only serves to annoy Ford and as the Kops finally make the rescue, Ford pretends to commit suicide, but as the crowd mourns his passing, he gets up and sneaks away. . . .

In spite of the fanciful stories about taking a crew and camera out to film a comedy at the drop of an idea, some form of production organization was necessary to produce even these simple comedies, and with the advent of Keystone's move to full-reel subjects in early 1913 the need for such organization became even more pressing. Once a basic premise was decided upon, locations had to be selected and camera positions marked off for use. Some rudimentary form of rehearsal was required to keep the action within a suitable camera range and prevent the comics from moving beyond the camera's field of view. Sennett usually plotted these things himself, with a secretary following closely behind him to jot down notes, thoughts and ideas that would later be incorporated into a script of sorts. While the casual, off-the-cuff manner of filming associated with the Keystone Legend makes a much more colorful story, when analyzed the comedies themselves implicitly deny this approach.

Filmed in February 1913, *A Strong Revenge* (released March 10, 1913) was the third of the full-reel Keystones to be released, and a high degree of continuity in both plot and action is exhibited in this story of two rivals for Mabel's hand. When Sterling throws a party for her to announce their engagement (he hopes), Sennett pops in to press his case at Ford's expense. But a piece of limburger cheese which Sterling has cleverly deposited in his rival's back pocket quickly alienates those present and Mack is ejected. Once he discovers the source of the unpleasant odor, he returns to extract his revenge for the embarrassment and the party quickly dissolves into a two-man chase.

Production planning was clearly evident in the matching of interior and exterior shots for correct lighting and balance. The composition of the interior shots was too well balanced not to have been carefully pre-planned, and the intercutting of medium, medium close-up and close-ups to form a sequence showed a sophistication of camera work that could not have been accomplished by shooting "off-the-cuff." In a few instances, Sennett did send camera crews out with one or two lead comics to take advantage of some event that could be used to good advantage in a comedy; the draining of a city lake provided an opportunity for the Keystone Kops to enjoy a mud bath. When this footage was brought back and screened, Mack would decide whether or not it had merit, and if it did, a comedy was constructed around it. In a limited number of circumstances, such as this one, it could truthfully be said that although the central comic action was shot spontaneously, the comedy in which it appeared was nevertheless still the result of planning. . . .

Sennett's world of Keystone was fundamentally one of absurdity, in which dignity and refinement were revealed as a sham and replaced by vulgarity and ridicule. His comedians thumbed their noses at convention, and life on the Keystone screen was stripped of the masks society had imposed upon human behavior. Impulse and emotion replaced reason and rationality as the motivators of human action, and the hypocrisy of society's sacred institutions was laid bare for all to see. Married men flirted with other women while their spouses sought the attentions of other men; any criminal fresh from prison could easily pass as a pious clergyman (and did) with as much authority as the real article could command; the human frailties that cause us to hire police for protection from ourselves and our fellow men were just as much a part of their nature; the badge and uniform didn't really change the man in Keystone's view. . . .

Keystone did not share the worshipful reverence toward the machine that characterized the progress man was making in altering his environment. Elevators and escalators were as dangerous as revolving doors, which in Sennett's world could turn the simple act of exiting or entering into an obstacle course that threatened life and limb. Automobiles and aeroplanes were sublimely ridiculous devices whose utility was questionable, yet Henry's Ford refused to be conquered by mere man, often playing a large role in the frenzied on-screen follies, but inevitably ending as it began its existence — a jumble of metal parts reposing peacefully at the base of a tree, telephone pole or other immovable object. Sometimes meeting head-on, sometimes sailing over a cliff or from the end of a pier into the ocean, flivvers became comic objects in themselves, thus foregoing the dignity man had bestowed upon his mechanical horse in real life. . . .

Sennett was at his best in the cutting room, where he exercised a near-total control over what went into a finished comedy during the early years. While Mack's judgment in this area was exceptional, it must be remembered that his taste in humor sprang from the same roots as that of his audience. But Mack also possessed what seemed to be an innate sense of pacing and unity unmatched by most other producers during 1912-15. This quality was exercised with a finite touch by Sennett, who was well known for his ability to improve a sequence by additional (and occasionally drastic) editing. While Mack claimed to be "ruthless" at the cutting table, throwing away five feet of film for every foot he approved, detractors could as easily say that his directors were overly extravagant in giving him material to cut. . . .

An unusual lot, the majority of his early directors were promoted from within, in keeping with Sennett's frequent public announcements that he had developed his directoral staff from the ranks to make certain they were keenly attuned to the requirements of the Keystone comic style. Charles Avery, Nick Cogley, Dell Henderson, Wilfred Lucas, George Nichols and Glen Cavender were primarily actors, as were Mabel Normand, Ford Sterling and Roscoe Arbuckle, who directed the majority of their own films after 1913. Harry Williams was a songwriter-turned-gagman, William Campbell also earned his keep as a comedy writer, Ed Frazee came from the property department and Fred Fishback turned in his Kop uniform for the megaphone.

But as time passed and the company grew, the situation changed. The Triangle period found Walter Wright, Frank Griffin, Clarence Badger, Victor Heerman, Harry Edwards, Eddie Cline and F. Richard Jones joining the ranks from other companies, turning in consistently acceptable work without an apprenticeship as a Kop or supporting comedian. In fact, the latter three men still rank high on any list of outstanding comedy directors of any era.

The irreverence and near-total improbability of the earliest Keystones was gradually tempered as longer comedies became the accepted pattern, and by mid-1913, the formula Keystone was rapidly evolving from a frenzied study of movement into a more durable format which allowed time for study and reflection. *Fatty Joins The Force* (November 24, 1913) is an excellent example of a majority of the basic Keystone precepts coming together at one time to form a highly structured end product.

Directed by George Nichols, who did some fascinating things with Roscoe Arbuckle and from whom Fatty learned the rudiments of comic screen direction, this little jewel found Arbuckle and Dot Farley strolling along the water's edge, enjoying the scenery at the park. Tragedy threatens when a little girl falls into the water. Not about to risk his life to become a hero, Fatty is pushed in by Dot, and in saving himself accidentally rescues the child, who turns out to be the police commissioner's daughter. Learning of her identity, Arbuckle reacts as though he had committed a ghastly crime, giving the distinct impression that he and the law have tangled before. But the temptation to see how the other half lives is too great and Fatty accepts his reward, becoming a genuine policeman.

The measure of his mistake becomes clear when Arbuckle tries to break up a fight in the park and is suddenly forced to defend himself against both parties involved, who make it clear that no oversized representative of justice should interfere in man's God-given right to brawl. The pace then breaks as Fatty relaxes and nurses his bruised ego on a park bench with Dot, at peace with the world and himself, but resumes once more when a gang of kids intrude for a touch of their favorite sport — Kop baiting. The sequence ends with a thoroughly demoralized Arbuckle wearing a pie on his face.

Disregarding the "No Swimming" sign, Fatty takes a refreshing dip in the lake to clean up, but while he enjoys this idyllic interlude, our hero's uniform is picked up and turned in to the station, bringing the Keystone Kops into action to drag the lake for his body. Meanwhile, Fatty has discovered his loss and hides in the bushes, scaring the wits out of little old ladies, who report a wild man loose in the park. For once, the Kops emerge the victors; they capture the "wild man" and haul him off to the station house, where they discover the culprit to be their newest member. Enraged at finding the dead hero a live coward, the Chief locks him up, throws away the key and turns his attention to a neglected Dot.

Using the comic techniques of violence, improbability, vulgarity and absurdity in the best tradition, but moving at a rather modest speed for a Keystone, *Fatty Joins The Force* contained four distinct sequences, each separated by a break in pacing; taken as a whole, it signaled a change in Sennett's comic format. His comedies would undergo further evolution in pacing until the Triangle period, when more carefully developed stories required a degree of comic characterization impossible to achieve in the hustle and bustle of the earlier farces.

DONALD W. McCAFFREY
The Sennett Comic Pudding

Between the "polite poke" at Victorian standards expressed in John Bunny's little plays and the "child-like spirit of fun" in Barney Oldfield's Race for a Life, Professor McCaffrey clearly prefers the fast-moving Sennett burlesque of melodrama. He then shares with us in some detail his enjoyment of the slapstick episodes in Tillie's Punctured Romance (1915) probably the first feature-length comedy.

Mickey, made the following year, had quite a different tone, closer to the comedies of Mary Pickford and Harold Lloyd, which tended to bridge the gap between the "genteel" Drew stories and Sennett. Such plotted comedies of character were preferred by many of the critics of the time, including those writing for movie trade papers.

McCaffrey teaches in the English department at the University of North Dakota and was one of the first to make early comedy a subject for classroom study. The selections are from the first chapter of his book, Four Great Comedians: Chaplin, Lloyd, Keaton, Langdon *(A.S. Barnes & Co., 1968).*

The labour and birth of silent screen comedy could be chronicled with many conjectures and the positing of many views on the contributions that made this lively film form a full fledged *enfant terrible* of the arts. Some historians discover its origin springs from the primitive horseplay of the laboratory scientists (who produced burlesque skits before crude cameras) or find this genre evolving from the fertile, whimsical, theatrically oriented little farces of Melies. Other speculators may place the emphasis on the embryonic comic films of the Italian and English "trick films." Furthermore, a film scholar may search out the efforts of the early vaudeville comedian's routine before the camera and see this comedy "turn" as a strong contribution to the growth of the comic film.

After an apprenticeship as an actor with D.W. Griffith and a comedy director for Biograph, Sennett became the fountainhead for the comic film in the 1910's. When he decided to produce his own comedies, he formed his own comedy troupe with the backing of Adam Kessel and Charles Baumann. One of his earliest Keystone Company products, *Cohen at Coney Island*, a one-reel work, was released on September 23, 1912, featuring comedians Ford Sterling, Mabel Normand, and Fred Mace. Writer, director, and actor, totally involved in his works, Sennett existed a world apart from the genteel, theatrical comedies of John Bunny, one of the first comedy stars of motion pictures. Also, Sennett's comedy was a world apart from the light comedy of Mary Pickford, Douglas Fairbanks, and the team, Mr. and Mrs. Sidney Drew. These actors embraced the genteel tradition, with very small dashes of slapstick. With Sennett, on the other hand, the spice became the pudding. His works had all the wild antics of the chase and trick films of the early French and Italian producers. But Sennett developed his own brand of slapstick. He often burlesqued the serious films of his day, and in doing so, evolved a type of comic film which established a tradition.

The recipe for the Sennett comic pudding was essentially simple and straightforward. His Keystone films brewed up a *potpourri* of broad physical actions: fights, chases, accidental falls, relentless pursuits, and bungled rescues. Keystone peopled its one- and two-reel comic world with caricatures; the fat, the skinny, the rich, the poor, the stupid, the pompous, the shy, the aggressive. These cartoon-like portraits became embroiled in misunderstandings, misrepresentations, meaningless altercations, and even clandestine affairs. The plotting of the little farces sprang from material as uncomplicated as a *commedia dell' arte* scenario of the 17th century. One quality dominated the films — a nose-thumbing, anti-sentimental treatment of character and situation.

Sennett overrated the significance of his comic pokes at authority by declaring that when his comedians kicked a policeman or a society matron "the common people took a lick at all the upstarts, or intrenched, or pretentious people . . . the downfall of pretension runs through most great comic works, emphatically including Shakespeare." Such a justification for slapstick comedy seems in itself pretentious. Nevertheless, Sennett's lusty comedy did not depend on his application of comic theory: it just *was*. It did not have time to follow rules. Fortunately it did not have the saccharine politeness of much of the light comedy of the time; such works cleared a pathway for a more lively, honest comedy that was to follow.

Many of Sennett's works were burlesques of serious films, novels, and events of the times. For example, the climactic fight and chase sequences were embraced by serious film-makers in the 1910's and 1920's. It took a man like Sennett to lampoon the excesses in the treatment of such material. The heroic and sentimental poses of the protagonists of the popular fiction of the time needed deflation. The irreverent kick on the rump which Sennett directed at many *mores* of the times provoked a cool, refreshing breeze in the world of popular entertainment.

With great drive and the obsession of a Fuller Brush salesman, Sennett established a comedy mill that turned out a mass produced product. As many as nineteen comedies were in various stages of completion at one time, a production procedure that parallels, in a sense, today's method of creating films for television series. As with many mass produced items, there was a shortage of quality. The strange fruit of Sennett's mill was ground out — one-reel comedies were thrown together in a week or even a few days; the six-reel feature, *Tillie's Punctured Romance* (1915), was shot in forty days according to Sennett's recollection.

The self-named "King of Comedy" was an enterprising producer who by personality and design could only loosely be called a creator. He was more of a manager or ringmaster and, at best, an entrepreneur. He gathered a battery of actors, acrobats, animals, gag writers, and directors to his bosom. True, he supervised the handling of the story material for practically all of his films, but it would be difficult to determine how much credit he can be given for a raucous film genre of which he has been called "creator." The contributions of others, such as Hal Roach and Al Christie, should not be overlooked. These men and others, chiefly the four great cinema comedians, Chaplin, Lloyd, Keaton, and Langdon, were to develop that genre which Sennett promoted with all his considerable energy and dogged effort.

A taskmaster with a giant ego, Sennett ruled his kingdom with all the authority he could muster. To his odd collection of low-brow clowns and hack writers he was just short of being a slave driver. According to biographer Gene Fowler, he did not like to argue or be contradicted. . . .

The exact nature of Sennett's films can be seen by comparing one of his works with John Bunny's *A Cure for Pokeritis*, a 1912 one-reel comedy replete with gentility. While Bunny's development of a comic character and his skill in acting may be applauded, the story and comic invention of his film are trite, laboured, and superficially sentimental. The humour of this work leans heavily on the minor foibles of a husband who is addicted to card playing. The husband's attempts to outwit his wife in order to carry on his vice are thwarted when a kindly young man called Cousin Freddie gets his Bible class to imitate policemen and raid the poker playing den of erring husbands. Since the wives of the offenders are a part of this conspiracy, they stage a feigned rescue after their husbands are collared by Freddie's mock police force. The "sinners" are grateful and repent as the last scene of the film fades to black. By today's standards, this work is so bland that it scarcely produces a flicker of a smile from

from a viewer. It is slow moving and theatrically oriented. The humorous situations obviously reflect an age in the grips of Victorian codes of behaviour. At best, the film could be designated as a polite poke at such standards; but, there seems to be a half-caress in the jab — sentiment produces creampuff humour.

In sharp contrast, Sennett's *Barney Oldfield's Race for a Life*, made only a year later in 1913, is a lively, humorous work far removed from the comedies of the genteel tradition. This one-reel film employs three times as many shots as Bunny's 1912 work and uses a fast paced comic rescue scene for its closing episode. It burlesques the melodrama, especially the type produced by the Eclectic Company which in 1913 turned out works with such excessive titles as *Doom of the Ocean, Fatal Plunge, Message of the Dead, His Fateful Passion,* and *Toils of Villainy*: later, in 1914, this company produced the famous serial *The Perils of Pauline*, starring Pearl White. Sennett's take-off of such works has many crude, stock devices of burlesque, but the film cannot be accused of dullness. The acting is artless even for this formative age of cinema when actors in serious films often aped the broad style of the stage. Ford Sterling as the comic villain struts and hops around as if he were playing to a theatre audience of four thousand. Mack Sennett as the country bumpkin who loves the heroine (played by Mabel Normand) slips in and out of character with each changing of locality and situation. Nevertheless, there is a broad, child-like spirit of fun that lifts this work above the polished, well-acted efforts of *A Cure for Pokeritis*. Action is cinematic — the actors move in depth, toward and away from the camera; the editing of the rescue scene assists the pace greatly. Three parallel actions are skillfully blended in this chase; the villain is shown trying to kill the heroine; the rescuers, Barney Oldfield and the comic oaf (Sennett's character), speed in a racer; and the embryonic Keystone Cops struggle with a railroad handcar to get to the scene of the assault.

Interestingly enough, Sennett's fresh, vivacious comedy may have achieved many of these cinematic techniques because of the method he used to shoot his films. He often filmed his early works without the benefit of elaborate sets and costumes. But his movies developed a liveliness that can be found in a spirited, devil-may-care amateur who decides to establish a little theatre or shoot a movie on a shoe string.

A look at a later work, *Tillie's Punctured Romance* (1915) reveals even more characteristics of the Sennett movie. This work gave the comedy prestige in an age of one- and two-reelers by extending the film to the unheard of length of six reels. This film might be called a prototype for many feature comedy works. A detailed examination of this movie, therefore, becomes an important springboard for this study of the leading clowns of the silent screen comedy.

Freely adapted from Marie Dressler's successful musical comedy, *Tillie's Nightmare*, Mack Sennett's movie version is a burlesque of the Cinderella story. It contains much-used plot elements from the stage and popular literature of the times. A crafty dandy lures an innocent country girl to the big city, rejects her after he has stolen her money, and rushes back to marry her when he hears she has inherited a fortune. During the 19th century such material would be treated sentimentally in the popular stage melodrama. Sennett's treatment, however, is anti-sentimental, although it retains some of the intrigue of such a plot line to hold the interest of the audience.

At the outset of the film, the burlesque treatment can be readily realised by the establishment of the comic characters. The City Slicker, a comic villain played by Charles Chaplin, is diminutive in size and cunning; he strikes seedy, flamboyant poses as he tries to charm the ladies. The victim of his scheme, Tillie, a farmer's daughter (played by Marie Dressler), is the antithesis of the sweet charming country maid. The character is not shy, but a horse of a woman who walks over clods in the field like a waddling bear. When she is wooed, her affectionate touches are as gentle as the rabbit punch of a lady wrestler. Other personalities in this early portion of the film are bucolic caricatures from vaudeville of the 1910's and the late 19th century stage comedy.

The plot is unified by a triangle situation that results in a rivalry between the City Slicker's girl friend and Tillie — a complication that develops in the second sequence of the film when the comic villain lures Tillie to the city. This conflict continues until the resolution of the film; the dandy is rejected and the two rivals become warm friends.

Above all, the meat of this prototype of the feature length comic film lies in a whole gamut of slapstick. Most noticeable in the early sequences of the film is the broad physical humour of abuse. Brickbats fly through the air, thrown intentionally or accidentally, and send the victim sprawling. Minor insults promote a cuff to the side of the face or the jaw; and kicks on the rump abound. More cleverly motivated than such stock comedy producing devices, Tillie's gesticulations account for some of the best slapstick. When she waves her arms to express her joy, one of her hands inevitably hits the end of the City Slicker's nose. Crude as it may seem, Tillie often produces a swing of her hips that strikes the little man and sends him teetering and crumpling to the ground. Affectionately, the country maid tosses a bouquet of flowers in the dandy's face with enough force to bowl him over; he smiles tightly and counters with a brickbat which evidently hurts but barely moves her bulk.

In the second sequence of the film, Tillie gets drunk in a restaurant and creates a grotesque spectacle as she is taken to the police station. She tries to dance with her escorting policeman and joyfully, affectionately slaps him. In the jail she bites the chief of police's finger.

Physical indignities are heaped upon the servants of Tillie's inherited mansion in sequence four of the work. In one of the longer, sustained pantomime routines of the film, Chaplin's genius in portraying the crudities of the *nouveau riche* produces a sparkling scene. A detailed quote from a scenario which I've prepared in the study of this film will best illustrate how rich with insult humour this work becomes:

> 246 LS — Charlie and Tillie walk into the plush room of the mansion from the background left. Servants stand at attention right and left, showing the new owners the way. One servant, on the left side — where Charlie stops — extends his arm. Charlie hangs his cane on the outstretched arm and places his hat in the servant's hand. Tillie points out that the other servant has nothing. Charlie gives him the hat and then leans back on the servant's chest. He then turns to this man and blows smoke from his cigarette into his face. He takes out the servant's lapel handkerchief and blows his nose on it — returns it by draping it over his hand. Charlie leans his elbow on the chest of the servant, crosses his legs nonchalantly, and listens to Tillie talk. Tillie leans against the other servant's chest — the one on the right. Again Charlie blows smoke in the servant's face; the servant sneezes; Charlie glares at him. Tillie comes over to this "offending" servant and slaps his face. Then for no particular reason at all, she goes to the servant on the right and gives him a short jab to the chin with the palm of her hand. . . .

A variation on such slapstick of abuse is used in sequence five. Much of the comedy focuses on the bungled attempts of Tillie and her husband to become society lions. Drinking too much punch, they try imitating the dance steps of two professional entertainers who have been hired for their party. Tillie drags her husband about the dance floor and dances with a vigour that sends Charlie twirling into a dizzy collapse.

Sequence six, the last one of the film, shows characteristics of the final portion of the two-reel comedies of the time. Fight and chase situations compose the material for this lively sequence. A rich gentleman, Mr. Woozis (played by Chester Conklin), and Charlie get into a "knock-'em-down-and-drag-'em-out" fight. The "little tramp," slightly tipsy from too much punch, puts his right foot on the gentleman's lap — an act which incites the wild fight. Charlie is the victor of the combat because of the energy of his dogged assault and the deft french kicks which he places soundly on Mr. Woozis's chest. The ease and mock dignity with which Chaplin executes his dance-like moves show excellent use of knockabout comedy. Clearly, such pantomime illustrates Chaplin's training in the music hall stages of London.

Far more cinematic in treatment, the final chase portion of the film shows Charlie and his girl friend, Mabel, being pursued by a wild-eyed, furious Tillie who blazes away at them with a pistol. Bungling policemen rush to the scene of the altercation. Typical frantic actions of the Keystone Cops fill the screen with a madcap rush and tumble. Sennett shows the running policemen bumping into pedestrians, falling from a speeding, open-topped automobile, and driving their car crazily down the street. The car finds its mark and knocks Tillie off a pier into the ocean. Then, the would-be rescuers have the driver of the vehicle back away from the accident, but argue over the wheel so vehemently that the automobile weaves to the end of the pier again and plunges into the water. More police arrive and after three blundering attempts to lift the elephantine Tillie from the ocean (where she is fighting off crabs and fish), they finally rescue the weary, water-logged comic heroine. . . .

> Burlesque and farce are becoming less and less popular, and there is no real demand for stories of this type. The comedy producers are desirous of polite, plausible situation comedies, preferably founded upon an amusing situation that might very naturally occur in the life of almost any spectator.

Frederick Palmer expressed this view in 1922 as he criticised a two-reel Christie comedy called *Her Bridal Nightmare* in a book which was intended to be a guide for scenario writers. If this statement is viewed with the historical perspective of today, it is obvious that Palmer overstated the situation. Many slapstick-filled burlesques and farces were ground out by the Mack Sennett and Hal Roach comedy mills even in the late Twenties. There was a trend, however, which formed the basis for this overstatement.

Genteel comedy's invasion of the screen world was helped greatly by the success of the short films of John Bunny and the comedy team of Mr. and Mrs. Sidney Drew. As this type of

drama took a firm grip in the 1910's, a wealth of light comedy actresses came into the limelight. Such famous women as Mary
Pickford, Dorothy Gish, Zasu Pitts, and Mabel Normand found
light comedy features their province. Mary Pickford had pre-
ceded Bunny and the Drews in her exploitation of polite comedy
filled with sentiment. . . . But by far the most interesting comedienne to embrace the genteel tradition was Mabel Normand.

Miss Normand was schooled by Mack Sennett in the rough
and tumble world of slapstick. She was known as a deft thrower
(and receiver) of the custard pie. In August, 1916, Sennett had
Bob Jones, a heretofore slapstick director and stunt man, launch
into a full-length film that was spiritually far removed from the
wild capers of *Tillie's Punctured Romance*. It was a sentimental
rags-to-riches movie that would have fitted Mary Pickford perfectly. A brief synopsis of the film's story from a contemporary
review reveals the well worn Cinderella story from the popular
magazine fiction of the age:

> Mickey has been brought up with little regard for conventions out
> West. Her aunt, believing she owns a gold mine, invites her East, but
> upon finding she has no money, puts her to work as a servant. While
> West, Mickey has met and fallen in love with a wealthy young man
> her aunt had intended to marry her daughter to, but he had, instead
> been captured by Mickey, so when he, too, comes East, he manages
> to free himself from aunty's designs and marries Mickey instead.
> [*Dramatic Mirror*, August 17, 1918.]

As Eileen Bowser, Assistant Curator of the Museum of Modern Art Film Library, so aptly observes, the film employs material like that used by Mary Pickford: "In *The Foundling*, made the
year before *Mickey*, Miss Pickford had played a similar and typical part, that of the mischievous and innocent little orphan, loved
by all right-thinking people and abused by the evil ones."*

What, one may ask, is funny about such material? The answer
may be a simple: "Not much." The basic material for the polite or
genteel comedy is often lacking in a strong central comic idea.
Comedy seems grafted onto a serious plot. After viewing such
works I believe that the actor or director has often injected comic
routines or simple comic business during the shooting of the
scenes, but some humorous elements are obviously written into
the script. In *Mickey*, for example, some comic traits of a mild, humorous nature can be observed in the tomboyish activities of the
title character. When the heroine is going to be spanked for her
misbehaviour, she feeds the instrument for punishment, a razor
strap, to a donkey. Also, in high society, Mickey's bad manners

are a subject for comedy. The film nearly engages in slapstick, but restrains itself, when Mickey's Western "parents," Joe and his fat Indian housekeeper, get into altercations with high society. In a final melodramatic fight between the hero and the villain, a burlesque treatment in the one- and two-reel Sennett tradition would seem a likely direction for the film. But director Bob Jones seems to have held back his natural inclinations. He designs the sequence to be taken seriously.

With all its faults, curiously enough, the film has a flair. By modern standards, it cannot be considered a comedy of great merit. Mabel Normand's skill as an actress, her spark and charm, however, save *Mickey*.

Women were not, of course, the most important promoters of the genteel comedy. Light comedians like Douglas MacLean, Charles Ray, Wallace Reid, and Johnny Hines advanced this type of film both in theory and practice. Each of these comedians dealt with material that Harold Lloyd was to employ with considerably more skill.

Johnny Hines, for example, created a two-reel Torchy series in the late 1910's in which light comedy situations revolved around the trials of the "average American boy next door." In the Twenties, Hines acted in many feature length works with such titles as *Burn 'Em Up Barnes*, *Luck*, *The Early Bird*, and *Live Wire* — comedies which, as the titles indicate, displayed the comedy of a young man trying to make good. Bernard Sobel's review of Hines's *Burn 'Em Up Barnes* reveals the nature of the material used in this film. Evidently the film used slick magazine story material involving a devil-may-care protagonist who was addicted to speeding around town in a racing car. An advertisement in *The Film Year Book 1925* makes capital of this quality by pointing out the virtues of Johnny Hines's comic character. Hines "typifies the American Go-getter," the advertisement reads as it announces that Hines's films offer "clean, smart, wholesome comedy that will be an inspiration to the youth of the land." . . .

In 1919 comedian Charles Ray appeared in a feature-length film, *The Sheriff's Son*, a work which displays many similarities to Lloyd's *Grandma's Boy* (1922). In theme, the two works are strikingly similar. In *The Sheriff's Son*, Ray plays the role of a meek, cowardly boy who overcomes a gang of outlaws despite his reputation for cowardliness. A year later Ray appeared in a feature-length comedy called *Homer Comes Home*, a work which related a tale of a young man going to the big city to gain employment as a clerk; he becomes successful enough to be given a managerial post in his home town, and he wins the girl friend who has waited for him back home. . . .

Although Wallace Reid was not considered a high-ranking comedian in the late 1910's and the early Twenties, he was a popular star who was versatile enough to play in both serious and comic works. In 1920 he applied his talents to a comic film with all the ingredients of the Hines, Ray, and MacLean features. From the popular literature of the time, Reid's enactment of a rural comic type, called Sylvester Tibble, provided another portrait of a young man striving for success. In this film, *The Dancin' Fool*, the young man from the country looks for his fortune in the big city. With the ambition characteristic of the Horatio Alger hero, he sets his uncle's business on a profitable basis by putting his ingenuity to work over his uncle's resistance to a country lad who, the uncle feels, is not a responsible addition to his factory.

Like *Mickey*, *The Dancin' Fool* incorporates sympathetic roles that an audience feels are close to their own lives. At least, it provides the illusion of characters that are known or might be encountered even though personal identification is not present. Such characters are warm and gentle; they have ambitions and tastes similar to those of the average man. They are not the odd, outcast protagonists of the slapstick tradition.

Three of the major comedians of the Twenties, Lloyd, Keaton, and Langdon, were influenced by the genteel tradition but were generally able to avoid its fault by retaining the spirit of and much material from the slapstick tradition. Lloyd, more than the other two, drew heavily on both the story material and the characterisations of the genteel comedy. . . .

But Lloyd did not create a sentimental portrait. He blended many facets which the polite comedians used and many that were different. In the shy young man there was a degree of will or determination that took on some of the characteristics which Douglas MacLean and Johnny Hines employed in their comic portraits. Furthermore, and probably most important of all, he did not reject as many of the facets of the slapstick character. He retained an aggressiveness in his comic character that was similar to the comedian's bold spirit when he faced opposition in his early one- and two-reel comedies. In moments of desperation in the feature-length works of the 1920's, Lloyd's character took drastic steps — he even stole a car or struck a policeman to achieve his goal.

Lloyd, therefore, was eclectic in the development of his comic character. The added dimension and flexibility of comic portrayal which resulted from such a practice may account in part for his eclipsing of the "country boys" and "go-getters" in popularity.

To a lesser degree, Keaton and Langdon changed their comic characters under the influence of the genteel comedy. When Keaton turned to features, his portrayal was altered to provide a broader basis for comic variety and story development. His John McKay of *Our Hospitality* (1923) takes on the facets of a determined young man who desires to claim his inheritance and win the affection of a girl. In his one- and two-reel works, Keaton's character was usually that of a little outcast without connections — without a family or a place to go. His *Sherlock Jr.* (1924) and *The General* (1927) feature comic protagonists who are small town boys with some of the same traits and problems of the genteel comedy character. Langdon retained modified traits of the little tramp in his *Strong Man* (1926) and turned toward the country lad in his *Long Pants* (1927). However, his modulation of character under the influence of genteel comedy was not as strong as either Lloyd's or Keaton's.

All three comedians dipped heavily into the plot materials of the genteel comedy. Lloyd's works, *Grandma's Boy* (1922), *Safety Last* (1923), and *The Freshman* (1925) are comic variations on the success story. Personal, business, and social achievement are essayed in a laughable way. Keaton's comic character was driven by child-like desire to be a detective in *Sherlock, Jr.* and a soldier in *The General*. Such desires were the mainspring of the plot development in his films. Less endowed with will than the comic portraits of Lloyd and Keaton, Langdon's character wistfully desired to be a man and a great lover in *Long Pants*.

While these three comedians used some of the same type of story material employed by Charles Ray, Douglas MacLean, and Johnny Hines, they handled their material differently. They did not directly adapt material from the literature of the day, nor did they employ a scenario as did these light comedians. Their working method remained more flexible by the retention of the off-the-cuff story plotting and shooting methods of the one- and two-reel comedies of the 1910's. On the other hand, Ray, MacLean, and Hines were often bound to the incidents of the magazine short story or the comic stage play. Such works as Hines's *The Live Wire*, MacLean's *One a Minute*, and Ray's *The Sheriff's Son* and *Homer Comes Home* are adaptations.

This more flexible method of handling story materials allowed Lloyd, Keaton, and Langdon greater latitude in developing their comedies. The story could be patterned to their acting abilities and to the characters they were portraying. Gags could arise from improvisation while shooting a scene. It would seem that such a working method would lead to episodic story development, but the comedians were usually able to prevent this by their strong control on production details and by constantly reminding themselves and their writers of the total flow of the dramatic story.

* From Eileen Bowser's unpublished programme notes on *Stenographer Wanted* (1912), *Goodness Gracious* (1914) and *Mickey* (1916-1918).

MACK SENNETT
The Psychology of Film Comedy

Here is some heavy thinking by the boss of the Keystone studio about what makes people laugh. Sennett is a lot more sweeping and simplified on this subject than Chaplin, whose writing style is also more ingenious and involving. Sennett decides to pick two main themes, the fall of dignity and mistaken identity. One gets the idea that he and the publicity man who helped him write this might have picked some other themes on some other day.

He sounds like an experienced producer, though, when he tells us there are unacceptable targets: the audience will not accept pies thrown at pretty girls or Shetland ponies. His opening example proposes that a gag needs space around it. It is particularly informative for aspiring funmakers and reveals some of his personal directorial skills in the editing room.

This piece appeared in a magazine called Motion Picture Classic *in November 1918.*

There was no doubt about it; the comedy looked like a flop.

In the scenario, it read like a yell. In rehearsal, it was still better. When they were taking the picture it seemed as tho there would be a laugh in every foot of film. Even the camera-man laughed, beyond which there is no possible tribute.

But when I saw it in the projecting room, the thing went bla-a-a — Especially the big scene with the china closet.

It was a very funny idea. Paddy McGuire and Chester Conklin were papering a room. One end of their scaffolding rested on the top of a cabinet of fancy china. Suddenly the end of the plank slipped and crashed into the Limoges; it took another bump and smashed all the Haviland on the next shelf. And so it went, bump, bump, bump, thru all the grades of fancy crockery to the floor.

In front of the camera it had been uproariously funny — frightfully comic, as our overseas Allies say. In the projecting-room it fell flat.

Comedies are not like murderers, however. They get more than one trial.

When one of our comedies is finished, it is usually about five times as long as it is when the public finally sees it. During the period of cutting it, we give many little performances in the projecting-room. Sometimes the projecting-theater is crowded. Sometimes there is an audience of only half-a-dozen scene-shifters and mechanics — a very discriminating audience, I may remark by the way.

We tried this gag on all of them. It didn't get over. Yet I knew that it was funny.

At last the reason dawned upon me. I cut the film and tried it again on a mixed audience made up of actors, scene-shifters, directors, mechanics and counting-room clerks. This time they yelled their heads off.

The reason the gag was not funny in its original form was due to the way it was placed in the film. Just before the scaffold broke thru the china there was a very exciting chase. Two or three men were pursuing a scared ltitle fellow around a swimming tank, shooting at him with guns. It was funny, but it was too long. In order to really "get" that scene with the china you had to be paying very close attention. You had to see and appreciate the fact that it was expensive china before the scaffolding began bumping into it. Chester Conklin was trying to surprise his wife by papering a room of their house. You can imagine the lady's surprise when she came home and found what had happened to her china. To thoroly "get" this gag you had to very clearly appreciate the fact that it was her treasure and pride. The shooting scene left you a little tired, mentally, and in no mood to give the close concentration necessary.

It is a curious thing to say that a noise spoiled the gag; but it really did. You failed to hear the imaginary crash of china on account of the greater imaginary noise of the shooting.

I took out most of the chase and transposed the position of what remained. Then the gag got over. I didn't make it any funnier. It had been funny all the time. All I did was to give it a chance to make itself heard.

Gozzi, the famous Italian dramatist, demonstrated conclusively, as the result of examining thousands of plays, that there are only thirty-six possible dramatic situations. There are only a handful of possible jokes.

The chief members of this joke band may be said to be:

The fall of dignity.

Mistaken identity.

Almost every joke on the screen belongs, roughly, to one or the other of these clans.

For instance, here are some of the old, reliable veterans:

Two detectives masquerade as burglars to catch another burglar and catch each other. Mistaken identity.

Rich old uncle comes to visit his nephew, to whom he is to give a hundred thousand dollars on condition that nephew marries and produces an heir. Uncle, on arrival, is mistaken for a servant and put to work in the kitchen. Mistaken identity again.

Young hubby plans to scare his wife by masquerading as a burglar. She finds out the scheme and entertains a real burglar under the impression it is her husband. Mistaken identity.

Hotel clerk gets room numbers mixed. Young hubby comes home unexpectedly and finds a man in the room where he expected to find his wife. Mistaken identity.

Pie-throwing in comedy is based directly or indirectly upon the fall of dignity. There is nothing funny about hitting a man with a pie. The joke is in throwing a pie at one man and hitting another; in aiming at a tramp and hitting your rich, old aunt.

Parenthetically, it may be remarked that comedy directors often fail with a gag thru lack of discrimination. There are certain characters whom the public wants to see roughly handled; there are others who are immune from rough stuff. It is not always clear why.

For instance, you can always be safe in hitting a policeman, a comedy policeman, that is to say. There is no American who, as a boy, has not dreamed of caving in the helmet of a cop with a mighty swat that will send it down around his ears. Most of us have never gotten over the feeling. Nearly every one of us lives in the secret hope that some day before he dies he will be able to swat a policeman's hat down around his ears. Lacking the courage and the opportunity, we like to see it done in the movies.

The copper is fair game for pies, likewise any fat man. Fat faces and pies seem to have a peculiar affinity. If the victim is fat enough the movie public will tolerate any kind of rough stuff.

On the other hand, movie fans do not like to see pretty girls smeared up with pastry. Shetland ponies and pretty girls are immune.

It is an axiom of screen comedy that a Shetland pony must never be put in an undignified position. People don't like it. You can take any kind of liberties with a donkey. They even like to see the noble lion rough-housed, but not a pony. You might as well show Santa Claus being mistreated.

The immunity of pretty girls doesn't go quite as far as the immunity of the Shetland pony, however. You can put a pretty girl in a comedy shower bath. You can have her fall into mud puddles. They will laugh at that. But the spectacle of a girl dripping with pie is displeasing.

Preachers in comedy have to be handled with tact and sagacity. If the preacher has side-whiskers and goggles they like to see things happen to him. If he is young and smooth-shaven he is as immune as a blond young lady.

I will not attempt to analyze the reason, but American comedy fans are rather ruthless with old age. The worst mishaps often happen to old people in screen comedies. Especially if they are well-dressed old men. An elegantly dressed elderly man with whiskers is headed straight for misfortune in the movies. He hasn't a chance.

No doubt this is an evidence of the reluctant awe that young America feels for wealthy old age; it is very much like the secret resentment against the policeman. The attitude of a comedy audience toward a judge is very peculiar. For some reason I have never been able to fathom, they like to see them get into domestic scandals. The spectacle of a solemn, old judge being led away by the ear by his irate wife makes a movie audience hug itself with delight.

That pie targets so frequently wear side-whiskers and top hats is rather to be regarded as a convenience of stage mechanics rather than as a settled prejudice against people with zits.

Explanations must be Hooverized to as great an extent as possible in the movies. By custom side-whiskers and stove-pipe hats have come to be recognized as the badge of the official goat of the comedy. Just as a white lawn dress and curls are the sign of the heroine in drama.

These conventions are more marked in comedy than in other forms of movie-drama. In comedy the events are piled on too rapidly to admit of much character drawing. You can't go into the personality of a preacher to show the audience that he is not a proper candidate for sympathy. When you put side-whiskers on him and top him with a stove-pipe hat the movie fans understand the trade-mark. They know that he is due for disasters.

So much for the material out of which comedies are built. Most of the materials are old. All jokes are old, and there are only a few of them. One of the earliest inscriptions found in Egypt was a joke about a mother-in-law told in hieroglyphics.

Skillful comedy direction consists of arrangement of these comedy elements. And the arrangement involves a knowledge — either instinctive or studied — of the psychology of the man sitting out there in the dark in front of the screen. You must know how he thinks and how fast he thinks. The extent to which you get in tune with him is the measure of your screen success.

Like a diamond, a joke depends very largely upon the setting. Nine times out of ten if a gag fails it is because of the poor paving of the way up to it.

This is true of any joke. How many times have you seen a good story ruined because the teller chose a time when the audience was not in the mood to pay attention?

JOE FRANKLIN
Mabel Normand

Her declining years brought tragedy and regrets to Mabel Normand, but the best times at Keystone with Sennett and Chaplin were wacky and wonderful. No woman equalled her popularity, apparently, in the era of silent comedy, and not till Carole Lombard in the 1930s was there another comic personality of similar range. Joe Franklin's Classics of the Silent Screen *(N.Y., Citadel, 1959) offers this encomium on pages 210-211.*

That old movie plot about the clown who made millions laugh but never achieved happiness himself has a striking real-life parallel in the career of Mabel Normand. Perhaps it would be an exaggeration to say that Mabel was never happy; she lived life to the fullest, considering only the present, and having a wonderful time doing it. But her life was such a determined pursuit of a lasting happiness that somehow always eluded her, with tragedy stalking both her private life and her public career, that it seemed almost a mockery of the carefree spright that she played on the screen.

Mabel was a lively girl. "As beautiful as a Spring morning" is the way Mack Sennett once described her. And though she specialized in comedy — both violent slapstick, and gentler Cinderella whimsies — she had exceptional dramatic ability too. Many thought she could have been one of the screen's finest dramatic actresses had she been given the chance. Even in her comedies, there were often moments of pathos or drama that showed there were good foundations for this belief. Indeed, Mabel had started out under Griffith at Biograph as a straight actress. An athletic young lady, and something of a daredevil, she enjoyed doing roles that required a little more strenuous effort than usual. And Griffith, glad to oblige, cast her in films like *The Squaw's Love*, in which, as an Indian girl, she had to struggle with a rival atop some high rocks, dive into the river below, and swim under water to wreck the canoes of the her Indian pursuers.

While at Biograph, Mabel met Mack Sennett, then struggling along as a writer and actor, but with definite ideas of his own about making films — comedy films. Mabel and Mack were attracted to each other, and for a time it seemed that they would get married. Indeed, it seemed so on and off during the ensuing years — but unconsciously Mabel's restless nature seemed to rebel at the idea of settling down to marriage. Two wedding dates were set; both were called off. But when Sennett left Biograph to set up his own company, Mabel Normand came along with him as his leading star.

In the Keystone comedies that followed, Mabel worked like the proverbial horse. If it was for a laugh, nothing was too much trouble. She was manhandled and tied to the railroad tracks in *Barney Oldfield's Race for a Life*; dragged through a muddy lake by the Keystone Cops in *A Mud Bath*, and frequently plastered with goo of one kind or another by Ford Sterling or some other Keystone comedian. Occasionally, in films like *Mabel's Strategem*, in which she had an amusing sequence masquerading as a man and flirting with the boss's wife, she had an opportunity for a subtler kind of comedy, and when she began to be co-starred in Charlie Chaplin films she started to feel that she was worthy of something better than two-reelers. Mack Sennett agreed, and in 1917 put her into a charming seven-reeler called *Mickey*. It was a delightful combination of slapstick, whimsical comedy and pathos; Mabel had a glorious role as a tomboy from the mountains loosed on society, and the film had a jim-dandy melodramatic climax with Mabel fighting off the villain (Lew Cody), and clambering over the roof of a crumbling old mansion until rescued by the hero (Wheeler Oakman), who gave the villain his come-uppance in a terrific fistic set-to.

Mickey was a wonderful picture, but somehow nobody seemed to want it. It lay on the shelf for over a year, and Mabel drifted away from Sennett, doing features elsewhere. She seemed bored with life, yet determined to find pleasure in every waking moment. She was an ice-cream-for-breakfast girl — and her parties went on late into the night. Rest and relaxation just weren't allowed for on her schedule. Then, suddenly, *Mickey* was released and was a tremendous hit. It made a small fortune for Triangle, and Sennett, sure he had found the right formula for Mabel, asked her to come back. But she was vague and evasive. It was to be some time before she was to make another feature for Mack.

And now stories of Mabel's wild living began to circulate around Hollywood. She was late turning up at the studio, sometimes disappeared for days at a time. Once she even took off unannounced for Europe. There were hints of scandals, but never anything more than rumors and hearsay. Then, suddenly, came the murder (still unsolved) of beloved and respected director William Desmond Taylor. Since the question of dope came up in the proceedings, the newspapers, still full of the Fatty Arbuckle-Virginia Rappe case, had a field-day. Mabel was involved — deeply — and though she was proved innocent of any connection with the murder, the damage done by yellow journalism was serious. Courageously, she fought back and continued with her work. Just as it seemed that she had risen above it all, she was involved in another scandal in which a prominent Hollywood personality was shot. She was tired and dispirited. And an appearance in a play in New York, for which she was rapped mercilessly by the critics, didn't serve to bolster her sagging spirit.

During all this time, she had been busy making movies. She had made a group for Sam Goldwyn, and had returned to Sennett for some good films — *Susanna, Molly O* and *The Extra Girl.* In the latter she had had some great material, including a still very funny scene where she leads a lion around the studio, fondly imagining that it is merely Teddy, the studio dog, in makeup. It was an unusual Cinderella story in which the small-town-girl *doesn't* make good in Hollywood, and was one of her best pictures since *Mickey.*

But the pace was beginning to tell on Mabel. It was known that she had turned to drugs, and her health was suffering badly. She put on a brave front, but she often looked tired and ill — and the camera eye is perceptive. Her popularity began to wane a little. She no longer felt up to doing features and the studios were unwilling to risk starring her until she was herself again. Almost overnight, she descended from the top rung of stardom and was back where she started. Her last films were two-reel slapstick comedies made not for Sennett but for his rival, Hal Roach. In a last, desperate measure to attain some kind of contentment, she married Lew Cody, an old friend. It was a curious marriage that puzzled all their friends, and it was an unhappy and a tragic one. Both stars were dying — Cody from a heart ailment, news of which he gallantly kept from his wife. Like a meteor which burns itself out by the very speed which gives it light, Mabel Normand had burned herself out. In 1930, she entered a health retreat, suffering from a tubercular condition accelerated by her exhausting and reckless living over the past thirteen years. There, a few months later at the age of 32, she died — just as the silent screen, of which she had been one of the brightest and most beloved stars, was dying too.

Mack Sennett and friend.

1969 Poster, University of Kansas,
by John Tibbetts

Chapter 2

Chaplin

Personally I hated a chase. It dissipates one's
personality; little as I knew about movies, I knew
that nothing transcended personality.
— *Charlie Chaplin.*[1]

Charlie Chaplin: total film author — producer, writer, director, editor, composer, performer, comedian. He was the only person in American history who had total creative control over every aspect of all his feature-length films (and many of the short ones). He also found out how to retain ultimate control financially. Each of his features reverted to his ownership five years after the first release. When he died in Switzerland in 1977 he was a very wealthy man.

During his lifetime Chaplin — as actor and as film maker — probably won more critical praise from a wider range of observers than anyone in the movie business ever has. Albert Einstein sat beside him at the *City Lights* premiere in 1931. Winston Churchill wrote an article about him for *Colliers* magazine in 1935. Bernard Shaw said he was "the only genius of motion pictures," and Thomas Burke called his fellow Englishman the first person in history to be truly world-famous. The American critics James Agee, Robert Sherwood, and

1   Charles Chaplin, *My Autobiography*, (1964) p. 141-2.

Gilbert Seldes called him, in that order, a poet, a great artist, and the one universal man.

Such encomiums make it difficult to write or speak of Chaplin today. There is the temptation on the one hand to be profound and find various symbols in his work, or on the other hand to belittle him in the usual fashion of historical revisionism and call him overrated.

For example, Chaplin today is often downgraded as a director because he did not do very much with editing or camera movement. But that was his very plain particular style. He wanted the camera to be quite calm and watch what Chaplin did. Theorists of cinematics tend to be puzzled by Chaplin or ignore him. Graham Petrie responds to that with irony in a valuable study of writings about Charlie Chaplin: How could a director said to be so ignorant of his medium produce some of the greatest films ever made?[2]

As pantomime artist and comedian, he has probably not been equalled. Combined with these talents for entertainment there was a yearning to do good. Like D.W Griffith and certain other American film makers — Vidor, Capra, Ford, especially — Chaplin had a recurring faith in the power of motion pictures to stir up ideas and change our minds. This occasional concern was most prominent in late films like *The Great Dictator, Modern Times, Monsieur Verdoux, A King In New York.*

"I am naturally pedagogic," he told the *Life* magazine photographer, Eugene Smith.[3] With just four years of schooling, two of them in an orphanage, he used to read John Locke and Schopenhauer in his dressing room, trying to pull himself up intellectually by his bootstraps. The underlying seriousness of some of his ideas, together with his intense, egotistic desire to be accepted by famous people, separated him from the other great clowns of his day.

Unlike Buster Keaton and Harold Lloyd, Chaplin grew up in oppressive poverty and misery. His parents were in show business, but not often. With his father usually missing, he and his mother lived for a time in a third floor London garret in an area much like the slum in his short film *Easy Street.*

2 Graham Petrie, "So Much and Yet So Little: A Survey of Books on Chaplin," *Quarterly Review of Film Studies,* November 1977.
3 *Life,* March 17, 1952.

Similar representations of his sufferings and wanderings can be found in *The Tramp, A Dog's Life, The Kid, City Lights,* and other stories.

Living as he could from odd jobs on the streets after his mother was sent once more to the insane asylum, young Charlie suddenly had a change of luck. He was summoned by a talent agent for a boy's part in a Sherlock Holmes play. In this and other parts he toured for four years until his half-brother Sydney got him a job with the music hall impresario, Fred Karno. This was big business, with buses carrying whole companies out for the day's work at theaters.

Karno had a company touring the U.S.A. and Chaplin went with them in 1910. Mack Sennett saw him perform in New York two years later on his second tour. In need of a new comic, Sennett offered Chaplin $150 a week to join the Keystone studio. Diffident, unsure of himself as he moved to Los Angeles and into films, the new recruit seemed to find his identity when he found his costume. "I wanted everything a contradiction: the pants baggy, the coat tight, the hat small and the shoes large."[4]

He made 35 films during his year at Keystone. Before long he realized that movie-goers were responding to his personality. The orders for his pictures were coming in fast, and he was given the right to direct his own performances. The Essanay Company offered him $1250 a week, and he directed 15 pictures for them. In 1916 his brother arranged for him a staggering deal with Mutual Films, the releasing company for *The Birth of a Nation.* He was to get a bonus of $150,000 and $10,000 a week, with freedom to make 12 two-reelers in his own way. Among the masterpieces he provided were *The Rink, The Pawnshop, The Floorwalker, One A.M., Easy Street, The Cure, The Immigrant, Behind the Screen.*

At about this time theater owners were gearing up to fight Adolph Zukor's near-monopoly of the star system at Famous Players. A new company called First National stole Mary Pickford from Zukor and Chaplin from Mutual — each for a million dollars. Having benefited thus from the corporate wars, Charlie decided to build himself a studio, giving it the exterior look of a series of English cottages. It was for many years a Hollywood landmark at LaBrea and Sunset.

4   Chaplin, p. 144.

From 1918 to 1922 he delivered eight films to First National, three of them longer than two reels: *A Dog's Life, Shoulder Arms,* (a sad/funny dream story of World War I), and *The Pilgrim,* in which he is on the run, has to impersonate a preacher, and pantomimes the whole David and Goliath story at the podium. Another for First National was the first of his that was close to feature length: *The Kid,* (1921, 6 reels) with five-year-old Jackie Coogan. It turned out to be his most successful combination of slapstick and pathos.

Meanwhile in 1919, Chaplin had agreed to join his close friends, Mary Pickford and Douglas Fairbanks, along with D.W. Griffith, a director he had always admired, in forming the United Artists Corporation. He was very slow in delivering product for them, and in later years became (in Mary's eyes) a stubborn and unpredictable partner. But from 1923 to 1940 he made his six greatest features: *A Woman of Paris, The Gold Rush, The Circus, City Lights, Modern Times, The Great Dictator.*

In 1921, Chaplin was starting a new picture, complete with script, sets, and crew, about a wealthy plumber. He was to arrive in a limousine and take tea with his lady customer. Then he would bring out a stethoscope to listen to the ailing pipes.[5] It was a promising premise. But he suddenly realized he was totally exhausted and needed a vacation. He may have recalled the exhilarating surprise of his railroad trip to New York City in 1916 when he first discovered how popular he was. At every city on the way, there had been enormous crowds, shouting and waving just because he was on that train. Now he needed to feel again the waves of crowd approval.

He took off for London. A friend, the prominent writer, Edward Knoblock, went along to provide some introductions. It was to be a nostalgic trip to visit the places where he had grown up. Would it also be his last chance for public approval? Would he ever make another picture as popular as *The Kid?*[6]

---

5   According to David Robinson (*Chaplin: His Life and Art,* 1985, p. 273) the picture had the tentative title, *Come Seven.* The autobiography describes it more fully, p. 263. On his return from England, *Come Seven* became a story about construction workers, *Pay Day* (1922).

6   See Theodore Huff, *Charlie Chaplin,* 1951, p. 135.

In London his car was barely able to inch its way along through the crowds from the railroad station to his hotel. All England seemed to have turned out to welcome him. Like Griffith's earlier visit during the first world war, this was probably the most memorable event of Chaplin's public life. He met H.G. Wells, James Barrie, and other leading lights. When Knoblock took him to call on George Bernard Shaw, however, he was stricken with nervousness and refused to ring the bell.

Chaplin's autobiography offers a great many recollected conversations with famous people, including Shaw, whom he later met. The book was a best seller for a long time, although criticized by reviewers when it came out in 1964 because it laid such stress on reflected glory. The criticism was justified. Yet we can be glad he gave us so frank a picture of his mind, which was never rigorously logical or even especially well-informed. It is a fascinating story of a truly interesting person with wide-ranging interests reacting with many sharp insights to the currents of thought around him, to the world as he saw it revolving about him.

Chaplin was ever the meticulous observer, just as his mother was when she called his attention to passersby from their third-floor garret — guessing whether someone had left home without breakfast, noticing "a refined young man, but at the moment he's worried about the hole in the seat of his pants." He loved to spy on life. His films often had realistic backgrounds that evolved out of his curiosity about firemen, department stores, restaurants, factories, and circuses.

There is a deep and abiding class consciousness in the work of this British-born comedian, and it is often said that the Little Fellow, as Charlie Chaplin called himself, is also "the common man." But Michael Roemer, in a perceptive summation in the *Yale Review* in 1974, urges that "what we so continually recognize in his films are the feelings and experiences we had as children." He and other characters often fight like children and are often concerned with food, as children are. They are at the mercy, Roemer says, of those who are bigger and stronger. Of course in this simple sensory world, no one is ever vitally hurt physically, any more than they are in a comic strip.[7]

7   Michael Roemer, "Chaplin: Charles and Charlie," *Yale Review*, December 1974.

"Nowhere is Charlie more explicitly a child," Roemer adds, "than with women." At Keystone, there was naturally a good deal of innuendo, ogling, and fumbling around, but as his character developed, regressed, and steadied later on, he became the safe-sex object Americans were comfortable with in their comedies — far from the unstable public image his personal life reflected in the headlines of the time. His real-life unlucky affairs and marriages stemmed from a single tragic obsession.

We know from his autobiography that his first and greatest love was Hetty Kelly, a 15-year-old dancer he met during his English music hall days. He was nineteen. She was "a slim gazelle with a shapely oval face, a bewitching full mouth and beautiful teeth — and two large brown eyes sparkling mischievously." Hetty at first put him off because she was too young, and he more or less bungled his meetings with her by his own admission, wavering between put-on overconfidence and a kind of miserable self-deprecation. Years later, when he looked for her on his trip to London, he found that she had died. His wives and leading ladies were all more or less a memory of Hetty Kelly.[8]

Chaplin is an outstanding example of those creative workers whose lives are constantly intermingled with their art. The intense experiences of childhood, the disappointments of adolescent love — both are in his films over and over again. Of course as he acted them out he touched a universal nerve. Certainly his marriage to Mildred Harris in 1918 and the divorce two years later contributed to his exhaustion in 1921. Making *Sunnyside*, he said, was "like pulling teeth."[9]

Theodore Huff's biography, still one of the most valuable gifts to film history, parallels the life with the works. In a motion picture biography, *The Gentleman Tramp*, authorized by Chaplin himself shortly before he died, these parallels were also frankly explored.

As years passed, Chaplin made greater demands on himself and others. Eddie Sutherland, an experienced director who signed on as assistant to Chaplin for *The Gold Rush*, told Kevin Brownlow about his way of working, his habit of shooting scenes endlessly over and over. This perfectionism meant

8   Chaplin, p. 104-8.
9   Chaplin, p. 234.

that the picture was only two thirds finished after eighteen months, when Sutherland had to leave.[10] Often the crew would break for days while Chaplin re-worked his ideas.

Robert Parrish, who became a well-known editor and director, reported in *Growing Up in Hollywood* that he was selected as a child to play a small role in *City Lights* (1931). Chaplin first explained, then demonstrated, exactly how he was to move. After that he demonstrated how each of the other persons in the scene would act and react. Then he "reluctantly gave us back our parts. I felt that he would much rather have played all of them himself."[11]

Politics and economics interested Chaplin a great deal, and his yearning to make life as perfect as a film got him in all sorts of trouble. It was probably fortunate that he never undertook a proposed film based on the life of Napoleon, although Alistair Cooke was hired for a while to work on research for it, and it was actually announced in the trade papers.[12] *The Great Dictator* (1940) was of his own time and closer to the needs of his audience.

Chaplin was neither a political nor a military expert. It was unfortunate for him that he was called upon during World War II to fill in as a speaker at a huge rally in San Francisco urging an immediate second front in France. The rally was obviously intended to praise the role of Soviet Russia in holding off the Germans on the east front — and by implication a criticism of delays in American preparations. His impassioned plea was no doubt humane in purpose and came from the heart. It also pleased him as an exciting theatrical performance. He agreed to give further speeches in New York and Chicago. As a result of this rhetorical adventure, for the rest of his life he was widely believed to be a communist sympathizer.

When he left for a trip to Europe in September 1952, a national election was coming up, with Adlai Stevenson facing Dwight Eisenhower and a little known Vice Presidential nominee, Richard Nixon, who was making a career out of anti-communism. Harry Truman's attorney general, evidently

10 Kevin Brownlow, *The Parade's Gone By* (1968), p. 502.
11 Parrish, *Growing Up in Hollywood* (1976), pp. 39-44.
12 See for example *Exhibitors Herald and Moving Picture World* January 7, 1928.

to show that the Democratic administration was not "soft on communism," decided to withdraw Chaplin's re-entry permit. If he returned, the world-famous American comedian, still a British subject, would have to be reexamined as to his morals and his views on communism under the recently revised U.S. Code on aliens.

Thus Chaplin became an exile from his adopted country for twenty years. *Limelight*, (1953) a completely nonpolitical film, was picketed by the American Legion and banned by the Fox West Coast theater chain because of his supposed "communist" views.

Of course Chaplin was no "leveller" in the old-fashioned sense, no advocate or even prophet of class struggle by "the masses." Emotionally a rebel, he found things wrong with the world, as someone with his background of privation would be likely to. But his life was a supreme example of the immigrant who rises through talent, effort, and luck to fame and fortune — Horatio Alger individualism triumphant in a capitalist economy. No one knew that better than Chaplin. He told reporters in England in 1952, "I'm an individualist and I believe in liberty."

He felt himself caught, like so many Hollywood people in the thirties, in the contradiction between his wealth and his sympathy for those poor "huddled masses" mentioned on the Statue of Liberty. Like many others who have tried to think about liberty vs. equality, from Jefferson onward, he found no obvious solution. His struggle with these issues found its way into his public life and his films. But he was living evidence of the American dream of individual success.

As for the rack and ruin of his personal life — the awkward marriage to Mildred Harris (1918-1920), the public humiliation of the forced marriage to Lita Grey (1924-1927), the apparent dalliances with Peggy Hopkins Joyce and Pola Negri, the mystery of the supposed marriage to Paulette Goddard with whom he lived for nearly ten years, the bizarre episodes surrounding Joan Barry's paternity suit (in which a jury found Chaplin guilty even though blood tests proved him innocent) — these combined with his unwise political pronouncements to turn his popularity into notoriety.

Recognized as a comic genius, Chaplin was also noted for the wistful departures in some of his films — walking down the road away from the camera, alone. Within his structured slapstick stories were other unique moments of rejection and of pathos, ways of touching the hearts of his viewers which he learned many years before from his British employer, Fred Karno. Would his own life experience, with all its fame and high moments, end, as it began, in loneliness and sorrow?

In real life, like Horatio Alger, he won both wealth and the girl, as he did in *The Gold Rush*. He married Oona O'Neill (daughter of the great American playwright, Eugene O'Neill) a close approximation of his ideal memory, Hetty Kelly. They proceeded to have a large and happy family in Switzerland. Eventually he was welcomed back to America and to Hollywood: he was given a special Academy Award and a standing ovation in 1972 for his contributions to the art of the film.

Perhaps he remembered then his first trip to America, when he reacted (according to his autobiography) against the "ruthless" skyscrapers, the "slick tempo," the New York in which many people looked "lone and isolated" while others "swaggered as if they owned the place." Yet as he walked along the Broadway he was to conquer so soon and so easily,

> it began to light up with myriads of colored electric bulbs and sparkled like a brilliant jewel. And in the warm night my attitude changed. . . . "This is it!" I said to myself. "This is where I belong!"[13]

---

13 Chaplin, p. 121.

CHARLES CHAPLIN
I Come to America

This is the story of the self-discovery of a great talent. It begins in early childhood, against a dismal background of deprivation in London. His mother shows him how to observe and invent the lives of passers-by. She loses touch with reality and he is left alone. He finally finds work he can do well, as a child actor. His half-brother Sydney brings him along with music-hall sketches, and the Karno company takes him to the U.S. in 1910.

These early years are the best part of his bestselling My Autobiography, *written and rewritten by Chaplin over several years (NY, Simon & Schuster, 1964). As Michael Roemer points out, some people would be destroyed by such beginnings, but Charlie was able to use them as grist for his performances and his films. We have chosen certain passages that show his despair and his high hopes, his nervous fears at Keystone (starting in January 1914) and his gradual growth of confidence in his image and his art. (Pp. 67-72, 76-78, 140-144, 146, 151-153.)*

[May, 1903]

Now six weeks had elapsed and still Sydney had not returned. At first this did not alarm Mother, but after another week's delay she wrote to the officers of the Donovan and Castle Line and received information that he had been put ashore at Cape Town for treatment of rheumatism. This news worried Mother and affected her health. Still she continued working at her sewing machine and I was fortunate in obtaining a little work by giving a few dancing lessons to a family after school for the sum of five shillings a week.

About this time the McCarthys came to live in Kennington Road. Mrs. McCarthy had been an Irish comedienne and was a friend of Mother's. She was married to Walter McCarthy, a certified accountant. But when Mother was obliged to give up the stage we had lost sight of Mr. and Mrs. McCarthy, and not until seven years later did we meet them again, when they came to live at Walcott Mansions in the select part of Kennington Road.

Their son, Wally McCarthy, and I were the same age. As little children, we used to play at grownups, pretending we were vaudevillians, smoking our imaginary cigars and driving in our imaginary pony and trap, much to the amusement of our parents.

Since the McCarthys had come to live in Walcott Mansions, Mother had rarely seen them, but Wally and I had formed an inseparable friendship. As soon as I was through with school I would race home to Mother to find out if she needed any errands done, then race up to the McCarthys'. We would play theatre at the back of Walcott Mansions. As the director, I always gave myself the villain parts, knowing instinctively they were more colorful than the hero. We would play until Wally's suppertime. Usually I was invited. At mealtime I had an ingratiating way of making myself available. There were occasions, however, when my maneuvering did not work, and I would reluctantly return home. Mother was always happy to see me and would prepare something for me, fried bread in dripping or one of Grandfather's eggs and a cup of tea. She would read to me or we would sit together at the window and she would amuse me by making remarks about the pedestrians as they passed by. She would invent stories about them. If it was a young man with a breezy, bobbing gait, she would say, "There goes Mr. Hopandscotch. He's on his way to place a bet. If he's lucky today he's going to buy a secondhand tandem for him and his girl."

Then a man would pass slowly, moping along. "Hm, he's going home to have stew and parsnips for dinner, which he hates."

Then someone with an air of superiority would walk by. "Now there's a refined young man, but at the moment he's worried about the hole in the seat of his pants."

Then another with a fast gait would streak past. "That gentleman has just taken Eno's! [a mild laxative]." And so she would go on, sending me into gales of laughter.

Another week had gone by and not a word from Sydney. Had I been less a boy and more sensitive to Mother's anxiety I might have realized what was impending. I might have noticed that for several days she had been sitting listlessly at the window, had neglected to tidy up the room, had grown unusually quiet. I might have been concerned when the firm of shirtmakers began finding fault with her work and stopped giving it to her, and when they took away her sewing machine for arrears in payments, and when the five shillings I earned from dancing lessons suddenly ended. Through all this I might have noticed that Mother remained indifferent, apathetic.

Mrs. McCarthy suddenly died. She had been ailing for some time, and her health rapidly deteriorated until she passed on. Immediately, thoughts invaded my mind: how wonderful if Mr. McCarthy married Mother — Wally and I being such good friends. Besides, it would be an ideal solution to all Mother's problems.

Soon after the funeral I spoke to Mother about it: "You should make it your business to see a lot of Mr. McCarthy. I bet he'd like to marry you."

Mother smiled wanly. "Give the poor man a chance," she said.

"If you were all dressed up and made yourself attractive, as you used to be, he would. But you don't make any effort; all you do is to sit around this filthy room and look awful."

Poor Mother. How I regret those words. I never realized that she was weak from malnutrition. Yet the next day, by some superhuman effort, she had tidied up the room.

The school's summer holidays were on, so I thought I would go early to the McCarthys' — anything to get away from the wretchedness of our garret. They had invited me to stay for lunch, but I had an intuition that I should return home to Mother. When I reached Pownall Terrace, I was stopped at the gate by some children of the neighborhood.

"Your mother's gone insane," said a little girl.

The words were like a slap in the face.

"What do you mean?" I mumbled.

"It's true," said another. "She's been knocking at all our doors giving away pieces of coal, saying they were birthday presents for the children. You can ask my mother." . . .

The parish doctor was old and grumpy, and after hearing the landlady's story, which was similar to that of the children, he made a perfunctory examination of Mother. "Insane. Send her to the infirmary," he said.

The doctor wrote out a paper; besides other things it said she was suffering from malnutrition, which the doctor explained to me, saying that she was undernourished.

"She'll be better off and get proper food there," said the landlady by way of comforting me.

She helped to gather up Mother's clothes and to dress her. Mother obeyed like a child; she was so weak, her will seemed to have deserted her. As we left the house, the neighbors and children were gathered at the front gate, looking on with awe.

The infirmary was about a mile away. As we ambled along Mother staggered like a drunken woman from weakness, veering from side to side as I supported her. The stark afternoon sun seemed to ruthlessly expose our misery. People who passed us must have thought Mother was drunk, but to me they were like phantoms in a dream. She never spoke, but seemed to know where we were going and to be anxious to get there. On the way I tried to reassure her, and she smiled, too weak to talk.

When at last we arrived at the infirmary a young doctor took her in charge. After reading the note, he said kindly, "All right, Mrs. Chaplin, come this way."

She submitted obediently. But as the nurses started to lead her away she turned suddenly with a painful realization that she was leaving me behind.

"See you tomorrow," I said, feigning cheerfulness.

They led her away looking anxiously back at me. When she had gone, the doctor turned. "And what will become of you, young man?"

Having had enough of workhouse schools, I replied politely, "Oh, I'll be living with my aunt."

As I walked from the hospital toward home, I could feel only a numbing sadness. Yet I was relieved, for I knew that Mother would be better off in the hospital than sitting alone in that dark room with nothing to eat. But that heartbreaking look as they led her away I shall never forget. I thought of all her endearing ways, her gaiety, her sweetness and affection; of that weary little figure that used to come down the streets looking tired and preoccupied until she saw me charging toward her; how she would change immediately and become all smiling as I looked eagerly inside the paper bag she carried for those little niceties that she always brought home for Sydney and me. Even that morning she had saved some candy — had offered it to me while I wept in her lap.

I did not go straight home — I could not. I turned in the direction of the Newington Butts market and looked in shop windows until late afternoon. When I returned to the garret it looked reproachfully empty. On a chair was a washtub half-filled with water. Two of my shirts and a chemise were soaking in it. I began to investigate. There was no food in the cupboard except a small half-filled package of tea. On the mantelpiece was her purse, in which I found three halfpence, some keys and several pawn tickets. On the corner of the table was the candy she had offered me. Then I broke down and wept again.

Emotionally exhausted, I slept soundly that night. In the morning I awoke to a haunting emptiness in the room; the sun streaming in on the floor seemed to heighten Mother's absence. Later the landlady came up and said that I could stay on there until she let the room and that if I needed food I had only to ask for it. I thanked her and told her that Sydney would pay all our debts when he returned. But I was too shy to ask for food.

I did not go to see Mother the next day as promised. I could not; it would have been too upsetting. But the landlady saw the doctor, who said that she had already been transferred to Cane Hill asylum. This melancholy news relieved my conscience, for Cane Hill was twenty miles away and I had no means of getting there. Sydney would soon return and then we could see her together. For the first few days I neither saw nor spoke to anyone I knew.

I would steal out in the early morning and stay out all day; I always managed to get food somewhere — besides, missing a meal was no hardship. One morning the landlady caught me creeping downstairs and asked if I had had my breakfast. I shook my head. "Then come on," she said in her gruff way.

I kept away from the McCarthys because I did not want them to know about Mother. Like a fugitive, I kept out of everyone's way. . . .

[July, 1903]

Joseph Conrad wrote to a friend to this effect: that life made him feel like a cornered blind rat waiting to be clubbed. This simile could well describe the appalling circumstances of us all; nevertheless, some of us are struck with good luck, and that is what happened to me.

I had been news vendor, printer, toymaker, glass blower, doctor's boy, etc., but during these occupational digressions, like Sydney, I never lost sight of my ultimate aim to become an actor. So between jobs I would polish my shoes, brush my clothes, put on a clean collar and make periodical calls at Blackmore's theatrical agency in Bedford Street off the Strand. I did this until the state of my clothes forbade any further visits.

The first time I went there the office was adorned with immaculately dressed Thespians of both sexes, standing about talking grandiloquently to each other. With trepidation I stood in a far corner near the door, painfully shy, trying to conceal my weatherworn suit and shoes slightly budding at the toes. From the inner office a young clerk sporadically appeared and like a reaper would cut through the Thespian hauteur with the laconic remark, "Nothing for you — or you — or you" — and the office would clear like the emptying of a church. On one occasion I was left standing alone! When the clerk saw me, he stopped abruptly. "What do you want?"

I felt like Oliver Twist asking for more. "Have you any boys' parts?" I gulped.

"Have you registered?"

I shook my head.

To my surprise he ushered me into the adjoining office and took my name and address and all particulars, saying that if anything came up he would let me know. I left with a pleasant sense of having performed a duty, but also rather thankful that nothing had come of it.

And now, one month after Sydney's return, I received a postcard. It read: "Would you call at Blackmore's Agency, Bedford Street, Strand?"

In my new suit I was ushered into the very presence of Mr. Blackmore himself, who was all smiles and amiability. Mr. Blackmore, whom I had imagined to be almighty and scrutinizing, was most kindly and gave me a note to deliver to Mr. C.E. Hamilton at the offices of Charles Frohman.

Mr. Hamilton read it and was amused and surprised to see how small I was. Of course I lied about my age, telling him I was fourteen — I was twelve and a half. He explained that I was to play Billie, the pageboy in *Sherlock Holmes*, for a tour of forty weeks, which was to start in the autumn.

"In the meantime," said Mr. Hamilton, "there is an exceptionally good boy's part in a new play, *Jim, the Romance of a Cockney*, written by Mr. H.A. Saintsbury, the gentleman who is to play the title role in *Sherlock Holmes* on the forthcoming tour." *Jim* would be produced in Kingston for a trial engagement, prior to the tour of *Holmes*. The salary was two pounds ten shillings a week, the same as I would get for *Sherlock Holmes*.

Although the sum was a windfall I never batted an eye. "I must consult my brother about the terms," I said solemnly.

Mr. Hamilton laughed and seemed highly amused, then brought out the whole office staff to have a look at me. "This is our Billie! What do you think of him?"

Everyone was delighted and smiled beamingly at me. What had happened? It seemed the world had suddenly changed, had taken me into its fond embrace and adopted me. Then Mr. Hamilton gave me a note to Mr. Saintsbury, whom he said I would find at the Green Room Club in Leicester Square, and I left, walking on clouds.

The same thing happened at the Green Room Club, Mr. Saintsbury calling out other members to have a look at me. Then and there he handed me the part of Sammy, saying that it was one of the important characters in his play. I was a little nervous for fear he might ask me to read it on the spot, which would have been embarrassing as I was almost unable to read; fortunately he told me to take it home and read it at leisure, as they would not be starting rehearsals for another week.

I went home on the bus dazed with happiness, and began to get the full realization of what had happened to me. I had suddenly left behind a life of poverty and was entering a long-desired dream — a dream my mother had often spoken about, had reveled in. I was to become an actor! It had all come so suddenly, so unexpectedly. I kept thumbing the pages of my part — it had a new brown-paper cover — the most important document I have ever held in my life. During the ride on the bus I realized I had crossed an important threshold. No longer was I a nondescript of the slums; now I was a personage of the theatre. I wanted to weep. . . .

[1913 — 1914]

Eager and anxious, I arrived in Los Angeles and took a room at a small hotel, the Great Northern. The first evening, I took a busman's holiday and saw the second show at the Empress, where the Karno Company had worked. The attendant recognized me and came a few moments later to tell me that Mr. Sennett and Miss Mabel Normand were sitting two rows back and had asked if I would join them. I was thrilled, and after a hurried, whispered introduction we all watched the show together. When it was over, we walked a few paces down Main Street, and went to a rathskeller for a light supper and a drink. Mr. Sennett was shocked to see how young I looked. "I thought you were a much older man," he said. I could detect a tinge of concern, which made me anxious, remembering that all Sennett's comedians were oldish-looking men. Fred Mace was over fifty and Ford Sterling in his forties. "I can make up as old as you like," I answered. Mabel Normand, however, was more reassuring. Whatever her reservations were about me, she did not reveal them. Mr. Sennett said that I would not start immediately, but should come to the studio in Edendale and get acquainted with the people. When we left the cafe, we bundled into Mr. Sennett's glamorous racing car and I was driven to my hotel.

The following morning I boarded a streetcar for Edendale, a suburb of Los Angeles. It was an anomalous-looking place that could not make up its mind whether to be a humble residential district or a semi-industrial one. It had small lumberyards and junkyards, and abandoned-looking small farms on which were built one or two shacky wooden stores that fronted the road. After many inquiries I found myself opposite the Keystone Studio. It was a delapidated affair with a green fence round it, one hundred and fifty feet square. The entrance to it was up a garden path through an old bungalow — the whole place looked just as anomalous as Edendale itself. I stood gazing at it from the opposite side of the road, debating whether to go in or not.

It was lunchtime and I watched the men and women in their makeup come pouring out of the bungalow, including the Keystone Cops. They crossed the road to a small general store and came out eating sandwiches and hot dogs. Some called after each other in loud, raucous voices: "Hey, Hank, come on!" "Tell Slim to hurry!"

Suddenly I was seized with shyness and walked quickly to the corner at a safe distance, looking to see if Mr. Sennett or Miss Normand would come out of the bungalow, but they did not appear. For half an hour I stood there, then decided to go back to the hotel. The problem of entering the studio and facing all those people became an insuperable one. For two days I arrived outside the studio, but I had not the courage to go in. The third day Mr. Sennett telephoned and wanted to know why I had not shown up. I made some sort of excuse. "Come down right away, we'll be waiting for you," he said. So I went down and boldly marched into the bungalow and asked for Mr. Sennett.

He was pleased to see me and took me immediately into the studio. I was enthralled. A soft, even light pervaded the whole stage. It came from broad streams of white linen that diffused the sun and gave an ethereal quality to everything. This diffusion was for photographing in the daylight.

After being introduced to one or two actors, I became interested in what was going on. There were three sets side by side, and three comedy companies were at work in them. It was like viewing something at the World's Fair. In one set Mabel Normand was banging on a door, shouting, "Let me in!" Then the camera stopped and that was it — I had no idea films were made piecemeal in this fashion.

On another set was the great Ford Sterling, whom I was to replace. Mr. Sennett introduced me to him. Ford was leaving Keystone to form his own company with Universal. He was immensely popular with the public and with everyone in the studio. They surrounded his set and were laughing eagerly at him.

Sennett took me aside and explained their method of working. "We have no scenario — we get an idea, then follow the natural sequence of events until it leads up to a chase, which is the essence of our comedy."

This method was edifying, but personally I hated a chase. It dissipates one's personality; little as I knew about movies, I knew that nothing transcended personality.

That day I went from set to set watching the companies at work. They all seemed to be imitating Ford Sterling. This worried me, because his style did not suit me. He played a harassed

Dutchman, ad-libbing through the scene with a Dutch accent, which was funny but was lost in silent pictures. I wondered what Sennett expected of me. He had seen my work and must have known that I was not suitable to play Ford's type of comedy; my style was just the opposite. Yet every story and situation conceived in the studio was consciously or unconsciously made for Sterling; even Roscoe Arbuckle was imitating Sterling.

The studio had evidently been a farm. Mabel Normand's dressing room was situated in an old bungalow and adjoining it was another room where the ladies of the stock company dressed. Across from the bungalow was what had evidently been a barn, the main dressing room for minor members of the stock company and the Keystone Cops, the majority of whom were ex-circus clowns and prize fighters. I was allotted the star dressing room used by Mack Sennett, Ford Sterling and Roscoe Arbuckle. It was another barnlike structure, which might have been the harness room. Besides Mabel Normand, there were several other beautiful girls. It was a strange and unique atmosphere of beauty and beast.

For days I wandered around the studio, wondering when I would start work. Occasionally I would meet Sennett crossing the stage, but he would look through me, preoccupied. I had an uncomfortable feeling that he thought he had made a mistake in engaging me which did little to ameliorate my nervous tension.

Each day my peace of mind depended on Sennett. If perchance he saw me and smiled, my hopes would rise. The rest of the company had a wait-and-see attitude, but some, I felt, considered me a doubtful substitute for Ford Sterling.

When Saturday came, Sennett was most amiable. Said he, "Go to the front office and get your check." I told him I was more anxious to get to work. I wanted to talk about imitating Ford Sterling, but he dismissed me with the remark, "Don't worry, we'll get around to that."

Nine days of inactivity had passed and the tension was excruciating. Ford, however, would console me, and after work he would occasionally give me a lift downtown, where we would stop in at the Alexandria Bar for a drink and meet several of his friends. One of them, a Mr. Elmer Ellsworth, whom I disliked at first and thought rather crass, would jokingly taunt me: "I understand you're taking Ford's place. Well, are you funny?"

"Modesty forbids," I said squirmishly. This sort of ribbing was most embarrassing, especially in the presence of Ford. But he graciously took me off the hook with the remark, "Didn't you catch him at the Empress playing the drunk? Very funny."

"Well, he hasn't made me laugh yet," said Ellsworth.

He was a big, cumbersome man, and looked glandular, with a melancholy, hangdog expression, hairless face, sad eyes, a loose mouth and a smile that showed two missing front teeth. Ford whispered impressively that he was a great authority on literature, finance and politics, one of the best-informed men in the country, and that he had a great sense of humor. However, I did not appreciate it and decided I would try to avoid him. But one night at the Alexandria Bar, he said, "Hasn't this limey got started yet?"

"Not yet." I laughed uncomfortably.

"Well, you'd better be funny."

Having taken a great deal from the gentleman, I gave him back some of his own medicine: "Well, if I'm half as funny as you look, I'll do all right."

"Blimey! A sarcastic wit, eh? I'll buy him a drink after that."

At last the moment came. Sennett was away on location with Mabel Normand as well as the Ford Sterling Company, so there was hardly anyone left in the studio. Mr. Henry Lehrman, Keystone's top director after Sennett, was to start a new picture and wanted me to play a newspaper reporter. Lehrman was a vain man and very conscious of the fact that he had made some successful comedies of a mechanical nature; he used to say that he didn't need personalities, that he got all his laughs from mechanical effects and film cutting.

We had no story. It was to be a documentary about the printing press done with a few comedy touches. I wore a light frock coat, a top hat and a handlebar mustache. When we started I could see that Lehrman was groping for ideas. And of course, being a newcomer at Keystone, I was anxious to make suggestions. This was where I created antagonism with Lehrman. In a scene in which I had an interview with an editor of a newspaper I crammed in every conceivable gag I could think of, even to suggesting business for others in the cast. Although the picture was completed in three days, I thought we contrived some very funny gags. But when I saw the finished film it broke my heart, for the cutter had butchered it beyond recognition, cutting into the middle of all my funny business. I was bewildered, and wondered why they had done this. Henry Lehrman confessed years later that he had deliberately done it, because, as he put it, he thought I knew too much.

The day after I finished with Lehrman, Sennett returned from location. Ford Sterling was on one set, Arbuckle on another; the whole stage was crowded with three companies at work. I was in my street clothes and had nothing to do, so I stood where Sennett could see me. He was standing with Mabel, looking into a hotel lobby set, biting the end of a cigar. "We need some gags here," he said, then turned to me. "Put on a comedy make-up. Anything will do."

I had no idea what make-up to put on. I did not like my getup as the press reporter. However, on the way to the wardrobe I thought I would dress in baggy pants, big shoes, a cane and a derby hat. I wanted everything a contradiction: the pants baggy, the coat tight, the hat small and the shoes large. I was undecided whether to look old or young, but remembering Sennett had expected me to be a much older man, I added a small mustache, which, I reasoned, would add age without hiding my expression.

I had no idea of the character. But the moment I was dressed, the clothes and the make-up made me feel the person he was. I began to know him, and by the time I walked onto the stage he was fully born. When I confronted Sennett I assumed the character and strutted about, swinging my cane and parading before him. Gags and comedy ideas went racing through my mind.

The secret of Mack Sennett's success was his enthusiasm. He was a great audience and laughed genuinely at what he thought funny. He stood and giggled until his body began to shake. This encouraged me and I began to explain the character: "You know this fellow is many-sided, a tramp, a gentleman, a poet, a dreamer, a lonely fellow, always hopeful of romance and adventure. He would have you believe he is a scientist, a musician, a duke, a polo player. However, he is not above picking up cigarette butts or robbing a baby of its candy. And, of course, if the occasion warrants it, he will kick a lady in the rear — but only in extreme anger!"

I carried on this way for ten minutes or more, keeping Sennett in continuous chuckles. "All right," said he, "get on the set and see what you can do there." As with the Lehrman film, I knew little of what the story was about, other than that Mabel Normand gets involved with her husband and a lover.

In all comedy business an attitude is most important, but it is not always easy to find an attitude. However, in the hotel lobby I felt I was an impostor posing as one of the guests, but in reality I was a tramp just wanting a little shelter. I entered and stumbled over the foot of a lady. I turned and raised my hat apologetically, then turned and stumbled over a cuspidor, then turned and raised my hat to the cuspidor. Behind the camera they began to laugh.

Quite a crowd had gathered there, not only the players of the other companies who left their sets to watch us, but also the stagehands, the carpenters and the wardrobe department. That indeed was a compliment. And by the time we had finished rehearsing we had quite a large audience laughing. Very soon I saw Ford Sterling peering over the shoulders of others. When it was over I knew I had made good.

At the end of the day when I went to the dressing room, Ford Sterling and Roscoe Arbuckle were taking off their make-up. Very little was said, but the atmosphere was charged with cross-currents. Both Ford and Roscoe liked me, but I frankly felt they were undergoing some inner conflict.

It was a long scene that ran seventy-five feet. Later Mr. Sennett and Mr. Lehrman debated whether to let it run its full length, as the average comedy scene rarely ran over ten. "If it's funny," I said, "does length really matter?" They decided to let the scene run its full seventy-five feet. As the clothes had imbued me with the character, I then and there decided I would keep to this costume, whatever happened.

That evening I went home on the streetcar with one of the small-bit players. Said he, "Boy, you've started something; nobody ever got those kind of laughs on the set before, not even Ford Sterling — and you should have seen his face watching you, it was a study!"

"Let's hope they'll laugh the same way in the theatre," I said, by way of suppressing my elation.

. . . I found that the placing of a camera was not only psychological but articulated a scene; in fact, it was the basis of cinematic style. If the camera is a little too near, or too far, it can enhance or spoil an effect. Because economy of movement is important you don't want an actor to walk any unnecessary distance unless there is a special reason, for walking is not dramatic. Therefore placement of camera should effect composition and a graceful entrance for the actor. Placement of camera is cinematic inflection. There is no set rule that a close-up gives more emphasis than a long shot. A close-up is a question of feeling; in some instances a long shot can effect greater emphasis.

An example of this is in one of my early comedies, *Skating*. The tramp enters the rink and skates with one foot up, gliding and twirling, tripping and bumping into people and getting into all sorts of mischief, eventually leaving everyone piled up on their backs in the foreground of the camera, while he skates to the rear of the rink, becoming a very small figure in the background, and sits among the spectators innocently reviewing the havoc he has just created. Yet the small figure of the tramp in the distance was funnier than he would have been in a close-up.

When I started directing my first picture, I was not as confident as I thought I would be; in fact, I had a slight attack of panic. But after Sennett saw the first day's work I was reassured. The picture was called *Caught in the Rain*. It was not a world-beater, but it was funny and quite a success. When I finished it, I was anxious to know Sennett's reaction. I waited for him as he came out of the projection room. "Well, are you ready to start another?" he said. From then on I wrote and directed all my own comedies. As an inducement, Sennett gave me a twenty-five-dollar bonus for each picture. . . .

There was a lot Keystone taught me and a lot I taught Keystone. In those days they knew little about technique, stagecraft or movement, which I brought to them from the theatre. They also knew little about natural pantomime. In blocking a scene, a director would have three or four actors blatantly stand in a straight line facing the camera, and, with the broadest gestures, one would pantomime "I-want-to-marry-your-daughter" by pointing to himself, then to his ring finger, then to the girl. Their miming dealt little with subtlety or effectiveness, so I stood out in contrast. In those early movies, I knew I had many advantages, and that, like a geologist, I was entering a rich, unexplored field. I suppose that was the most exciting period of my career, for I was on the threshold of something wonderful.

Success makes one endearing and I became the familiar friend of everyone in the studio. I was "Charlie" to the extras, to the stagehands, the wardrobe department, and the cameramen. Although I am not a fraternizer, this pleased me indeed, for I knew that this familiarity meant I was a success.

Now I had confidence in my ideas, and I can thank Sennett for that, for although unlettered like myself, he had belief in his own taste, and such belief he instilled in me. His manner of working had given me confidence; it seemed right. His remark that first day at the studio: "We have no scenario — we get an idea then follow the natural sequence of events . . ." had stimulated my imagination.

Creating this way made films exciting. In the theatre I had been confined to a rigid, nondeviating routine of repeating the same thing night after night; once stage business had been tried out and set, one rarely attempted to invent new business. The only motivating thing about acting in the theatre was a good performance or a bad one. But films were freer. They gave me a sense of adventure. "What do you think of this for an idea?"

Sennett would say, or "There's a flood downtown on Main Street." Such remarks launched a Keystone Comedy. It was this charming alfresco spirit that was a delight — a challenge to one's creativeness. It was so free and easy — no literature, no writers — we just had a notion around which we built gags, then made up the story as we went along.

For instance, in *His Prehistoric Past* I started with one gag, which was my first entrance. I appeared dressed as a prehistoric man wearing a bearskin, and, as I scanned the landscape, I began pulling the hair from the bearskin to fill my pipe. This was enough of an idea to stimulate a prehistoric story, introducing love, rivalry, combat and chase. This was the method by which we all worked at Keystone.

I can trace the first prompting of desire to add another dimension to my films besides that of comedy. I was playing in a picture called *The New Janitor*, in a scene in which the manager of the office fires me. In pleading with him to take pity on me and let me retain my job, I started to pantomime appealingly that I had a large family of little children. While I was enacting mock sentiment, Dorothy Davenport, an old actress, was on the sidelines watching the scene, and during rehearsal I looked up and to my surprise found her in tears. "I know it's supposed to be funny," she said, "but you just make me weep." She confirmed something I already felt: I had the ability to evoke tears as well as laughter.

THEODORE HUFF
The Classic Mutual Comedies

Still a most perceptive evaluation of Chaplin's life and films — and especially of the frequent relationship between the two — Huff's Charlie Chaplin *(N.Y., Henry Schuman, 1951) was for many years the only American biography. Huff was a critic and teacher of motion picture history at a time when there were no departments of film in the colleges. He shared his talents and knowledge, no doubt for a meager fee, with New York University, the College of the City of New York, the University of Southern California, UCLA, and the Museum of Modern Art.*

His descriptions of the Mutual short subjects on pages 67-83 are a service to those who lack the opportunity to see them all.

The idea for his first Mutual comedy came to Chaplin while visiting a New York department store. Going up an escalator, he saw a nervous man slip, and at once grasped the comic possibilities of the moving staircase. On his return to Hollywood he ordered a department store set built and wrote a comedy around it — *The Floorwalker*, released May 15, 1916.

Except for some clever gags and more elaborate properties, this first Mutual comedy stays in the slapstick tradition.

Charlie enters, picks up an artificial limb (which he is told is not for sale), knocks over boxes with his cane, mismanages the drinking fountain from which he emerges, his face adrip, and is worsted in his first bout with the moving staircase. About to kick a clerk he changes his mind when a store detective appears, and stoops to brush off his pants.

Upstairs the floorwalker double-crosses the manager with whom he was to abscond with the store receipts, hits him over the head, and goes off with all the loot. In the anteroom he encounters Charlie who is almost his double in appearance.

Imagining they are looking in a mirror, their hands touch, they scratch their heads together and raise and lower their arms in unison (ancestor of the similar stunt in the Marx Brothers' *Duck Soup*, years later). The confusion ends when Charlie notices that the other is carrying a satchel instead of a cane.

The floorwalker bribes Charlie to change places with him only to fall into the cop's hands and get a billy over the head as Charlie, just in time, doffs his derby. When Charlie picks up the satchel of money he gets a scare as a dummy's hand falls on it.

The stunned manager comes to and rushes at Charlie but stops as the detectives turn to see and his lunge changes to an af-

fable handshake with the surprised Charlie. But the assault resumes upstairs where Charlie's efforts to fend off his assailant
with some exquisite ballet steps go unappreciated. He is picked
up by the neck and given a shaking. Managing to slip out of the
other's grip Charlie dives under his legs and a minor chase goes
into a major one as the police swarm in.

The chase proceeds down the "up" escalator. Charlie slipping
when he reaches bottom is pulled up again. Then another mechanical monster, the store elevator, joins in the free-for-all. It
cracks the crooked store manager on the head and brings the
comedy to an end.

The Floorwalker's mirror and ballet scenes are its high points.

The Fireman is perhaps the least interesting of the Mutuals
since it depends most on violence and slapstick. But it is re-
deemed by several outstanding touches to which George Jean
Nathan, no lover of the movies, has paid tribute.

Fireman Charlie, still abed, mistakes a drill bell for a fire
alarm, slides down the pole and upsets the whole fire company
by driving the engine out, single-handed. The tough fire chief administers heavy-handed punishment. Ordered to serve breakfast,
the coffee and cream for which are extracted from the engine
boiler, Charlie's clumsiness earns him some more knock-down
punishment.

As he lies prostrate, the chief becomes remorseful and lifts him
up. Charlie kicks him into a bucket of water, shins up the pole,
and resorts to prayer as he sees the chief working his way up after him. Charlie is saved by the timely entrance of the chief's
sweetheart and her father, who takes him aside to whisper, "Let
my house burn. I'll get the insurance. You wed my daughter."

Later when an alarm interrupts Charlie and another fireman at
a game of checkers Charlie stuffs a handkerchief in the bell as a
silencer. When the owner of the burning house calls, Charlie nonchalantly picks up the phone, shrugs as he confuses his pipe and
the earpiece, and ends by ripping out the telephone wire. The
frantic owner storms into the firehouse and falls, sobbing, on
Charlie's shoulder. Charlie, moved, also begins yelling "Help!
Fire!" Handing the owner a book to relax with, he goes to fetch
the captain from the girl's house.

Back at the firehouse the fire victim pores over the book, ab-
sentmindedly looks up, recalls the fire, and starts raving again.
Upstairs the firemen jump out of bed, rush out of the camera
frame, to return, immediately, in uniform. The engine strews
men and equipment all along the road. Before the burning house

the men go into a musical comedy fire drill, passing axes from left to right shoulder and executing dance steps.

Meanwhile the insurance-hungry father sets his house afire, unwittingly trapping his daughter on the third floor. Frantic, he hunts for the firemen, finally locating them at the other fire. Charlie, on the driver's seat, rides like the wind, only to lose most of the engine turning a sharp corner. Little is left except the seat when he arrives at the fire; but he makes up for it by climbing up the face of the building to make a heroic rescue.

The Vagabond, on the other hand, is almost straight drama. This unique little picture is a prototype of *The Kid* and *The Circus*. It has many enthusiasts though others find the emotional scenes awkward. They feel that Chaplin, as a director, was then not quite up to the effects he was to get so masterfully later on. Nevertheless *The Vagabond*, in which Chaplin ventures into a new realm, is an important picture.

It opens with a shot of Charlie's familiar feet under the swinging door of a saloon. He is playing a violin but yields to a competing German brass band. Moving over to the free lunch, he switches signs so that an old Jew can help himself to some ham. Then he passes the hat, ostensibly for the brass band. He is caught and chased away.

Out in the country he plays for a pathetic gypsy drudge weeping over a washtub. As his tempo rises in a rhythmic gypsy number, the girl's rubbing speeds up until the tub upsets. Charlie bows like a maestro taking curtain calls, but gets no applause from the brutal chief who chases him and gives the girl a beating. From a refuge in a tree Charlie fells the pursuing gypsies, one by one, and makes an escape with the girl in the gypsies' wagon. Camping out happily, Charlie washes the girl's hair in a bucket, uses a hammer to open eggs, executes offending flies by making his pocket their death chamber. An artist meets the girl and paints her portrait. "His romance fading," Charlie makes pathetic competitive attempts at drawing but cannot wake the girl out of her dream of the handsome artist.

Taking first prize at an exhibition, the portrait is publicized. In it the girl's wealthy mother recognizes her daughter, abducted as an infant. "That birth mark — my child!" Arriving at Charlie's camp to claim her daughter the mother acknowledges Charlie's existence with a shoulder-high society handshake. Charlie refuses a money reward and bids the girl a fond goodbye. Watching the auto drive off Charlie tries unsuccessfully to perk up by flipping his heels, then disconsolately leans against the wagon.

Seated between the artist and her mother, the girl undergoes "the awakening of the real love," has the car turned back, flings her arms around Charlie, and pulls him into the automobile. This ending supplanted another in which the despairing Charlie, saved from a watery suicide by a homely farm woman (played by Phyllis Allen), plunges in again after one look at his rescuer.

One A.M., which came next, was also an experimental departure from previous practice. Unlike *The Tramp* it provides no model for future films. In it, except for a brief passage with a taxi driver, Chaplin appears alone. *One A.M.*, however, is a rare piece of virtuosity, a tour de force in which Chaplin successfully holds the screen with pantomime alone for two reels. Though some of the comic business, especially with the folding bed, is rather repetitious, most people find this picture very choice. Chaplin himself evidently did not think too highly of it. He never gave it the compliment of imitating it. And he is reported to have remarked, "One more film like that and it will be goodbye Charlie."

Yet *One A.M.* ranks with Chaplin's cleverest pictures. In full evening dress and high silk hat Charlie returns, after a night out, to a nightmarish home cluttered with stuffed animals and other horrors. Above the double staircase swings a huge pendulum. The walls are covered with a livid, striped wallpaper. The whole has an almost surrealist — or delirium tremens — look.

Charlie skids on rugs, shrinks from the stuffed animals, chases a drink around a revolving table, pours liquor into a bottomless decanter, is knocked down one staircase by the pendulum and is cascaded down the other, rolled inside the stair carpet, climbs a teetering rubber clothes tree, and ducks under the pendulum to get into the bedroom.

Here he presses a button to bring out a folding bed but it sticks halfway, then catching him in it, spins him into the closet. Several other attempts end in bringing the bed down on his head. Finally settled in it he leans over to pick up a cigarette, only to have the bed shed him and retire back into the wall.

At later attempts to mount it the bed bucks like a colt under his first saddle, pins him to the wall, then flops down and turns over. Suddenly the bed falls out right side up. Charlie dives into it only to have it collapse. Giving up, Charlie retires to the bathroom. After a mishap under the shower he finally succeeds in making his bed in the tub.

Throughout all of it he maintains the utmost dignity. This draws more laughs than if he had played the hilarious drunk.

The Count marks a return to more standard comedy. An expansion of, but also, in a sense, a regression to earlier manners, this picture is marked by fast action, slapstick, and clever pantomime.

It begins with blundering Charlie being fired by his huge boss, a tailor. Finding a note from Count Broko regretting his inability to attend a reception given by Miss Moneybags, the tailor decides to impersonate the count. At the Moneybags mansion, he encounters Charlie who is visiting the servants' quarters. Riding up the dumb-waiter his head appears between two curtains and he is at first taken for a painting by his startled ex-boss. With the aid of some crushing nudges, against which Charlie uses a tall chair as a shield, the tailor persuades Charlie not to expose him and to join in the imposture by posing as his secretary.

Subsequent funny business includes Charlie's interruption of the tailor's noisy ingurgitation of soup long enough to hear Miss Moneybags' questions, his parlor magic with the tailor's disappearing spaghetti, cascades of stolen silver when he is slapped on the back, and his quick recovery by a peek under the tailor's vest and administering a scolding to him. Other comic business follows on the slippery dance floor, including splits and elevations from the floor after a fall by hooking his cane on the chandelier, undercover exchanges of kicks with his obese rival, coyly flirting his cane at a harem-costumed girl with a wiggling rear, then spearing, instead, a roast fowl which he forward-passes to the butler, and "driving" gobs of icing off a large cake upon the other guests.

The comedy reaches its climax with the arrival of the genuine Count Broko. In the ensuing chase Charlie slides among the dancers, where his feet churn in one spot like a stalled locomotive. It winds up in the arrest of the tailor, and Charlie's escape and fadeout running up a sidewalk.

The Pawnshop, which followed *The Count*, is a little masterpiece. It contains all of Chaplin's choicest ingredients: irony, pity, fantasy, and comic transpositions. Chaplin demonstrates his genius for comic invention by overcoming the handicaps of the restricted locale and extracting humor out of everything in it. The slapstick world obliquely reflects life but makes no attempt at realism. Here Charlie takes advantage of the suspension of reality for some marvelously imaginative touches, by fantastic distortion of the familiar.

The story is simple. Its humor turns on a comic rivalry with another clerk, encounters with eccentric customers, and the foiling of a robbery. The comic business used in their development is extraordinary.

With his rival helpless between two steps of the step-ladder they are carrying, Charlie "boxes" him. When a cop arrives, he dances innocently back into the store, past the boss and out again, On top of the ladder Charlie "shoe polishes" one of the golden balls after bouncing it on the rival's head. In an attempt to clean an inaccessible sign he tips the ladder and goes through a magnificent balancing act before the ladder falls. Rising, Charlie's first thought is to see if his watch is still running.

Another bout with the clerk exhausts the boss's patience. Fired, Charlie pleads for his job, pantomiming that he has six children. The boss has his hands clasped behind his back but Charlie manages a farewell handshake. As the boss relents Charlie catapults upon him in gratitude. Immediately after, the wrestle with the rival clerk resumes. Charlie is giving his enemy a beating when the boss's daughter enters. Charlie drops down and pretends to be the victim, getting her consolation while his rival gets the scolding. When her consoling hand strays off, he hauls it back. Taken to the kitchen, he is further consoled with a home-baked doughnut so heavy that he uses it for dumbbell exercises, and it breaks the plate it is dropped on. Other comic business includes passing a plate, a cup, and his hands through a dry-wringer; a flash-length impersonation with a lei made of dough around his neck, strumming a ladle ukulele, and a show of innocent preoccupation by passing dough through the wringer to make pie crust when the boss's sudden entrance interrupts another altercation.

Into the shop staggers an old man — the broken-down Shakespearean-actor type. With quivering emotion and tragic gestures he offers his wedding ring for pawn. Charlie, reduced to tears, can find only a ten-dollar bill in the register. Told to keep the ring, the old man puts the bill in his mouth, pulls out a big wad of money, and counts the change over to Charlie. As he exits Charlie blinks and slaps his face with a hammer. Next follows a typical transmutation. A rope on the floor defies all of Charlie's attempt to sweep it up. He tries straightening it, then does a tight-rope walk on it with all the teetering and panic of making one's way across a chasm.

Deservedly the most famous passage in *The Pawnshop* is the alarm-clock scene. The ailing timepiece is brought in. Charlie puts a stethoscope to it, taps it like a doctor examining a lung, raps it as if testing porcelain, snaps his thumb on the bell, starts drilling with an auger, opens it with a can-opener, takes a significant sniff at its insides; then, with the telephone mouthpiece in his eye like a jeweler's magnifying glass, he examines it, oils it, uses dental forceps for some necessary extraction, taps it with a plumber's hammer, listens for noises, then pulls out the spring, measures it like ribbon, snips off lengths with a plier, then empties the remaining contents on the counter, where he stops the worm-like wriggling of the springs by squirts of oil. finally sweeping the debris into the puzzled customer's hat, he solemnly shakes his head. (The scene is photographed in two long takes of several hundred feet each, separated by a two-foot flash of the customer's face.)

The final robbery scene is practically a ballet. As the thief backs out with the jewels, Charlie steps out of a trunk with a rolling pin, fells the robber, bows circus-fashion, embraces the girl, and delivers a back kick at his rival — all in one continuous movement.

Behind the Screen, not as well known as some other Mutuals, is an amusing satire on Keystone slapstick. The setting is a movie studio. The comedy department rehearses "a new idea" — which turns out to be pie-throwing — at which one of the actors quits in disgust over "this highbrow stuff." Much of its comic business repeats the older *Property Man*, but in reverse. Charlie is David, the stage hand Goliath's assistant. He does all the heavy work, while the loafing Goliath takes all the credit. Charlie carries eleven chairs at a time, and looks like a porcupine. With all the concentration of a hairdresser he combs a bear rug, applies a hair tonic, gives it a finger massage, parts its front hair, and hot-towels its face. At lunch hour, in defense against a comrade partaking of onions, Charlie clears the air with a bellows and dons a helmet, opening the visor just long enough to stuff bread in his mouth. Following the onions the stagehand goes to work on a meaty bone, an end of which projects into Charlie's face. Charlie, sandwiching his end between lids of bread, stealthily munches away. When caught, he imitates a dog.

Other comic business includes a miscuing which plunges Goliath, director, and leading lady down a trapdoor; a strike of stagehands, indignant over having been scolded for napping; by-play with a screen-struck girl in a stagehand's disguise, very convincing until Charlie spies her long hair; and double-entendres as Goliath catches her and Charlie kissing. The giant dances about skittishly, pinches their cheeks, and exits with a soubrette kick. Shortly afterwards the comedy director (wearing a long beard and smoked glasses) offers Charlie a job as an actor. Charlie, in his comedy role, ducks too successfully, and his boss and dignified actors on a neighboring set are hit with juicy pies. There is a chase, whose tempo increases until there is an explosion set by the vengeful strikers. Amid the collapsing sets Charlie and the girl kiss in the final close-up, where Charlie, flouting another convention, winks at his camera audience. (Chaplin often looks directly at the camera for intimate effects.)

Chaplin's next Mutual, *The Rink*, a popular and fast-moving comedy, exhibits his agility and grace. In this picture he is a waiter who spends his lunch hours at the roller-skating rink. At one skating session, spinning around gracefully, he observes Edna being annoyed by the flirtatious Mr. Stout, whom he upsets in what starts a general scramble. Later Mr. Stout and Edna, Mrs. Stout and *her* partner in flirtation, and Charlie (posing as Sir Cecil Seltzer) all turn up unexpectedly at a skating party. Consternation follows. The ensuing action rings in every variety of fall, every species of mayhem, and ends in a grand chase in which Charlie makes his escape by hooking his cane on an automobile rear and being towed to safety.

The fast but delightfully graceful action is flavored with delicious comic bits. In one scene he mixes drinks to a wonderfully apposite "shimmy" rhythm; in another he unknowingly places a broiler cover over a live cat which he serves to the startled diner. (Imitations and variations of this gag have been legion.) Then there is his super-gallant kissing of Edna's hand; his dashing party entrance, shoulders aslant and flicking ashes into his hat; his hat tipping by pressures against the wall. (It would be hard to say who invented this gag which was often later worked by W.C. Fields.) Other prime comedy bits occur in the melee when, falling upon Mrs. Stout (played by Henry Bergman), Charlie decorously pulls down her skirt; and his attempts to retain his balance by rotating his hands like an electric fan.

Easy Street, released in January 1917, is the most famous of the Chaplin Mutuals. Though not as hilariously funny as some, it has the most cleverly worked-out story, in which some have read social criticism and others a satire on puritanism. Charlie, a derelict, wanders into a Mission. Reformed by the minister and the angelic organ player, his first act is to return the collection box he had stolen.

Gang war on Easy Street, the toughest section of the city, rises to a crescendo, with policemen carried back on stretchers, like soldiers from a battlefield. Help is needed and Charlie gets a job on the force. The very first day on his beat he encounters the leading gangster, whose appearance alone is enough to clear the street. The giant bully and the new cop size each other up. Charlie, at the alarm box, nervously tries to put in a call with the bully listening in. To deceive him, Charlie "plays" the receiver like a musical instrument and "looks through" it like an eyeglass. When the bully picks it up to take a look, Charlie gets in a lick with his club. As the sneering bully bends his head for more futile blows, Charlie tries to pacify him. In another display of his strength, the bully bends the gaslight lamp-post. Climbing quickly on his back. Charlie fits the lamp over the bully's face to anesthetize him. With all the finesse of a physician, he feels the bully's pulse and turns on more gas.

The Easy Streeters are awed by the new policeman while regulars on the force continue to cringe before a neighboring kid. Other funny business includes Charlie's catching a poor woman stealing a ham — and then, overcome by her sobs, "borrowing" vegetables from a neighboring stand to round out her dinner. For thanks he receives a flowerpot dropped on his head from above. Dispensing charity with Edna, he visits a couple with ten small children all in one slum room. Eyeing the puny father Charlie feels his muscle and pins his badge on him. He then strews cornflakes before the children as if they were chickens in a barnyard.

Pursued by the bully, who has broken jail, Charlie finally subdues him by dropping a stove on his head. In another scene, Edna is trapped in a dive and Charlie thrown down a manhole into the same room. Their plight seems hopeless when a dope fiend knocks Charlie on his hypodermic needle. The accidental injection produces superman results. He KO's the attacker, spins around and embraces Edna; then, with flying leaps, subdues the mob that hems them in.

The subtitle, *Love Backed by Force; Forgiveness Sweet, Bring Hope and Peace, to Easy Street*, introduces the closing scene. The reformed Easy Streeters, including the bully and his wife in their Sunday best, walking sedately to the new Mission with Charlie and Edna joining in the procession.

The Cure is probably the funniest of the Mutuals, interlacing fast and hilarious action with subtle pantomime and agile grace. At times it resembles a ballet laid in a sanitarium. Charlie in a light coat and straw hat is wheeled to the spring to take the water cure. The first comic sequence is a mixup in a revolving door with a gouty man whose tender foot is caught. Charlie is given a shove and they go round and round unable to "get off." This is followed by a muscle-feeling sequence in which a pretty nurse is involved. Urged by an attendant to feel his muscle as proof of the effects of the water cure, Charlie also feels the nurse's muscle. Then considering leg muscles as important to feel as arm muscles, he reaches toward the girl — but playfully feels his shoe instead. In another scene Charlie spills his spa water — and blames the puddle on a toy dog.

The gouty man, who happens to wear a fantastic beard, reappears and starts a flirtation with Edna. Charlie, seated between them, mistakes the handwavings and the winks as meant for him. As he turns a love seat, spilling the giant on the floor, he is ordered out — until Edna intercedes for him.

Upstairs the bearded bellhop has been sampling Charlie's trunkful of liquor. The head of the institution orders another drunken bellhop to dispose of Charlie's liquor supply. He carries out the order by tossing the bottles into the spa whose waters then impart unexpected powers.

In a steamroom sequence Charlie assumes statuesque poses each time the gouty man opens the curtain, finally dancing out daintily on his toes into the pool. In the massage room Charlie, watching a patient being pounded, raises the masseur's arm and proclaims him "the winner!" When his time comes, Charlie turns the treatment into a slippery wrestling match.

Pepped up by the spiked "water," two male invalids chase Edna whom Charlie rescues by deft use of his cane; then gallantly moves one of the "bodies" so that Edna may pass. A sampling of the water has its effects on him. He rests his foot on Edna's lap, sends the gouty man head-first into the pool, gets caught again in the revolving door, which sends him spinning around (photographed in fast motion) until he falls into the pool. Next morning, Edna explains as he holds an ice cake on his head. After Charlie vows to reform, the couple stroll forward — to his last ducking in the pool.

The Immigrant is another Chaplin triumph which compares favorably with any of his later works. Sentiment and social satire are adroitly worked into the story. The entire last half is cleverly constructed around an elusive coin, in one of the longest variations on a single comedy incident ever portrayed on the screen, yet so skillfully managed that every moment seems natural and spontaneous. Slower paced than the other Mutuals, *The Immigrant* has drama in the comedy and comedy in the drama.

On a rocking ocean liner, jammed with immigrants, we first see Charlie from the rear, leaning over the rail. His head is down and his shoulders quiver in an apparent spasm of *mal de mer.* Then, with a sudden turn forward, he triumphantly displays a large fish he has just hooked. The next scene is dinner on the violently rocking boat, with the passengers tossed from one end of the room to the other, and soup plates sliding from person to person as each helps himself in turn.

To comfort two weeping women, mother and daughter, who have just been robbed by a gambler, Charlie slips his craps winnings in the girl's pocket. The suspicious purser catches him as he is tempted to retain a bill or two. But the girl, finding the money, frees him and gives him tearful thanks. "The arrival in the Land of Liberty." As the ship passes the Statue of Liberty, the passengers are shoved and roped in like cattle, and Charlie takes a quizzical second look at the statue.

Ashore, "Later — hungry and broke," he picks up a coin, which slips through his torn pocket. He enters a restaurant, where a bullying waiter orders him to remove his hat, which Charlie finally does by making it bounce up into the air. Then he pantomimes musical fruit (beans), which he delicately masticates one by one.

Suddenly he spies the girl sitting alone across the aisle. He hugs her and leads her over to his table. Clasping her hands, he discovers she is clutching a black-bordered handkerchief and so learns of her mother's death. With a look of infinite sympathy he lowers her hand. After a poignant pause their spirits revive. Officiously Charlie orders food for Edna. As they eat, six waiters manhandle a customer who, Charlie is informed, "was ten cents short." Just then he discovers his own loss. An old tramp who has picked up the coin enters. He hands it to the waiter, who drops it to the floor and steps on it. As he turns, it is deftly covered by Charlie's foot. The waiter, securing the coin, bites it and finds it to be counterfeit.

The slumped and despairing Charlie is given another lease on life when an artist, there in search of unusual models, takes an interest in the couple. When Charlie's bill is presented he and the artist wrestle for it with exaggerated Alphonse and Gaston courtesy. The artist gives way too soon and Charlie is stuck with the bill. He gets out of this dilemma by putting his check over the tip left by the artist. Outside the restaurant Charlie asks for and receives an advance of a couple of dollars from the artist. He promptly puts the money to use at a "marriage license" bureau, across whose threshold he carries the coyly protesting girl.

The Adventurer, the last and perhaps the most popular of the famous Mutuals, was photographed at and near Santa Monica in July 1917. It is old-time screen comedy at its best and most typical — all wild chases, slapstick, and clever pantomime.

Charlie, an escaped convict, emerges from the sand into a guard's rifle. He does a "double take" and buries his head again.

As the guard dozes, he scales a cliff with lightning rapidity (fast-motion photography), only to bump into other guards, whom he eludes with miraculous agility, sliding eel-like under their legs. In a borrowed bathing suit he rescues two women from drowning along with the hulking but cowardly suitor of the younger woman. The two women invite Charlie, "the gallant sportsman," to stay over at their house. Waking next morning in striped pajamas that flash a frightening reminder of his prison garb, he receives another chilling reminder as he touches the brass bars of the bed.

Downstairs a ritzy party is in progress. Charlie, thirsty for more refreshment, bumps his empty glass into another guest's full one, thus refilling his own, and apologizes grandly for the apparent collision. There is another reminder of his past when the butler uncorks a bottle. Charlie puts up his hands — then nonchalantly covers the gesture by smoothing his hair. Joining dancers upstairs, Charlie takes Edna to a balcony where they eat ice-cream. Charlie has a mishap with his portion, dropping the ball down his pants front. By his facial expression one follows its path downward. It lands on the bare back of the mother below. As it slides down her fashionable décolleté, the screaming woman slaps the man with her who tries to reach for the icy lump.

Prison guards arrive. During the chase up and down stairs Charlie, donning a lampshade, "freezes" as the guards rush by. Pinning the jealous suitor between sliding glass doors, Charlie leaps over the balcony. He kisses Edna's hand and apologizes. As a guard grabs him he introduces him politely to Edna; the guard lets go to shake her hand — and Charlie takes off again.

CHARLIE CHAPLIN
What People Laugh At

Fresh and young at 29, Chaplin was not cautious about sharing his secrets with readers of American *magazine in November 1918. His precepts remain insightful and valid today.*

Given a knowledge of human nature, he says, and a willingness to observe people in action, the comedian looks for ways to achieve contrast and surprise. In terms of content, it's always a likely situation when you can make someone who is trying to be dignified look foolish. If the character is rich, that's all the better, because "nine tenths of the people in the world are poor and resent the wealth" of the others.

Chaplin also notes how lucky he was to think of carrying a cane: it makes him a "dude," just ready to have his dignity interrupted. On the other hand, as "the little fellow" in trouble, he draws on "the sympathy of the mob." In general, he'd rather be "clever and original," noted for his restraint, and even "spread the laughs out" than try to get a laugh every minute. To accomplish his ideals of originality, restraint, surprise, and social observation, he has sometimes spent 60,000 feet of film to achieve the 2000 feet he really wants.

Whenever I meet people who ask me to explain the mystery of "making people laugh" I always feel uncomfortable, and begin to edge away. There is no more mystery about my antics on the screen than about Harry Lauder's ability to entertain people. We both happen to know a few simple facts about human nature, which we use in our business. And when all is said and done, at the bottom of almost all success is a knowledge of human nature whether one be a salesman, hotel man, editor, or actor.

The one point of human nature that I play upon more than anything else, for example, is that it strikes people as funny when they see someone else placed in an undignified and embarrassing situation.

It isn't the mere fact of a hat blowing off that is funny. It is the ludicrous sight presented by a man chasing up the street with his hair blowing and his coat tails flying that makes people laugh. When a man walks quietly along a street, he is not funny. Placed in an embarrassing and ridiculous situation, however, the human being provokes other humans to laughter.

All comedy of situation is based upon this fact. Comedy moving pictures were an instant success because most of them showed policemen falling down coal holes, slipping into buckets of whitewash, falling off patrol wagons, and getting into all sorts of trouble. Here were men representing the dignity of the law, often very pompous themselves, being made ridiculous and undignified. The sight of their misfortunes at once struck the public funny bone twice as hard as if private citizens were going through like experiences.

Even funnier than the man who has been made ridiculous, however, is the man who, having had something funny happen to him, refuses to admit that anything out of the way has happened, and attempts to maintain his dignity. Perhaps the best example is the intoxicated man who, though his tongue and walk give him away, attempts in a dignified manner to convince you that he is quite sober.

He is much funnier than the man who, wildly hilarious, is frankly drunk and doesn't care a whoop who knows it. Intoxicated characters on the stage are almost always "slightly tipsy" with an attempt at dignity; because theatrical managers have learned that this attempt at dignity is funny.

For that reason, all my pictures are built around the idea of getting me into trouble and so giving me the chance to be desperately serious in my attempt to appear as a normal little gentleman. That is why, no matter how desperate the predicament is, I am always very much in earnest about clutching my cane, straightening my derby hat, and fixing my tie, even though I have just landed on my head.

I am so sure of this point that I not only try to get myself into embarrassing situations, but I also incriminate the other characters in the picture. When I do this, I always aim for economy of means. By that I mean that when one incident can get two big, separate laughs, it is much better than two individual incidents. In *The Adventurer*, I accomplished this by first placing myself on a balcony, eating ice cream with a girl. On the floor directly underneath the balcony I put a stout, dignified, well-dressed woman at a table. Then, while eating the ice cream, I let a piece drop off my spoon, slip through my baggy trousers, and drop from the balcony onto this woman's neck.

The first laugh came at my embarrassment over my own predicament. The second, and the much greater one, came when the ice cream landed on the woman's neck and she shrieked and started to dance around. Only one incident had been used, but it had got two people into trouble, and had also got two big laughs.

Simple as this trick seems there were two real points of human nature involved in it. One was the delight the average person takes in seeing wealth and luxury in trouble. The other was the tendency of the human being to experience within himself the emotions of the people he sees on the stage or screen.

One of the things most quickly learned in theatrical work is that people as a whole get satisfaction from seeing the rich get the worst of things. The reason for this, of course, lies in the fact that nine tenths of the people in the world are poor, and secretly resent the wealth of the other tenth.

If I had dropped the ice cream, for example, on a scrub-woman's neck, instead of getting laughs, sympathy would have been aroused for the woman. Also, because a scrubwoman has no dignity to lose, that point would not have been funny. Dropping ice cream down a rich woman's neck, however, is, in the minds of the audience, just giving the rich what they deserve.

By saying that human beings experience the same emotions as the people in the incidents they witness, I mean that — taking the ice cream as an example — when the rich woman shivered the audience shivered with her. A thing that puts a person in an embarrassing predicament must always be perfectly familiar to an audience, or else the people will miss the point entirely. Knowing that ice cream is cold, the audience shivers. If something was used that the audience did not recognize at once, it would not be able to appreciate the point as well. On this same fact was based the throwing of custard pies in the early pictures. Everyone knew that custard pie is squashy, and so was able to appreciate how the actor felt when one landed on him.

Many persons have asked me where I got the idea for the type of character I play. Well, all I can say is that it is a composite picture of many Englishmen I had seen in London during the years of my life in that city.

When the Keystone Film Company, with which I made my first pictures, asked me to leave Karno's *Night in an English Music Hall*, a pantomime in which I was playing, I was undecided what to do about the offer, principally because I did not know what kind of a comedy character I could play. Then, after a time, I thought of all the little Englishmen I had seen with small black mustaches, tight-fitting clothes and bamboo canes, and I decided to model my makeup after these men.

Thinking of the cane was perhaps the best piece of luck I ever had. One reason is that the cane places me, in the minds of the audience, more quickly than anything else could. The other is that I have developed the cane until it has almost a comedy sense of its own. Often I find it curling itself around someone's leg, or rapping someone on the shoulder and getting a laugh from the audience almost without my knowing that I was directing its action.

I don't think I quite realized, when I first used the cane, how, in the minds of literally millions of people, a cane labels a man as somewhat of a "dude." A young fellow who appears with a cane is very likely to be asked if he isn't afraid of catching cold without it. So when I shuffle onto the scene with my little stick and my serious expression, I at once convey the impression of attempted dignity, which is exactly the thing I want to do.

When I made my first picture with the Keystone Company I was twenty-two years old. (I am now twenty-nine.) You may wonder what I knew about human nature at that age. Well, you must remember that I had been playing before the public ever since I was fourteen years old. It seems a little queer that my first important stage engagement should have been with William Gillette, an American actor, in *Sherlock Holmes*, an American play. Nevertheless, it was, and for fourteen months I played the part of Billy, the office boy, in the London production of *Sherlock Holmes*.

At the end of that engagement I went into vaudeville. There I did a song and dance act for a few years, giving it up, however, to join one of Karno's pantomime companies. Pantomime is very well liked in England; and having a fondness for the art myself I was very glad to have a chance to learn something about it.

If it had not been for my mother, however, I doubt if I could have made a success of pantomime. She was one of the greatest pantomime artists I have ever seen. She would sit for hours at a window, looking down at the people on the street and illustrating with her hands, eyes, and facial expression just what was going on below. All the time, she would deliver a running fire of comment. And it was through watching and listening to her that I learned not only how to express my emotions with my hands and face, but also how to observe and to study people.

She was almost uncanny in her observations. For instance, she would see Bill Smith coming down the street in the morning, and I would hear her say:

"There comes Bill Smith. He's dragging his feet and his shoes are not polished. He looks mad, and I'll wager he's had a fight with his wife, and come off without his breakfast. Sure enough! there he goes into the bake shop for a bun and coffee."

And invariably, during the day, I would hear that Bill Smith had had a fight with his wife.

This habit of studying people was really the most valuable thing my mother could have taught me; because it has been only in this way that I have learned what appeals to human beings as funny.

That is why, when I am watching one of my pictures presented to an audience, I always keep one eye on the picture and the other eye, and both ears, on the audience. I notice what people laugh at, and what they don't laugh at. If, for example, several audiences do not laugh at a stunt I meant to be funny, I at once begin to tear that trick to pieces and try to discover what was wrong in the idea or in the execution of it, or in the photography of the scene.

Very often I hear a slight ripple at something I had not expected to be funny. At once I prick up my ears and ask myself why that particular thing got a laugh.

In a way, my going to see a movie is really the same as a merchant observing what people are wearing or buying or doing. Anyone who caters to the public has got to keep his knowledge of "what people like" fresh and up to date.

In the same way that I watch people inside a theater to see when they laugh, I watch them everywhere to get material which they can laugh at.

I was passing a firehouse one day, for example, and heard a fire alarm ring in. I watched the men sliding down the pole, climbing onto the engine and rushing off to the fire. At once a train of comic possibilities occurred to me. I saw myself sleeping in bed, oblivious to the clanging of the fire bell. This point would have a universal appeal, because everyone likes to sleep. I saw myself sliding down the pole, playing tricks with the fire horses, rescuing the heroine, falling off the fire engine as it turned a corner, and many other points along the same lines. I stored these points away in my mind and some time later, when I made *The Fireman*, I used every one of them. Yet if I had not watched the firehouse that day the possibilities in the character of a fireman might never have occurred to me.

Another time, I went up and down a moving staircase in a department store. I got to thinking how this could be utilized for a picture, and I finally made it the basis of *The Floorwalker*. Watching a prize-fight suggested *The Champion*, in which I, the small man, knocked out a big bruiser by having a horseshoe concealed in my glove, In another picture I used an employment office as the foundation of the picture. In other words, it has paid me to be always alive to the comic possibilities of the people and the things I see in everyday life.

I was seated in a restaurant once, for example, when I suddenly noticed that a man a few yards away kept bowing and smiling, apparently at me. Thinking he wished to be friendly, I bowed and smiled back at him. As I did this, however, he suddenly scowled at me. I thought I had been mistaken in his intentions. The next minute, however, he smiled again. I bowed; but once more he scowled. I could not imagine why he was smiling and scowling until, looking over my shoulder, I saw he had been flirting with a pretty girl. My mistake made me laugh, and yet it was a natural one on my part. So when the opportunity came a few months ago to utilize such a scene in *A Dog's Life*, I made use of the incident.

Another point about the human being that I use a great deal is the liking of the average person for contrast and surprise in his entertainment. It is a matter of simple knowledge, of course, that the human likes to see the struggle between the good and the bad, the rich and the poor, the successful and the unsuccessful. He likes to cry and he likes to laugh, all within the space of a very few moments. To the average person, contrast spells interest, and because it does I am constantly making use of it in my pictures.

If I am being chased by a policeman, I always make the policeman seem heavy and clumsy while, by crawling through his legs, I appear light and acrobatic. If I am being treated harshly, it is always a big man who is doing it; so that, by the contrast between big and little, I get the sympathy of the audience, and always I try to contrast my seriousness of manner with the ridiculousness of the incident.

It is my luck, of course, that I am short, and so am able to make these contrasts without much difficulty. Everyone knows that the little fellow in trouble always gets the sympathy of the mob. Knowing that it is part of human nature to sympathize with the "underdog," I always accentuate my helplessness by drawing my shoulders in, drooping my lip pathetically and looking frightened. It is all part of the art of pantomime, of course. But if I were three inches taller it would be much more difficult to get the sympathy of the audience. I should then look big enough to take care of myself. As it is, the audience, even while laughing at me, is inclined to sympathize with me. As someone once said, it feels like "mothering me."

However, one has got to be careful to make the contrast clear enough. At the close of *A Dog's Life*, for example, I am supposed to be a farmer. Accordingly, I thought it might be funny for me to stand in a field, take one seed at a time from my vest pocket, and plant it by digging a hole with my finger. So I told one of my assistants to pick out a farm where this scene could be taken.

Well, he picked out a nice farm; but I did not use it, for the simple reason that it was too small! It did not afford sufficient contrast for my absurd way of planting the seed. It might be slightly funny on a small farm, but done on a large one of about six hundred acres, the scene gets a big laugh, simply because of the contrast between my method of planting and the size of the farm.

On almost a par with contrast, I could put surprise.

Surprise has always seemed interesting to me because it is somewhat like news. Whenever I read the newspaper, I am always being surprised at what has happened in the world since yesterday. If, however, before I pick up the newspaper I knew exactly what was going to be in it, I should not be surprised, and therefore not so interested.

I not only plan for surprise in the general incidents of a picture, but I also try to vary my individual actions so that they, too, will come as a surprise. I always try to do the unexpected in a novel way. If I think an audience expects me to walk along the street while in a picture, I will suddenly jump on a car. If I want to attract a man's attention, instead of tapping him on the shoulder with my hand or calling to him, I hook my cane around his arm and gently pull him to me.

Figuring out what the audience expects and then doing something different, is great fun to me. In one of my pictures, *The Immigrant*, the opening scene showed me leaning far over the side of a ship. Only my back could be seen and from the convulsive shudders of my shoulders it looked as though I was seasick. If I had been, it would have been a terrible mistake to show it in the picture. What I was doing was deliberately misleading the audience. Because, when I straightened up, I pulled a fish on the end of a line into view, and the audience saw that, instead of being seasick, I had been leaning over the side to catch the fish. It came as a total surprise, and got a roar of laughter.

There is such a thing, however, as being too funny. There are some plays and pictures at which the audience laughs so much and so heartily that it becomes exhausted and tired. To make an audience roar is the ambition of many actors, but I prefer to spread the laughs out. It is much better when there is a continual ripple of amusement, with one or two big "stomach laughs," than when an audience "explodes" every minute or two.

People often ask me if all my ideas work out, and if it is easy to make a funny picture. I sometimes wish they could follow the whole process of getting the idea, working out the characters, taking the film, editing and arranging it.

I am often appalled at the amount of film I have to make in getting a single picture. I have taken as much as sixty thousand feet in order to get the two thousand feet seen by the public. It would take about twenty hours to run off sixty thousand feet on the screen! Yet that amount must be taken to present forty minutes of picture.

Sometimes, when I find that, though I have worked hard over an idea, it has not yet taken final shape in my head, and is therefore not ready to be filmed, I at once drop it and try something else. I do not believe in wasting too much time on something that will not work out. I do believe in concentrating all your energies upon the thing you are doing. But if you can't put it across, after having done your best, try something else for a time, and then come back to your original scheme if you still have faith in it. That is the way I have always worked.

In my work I don't trust anyone's sense of humor but my own. There have been times when the people around the studio have screamed at certain scenes while the picture was in the making, and yet I have discarded those scenes because they did not strike me as being funny enough. It isn't because I think I am so much smarter than those around me. It is simply because I am the one who gets all the blame or credit for the picture. I can't insert a title in a picture, for instance, and say:

"People, I don't blame you for not laughing. I didn't think this was funny myself, but the fellows around me told me it was and so I let it go."

Here is another point that makes it difficult for me to trust the judgment of those around me. My camera man and other assistants are so used to me that they don't laugh very much at what I do in rehearsal. If I make a mistake, however, then they laugh. And I, not realizing perhaps that I have made a mistake, am likely to think the scene is funny. I didn't get onto this point until I asked some of them one day why they had laughed at a bit of business that I did not think was amusing. When they told me they had laughed because I had done something wrong, I saw how they might mislead me. So now I am glad they *don't* always laugh at my stuff.

One of the things I have to be most careful about is not to overdo a thing, or to stress too much any particular point. I could kill laughs more quickly by overdoing something than by any other method. If I made too much of my peculiar walk, if I were too rough in turning people upside down, if I went to excess in anything at all, it would be bad for the picture. Restraint is a great word, not only for actors but for everybody to remember. Restraint of tempers, appetites, desires, bad habits, and so on, is a mighty good thing to cultivate.

One of the reasons I hated the early comedies in which I played was because there *couldn't* be much "restraint" in hurling custard pies! One or two custard pies are funny, perhaps; but when nothing but custard pies is used to get laughs, the picture becomes monotonous. Perhaps I do not always succeed by my methods, but I would a thousand times rather get a laugh through something clever and original than through slapstick and horseplay.

There is no mystery connected with "making people laugh." All I have ever done is to keep my eyes open and my brain alert for any facts or incidents that I could use in my business. I have studied human nature, because without a knowledge of it I could not do my work. And, as I said at the very beginning of this article, a knowledge of human nature is at the foundation of almost all success.

JANET E. LORENZ
The Gold Rush

> *Probably Chaplin's best feature film, and supposedly his favorite, The Gold Rush offers a strong combination of danger, pathos, and comedy within a satisfactory plot. Janet Lorenz is on the staff of the Center for Motion Picture Study at the Motion Picture Academy. She gives us a good description of what happens and also of some of the funny scenes, suggesting that Charlie as loner-bumbler represents the isolation we all have to cope with in the midst of our hopes of conforming and getting approval.*
>
> *The review is from Frank N. Magill,* Magill's Survey of Cinema: Silent Films *(Englewood Cliffs, N.J., Salem Press, 1982).*

Released: 1925
Production: Charles Chaplin for United Artists
Direction: Charles Chaplin
Screenplay: Charles Chaplin
Cinematography: Rollie Totheroh
Length: 9 reels/8,555 feet

Principal characters:

The Lone Prospector	Charles Chaplin
Big Jim McKay	Mack Swain
Black Larson	Tom Murray
Georgia	Georgia Hale
Georgia's friend	Betty Morrisey
Jack Cameron	Malcolm Waite
Hank Curtis	Henry Bergman

Of the vast array of unforgettable images that films have given the world, few are as widely recognized or as well loved as that of the Little Tramp, Charlie Chaplin's inspired comic creation. Chaplin's popularity dominated the realm of screen comedy during the years of silent films, and never was his particular blend of humor and pathos put to more effective use than in *The Gold Rush*. Made in 1925, *The Gold Rush* has appeared repeatedly on critics' lists of favorite films and is considered by many to be Chaplin's finest comedy.

The film's story is set in Alaska during the Gold Rush. Chaplin's Tramp, described here as the Lone Prospector, goes north to search for gold. Forced by a blizzard to take refuge in an isolated cabin, Charlie discovers that it is owned by an outlaw, Black Larson (Tom Murray). Big Jim McKay (Mack Swain), another prospector seeking shelter, soon joins them. Black Larson tries to force both men to leave, and he battles Big Jim for possession of his shotgun, while Charlie scrambles frantically to avoid the swerving gunbarrel. Finally, Big Jim triumphs and Black Larson is forced to go off in search of help. When he fails to return, Charlie and Big Jim find that they are trapped with no food, and starvation soon becomes a very real possibility. Ever resourceful, Charlie prepares a meal of boiled boot and, in the film's most famous sequence, proceeds to eat the unpalatable meal as if he were dining on the finest of foods. Big Jim, however, becomes desperate for real food and begins to imagine that Charlie is a giant chicken. Charlie is saved from Big Jim's axe when he spots a wandering bear and shoots it. The blizzard stops, and Charlie and Big Jim, fortified by a feast of bear meat, leave the tiny cabin. Charlie heads for a nearby town, while Big Jim sets off to find the claim he had discovered before the storm. There he finds Black Larson, who knocks him unconscious with a shovel, but is then killed in an avalanche.

Charlie, meanwhile, has reached the town where he enters a saloon and falls immediately in love with a dance-hall girl named Georgia (Georgia Hale). She, however, has no interest in the ragged little tramp, who soon leaves and persuades one of the townsmen to take him in. While the man is away and Charlie is staying alone in the cabin, Georgia and her friends come to call. When a hidden photograph reveals Charlie's devotion to Georgia, she and her friends accept his invitation to New Year's Eve dinner, hoping to amuse themselves at his expense. Charlie works hard shoveling snow to earn money for the dinner, then sits alone in the cabin as the hours pass and Georgia fails to appear. Falling asleep, Charlie dreams that the girls have arrived and he is entertaining them by performing a clever skit using two rolls stuck on forks as dancing legs. He awakens to the realization that Georgia is not coming, and he leaves the town in despair. Georgia remembers the dinner and comes to the cabin only to find Charlie gone and the decorations for the party still in place. She realizes too late how much her thoughtlessness has hurt him.

Charlie soon encounters Big Jim again, but finds that he is suffering from amnesia, caused by Black Larson's blow with the shovel, and is unable to remember the location of his claim. Charlie agrees to help him and the two proceed to the mountains, where they are once again trapped in Black Larson's cabin by a storm. During the night, the cabin slides to the edge of a cliff, and when Charlie steps outside in the morning, he narrowly avoids plummeting to his death. He and Big Jim then engage in a hilarious struggle to get out of the cabin before it slips over the edge of the precipice. Succeeding at last, they discover that the cabin has left them on the site of Big Jim's claim.

Wealthy now, and elegantly dressed, Charlie and Big Jim are on board a ship preparing to sail from Alaska. Having changed back into his old clothes for the benefit of photographers, Charlie falls down a flight of stairs to the lower deck and discovers that Georgia is also on board. Believing Charlie to be a stowaway, she tries to hide him and is amazed to discover that he is a millionaire. Declaring his love for her, Charlie proposes to Georgia, and the two set sail for a new and happier life.

The Gold Rush contains scene after scene in which Chaplin demonstrates his comic virtuosity. Chaplin's inspiration for the film was the notorious Donner party, a group of nineteenth century settlers who were trapped in the Sierra Nevada mountains by winter blizzards and were forced to resort to cannibalism before help reached them. Chaplin was able to draw on this grim event and turn it to his own comic devices. The sequence of the film in which a hunger-crazed Big Jim chases Charlie with an axe is both horrifying in its implications and exceedingly funny in its execution.

This mixture of emotions lies at the heart of all of Chaplin's best work, giving it a richness and depth that are rare in silent comedy. Charlie's efforts to charm Georgia in the dance hall take on humorous dimensions when he unwittingly uses a dog's leash to tie up his pants — with the dog still attached. Audiences laugh at his predicament, but they are also saddened by his humiliation in front of the woman he loves. The famous "Oceana Rolls" scene, in which Charlie dreams he is entertaining Georgia and her friends, is a delight to watch; yet viewers know that he will soon wake up to discover he is alone.

The Tramp's vulnerability is offset, however, by his resourcefulness and determination. When he must think of a way to earn money for his New Year's Eve party, he shovels a huge pile of snow from one doorstep to the next, charging each occupant for its subsequent removal. He proceeds from house to house in this manner, collecting a fee at each door. The best embodiment of this quality of resourcefulness is the legendary shoe-eating scene. In Charlie's agile hands, the shoelaces become spaghetti and the nails are delicately nibbled like bones. With its combination of humor, cleverness, and the underlying seriousness of Charlie's situation, this scene stands among the finest moments of screen comedy.

A third aspect of Chaplin's artistry is also evident in *The Gold Rush*, that of his astonishing physical agility. Although he is frequently stumbling, struggling with inanimate objects, or leaping about to escape imminent danger, his actions are as graceful and as carefully choreographed as a dancer's. From his first appearance, teetering on one foot around corners on the icy mountain paths, to his final shipboard tumble down the stairs to Georgia, Chaplin's moments of slapstick are pure poetry.

Finally, *The Gold Rush* serves to demonstrate the universality of Chaplin's appeal. The Little Tramp, at first appearance, seems to be a hopeless bumbler. Upon closer examination, however, viewers see that his problems stem from the fact that he is at odds with society and is trying haplessly to fit in. The more he struggles to observe social conventions and proprieties, the more absurd and isolated he becomes. His actions are a reminder, albeit on a much less catastrophic level, of the universal frustration of trying to reconcile individuality with society's demands.

CHARLES J. MALAND
The Burdens of Being Funny: *The Circus*

Chaplin was not overly productive during the 1920s, much to the regret of his United Artists partners (Mary Pickford, Douglas Fairbanks, and D.W. Griffith). A Woman of Paris (1923) was his first United Artists release, and it was neither a comedy nor a moneymaker. The Gold Rush (1925) was more than satisfactory at the boxoffice, but his only other feature for the rest of the decade was The Circus (1928).

Charles Maland, professor of English and chairperson of the cinema studies program at the University of Tennessee, is a scholar trained in American studies. He offers us a unique and fascinating comparison of these two feature-length comedies. In his book, Chaplin and American Culture: The Evolution of a Star Image *(Princeton University Press, 1989, pp. 105-110) he shares some of Chaplin's behind-scenes hesitation in choosing his next subject. Then he suggests that Chaplin was cautiously and consciously "creating his own genre," following up the success of* The Gold Rush *with similar structure, characters, and scenes.*

Shortly after the opening of *The Gold Rush* in August 1925, Chaplin was back at work, planning another film. His choice of subject was crucial. On the one hand, in only one of his two previous films had his Charlie persona appeared. Chaplin's Olympian status among critics, as well as his own aspirations, encouraged him to follow Stark Young's advice from 1922 and take on something new and more ambitious. On the other hand, *The Gold Rush* had done far better at the box office than had *A Woman of Paris*, and Chaplin was both jealous enough of his independence and shrewd enough to know that keeping the Charlie persona at the center of his films would be an economically sound decision.

Chaplin was thus pulled in two directions about his new project: should he stick with Charlie or abandon him? In November an article in the *New York Times* commented on Chaplin's plans. It reported that Chaplin had toyed with the idea of making a film called *The Suicide Club* but had discarded that idea in favor of another film — contents unknown — called *The Dandy*. After completing that film, Chaplin would make *The Clown*, in which Charlie would appear in the costume of a circus clown except for his shoes, cane and bowler. "This story," continued the article, "was described as another dramatic comedy, and in its method something after the style of *The Gold Rush*, except that it was to have a tragic ending — the funmaker impersonated by Chaplin is supposed to die in the tanbark while the spectators are applauding the comic pantomime."[1] These descriptions suggest that Chaplin was compromising by planning one non-Charlie film, then a second featuring a close relative of Charlie.

As it turned out, however, Chaplin returned more quickly than the *Times* article suggested he would to the formula that succeeded in *The Gold Rush*. *The Dandy* disappeared into the rapidly filling bin of discarded Chaplin ideas and projects, and *The Clown* evolved into *The Circus*. The tragic ending of *The Clown* was deferred (it sounds much like the conclusion of Chaplin's 1952 film, *Limelight*). And instead of being disguised as a circus clown, Charlie looks quite familiar in *The Circus*, clad in much the same way he appeared in most scenes of *The Gold Rush* and in many earlier Charlie comedies.

For some reason, reviewers suggested when the film was released that *The Circus* (1928) was somewhat archaic. In the *New York Times*, Mordaunt Hall praised it and noted that it was "more like his earlier films than either *The Kid* or *The Gold Rush*."[2] In the *New Republic* Chaplin's old friend Young used almost the same phrasing, calling *The Circus* "purer in the old-style Chaplin than *The Kid* or *The Gold Rush*."[3] It is true that some gags recall those of earlier Chaplin films, as when Charlie quickly gulps down a baby's hot dog when his father is not looking, reminiscent of the lunch wagon scene in *A Dog's Life*.

Nevertheless, in *The Circus* Chaplin also very carefully builds on the success of *The Gold Rush* by following the narrative structure and the essential blend of comedy and pathos he had established in this earlier film. One could almost say that Chaplin was self-consciously creating his own genre, one that ensured his popularity and respect among a diverse audience and sustained his star image.

Consider the similarities between *The Gold Rush* and *The Circus*. In both films the central character is Charlie, dressed the same in nearly every scene. In both works Charlie is thrust into a new social situation — the Klondike, a circus — in which he must learn to function. In both settings human beings exhibit cruelty to others. In *The Gold Rush* both Black Larson and Jack cause problems for Charlie; in *The Circus* the circus owner is an unreasonable and often cruel character.

Both films develop a romance between Charlie and a heroine that creates joy and sorrow, and here they are especially similar. Charlie's joyous enthusiasm in Hank's cabin in *The Gold Rush* — he jumps around, swings from the rafters, and beats the feathers out of a pillow when Georgia accepts his invitation to a New Year's Eve dinner — is analogous to the scene in *The Circus* when Charlie dances gleefully after he believes that Merna loves him. Both films also create moments of pathos that stem from Charlie's unrequited love. The pathos that arises in *The Gold Rush* when Charlie wakes up from his dream of a successful party with Georgia, followed by his walk to the dance hall and his isolated look into the window at the others' celebration, functions in much the same way, albeit more powerfully, as the scene in *The Circus* in which Charlie overhears Merna tell the fortune-teller that she is in love with Rex, the tightrope walker. Chaplin shows Charlie's reaction in medium close-up, followed by a long shot of Charlie alone in the dressing room.. The isolation of Charlie in the frame recalls the similar isolation when Charlie stands alone outside of the Monte Carlo dance hall in *The Gold Rush*.

Both films also frequently use animals to generate comedy. *The Gold Rush* uses bears, dogs, and a mule, and for a time Big Jim even imagines Charlie to be a chicken. In *The Circus*, Charlie often has an intransigent circus mule chasing him. He swallows a horse pill while trying to blow it through a tube into a horse's throat. He has a comic scene when locked in with a lion, a circumstance exacerbated by a barking dog outside the cage. And in the comic climax of the film, monkeys clamber all over Charlie as he tries to walk the tightrope.

This final scene suggests yet another similarity. In both films, the final long *comic* scene places Charlie in extreme danger, either balancing tenuously in a cabin at the edge of a precipice or walking a tightrope, high above the circus crowd, when he doesn't really know how. Taken collectively, these similarities in the areas of central character, setting, handling of romance, use of animals to generate comedy, and climactic comic scenes suggest that however different the films are in other ways, they possess a very similar structure, one with which Chaplin's approving audience was becoming familiar and with which Chaplin's star image was becoming associated.

There are, of course, dissimilarities in the two films. (A central dynamic of popular cinema generally is the equipoise between similarity and differentiation from film to film.) One of the most prominent differences lies in the conclusions. Most simply, in *The Gold Rush* Charlie gets the girl and in *The Circus*, he does not. More precisely, he realizes in *The Circus* that he is not right for Merna and that Rex is, so he sacrifices his own desires for the well-being of the other two. The final shots of *The Circus* contrast significantly to the final shots of *The Gold Rush*. At the end of *The Circus*, Charlie picks up a torn paper with a star on it that had once been the center of the hoop Merna jumped through in the film's first shot. He looks at it, apparently musing on how transitory stardom is (even he himself had been a star "funny man" in the circus for a time). He then crumples it into a ball, begins walking away from the camera, tosses the ball into the air, and kicks it sideways as it falls toward the ground. After a few heavily burdened steps, he takes a sprightly bounce, much like at the end of *The Tramp*, and walks away from the camera with renewed resolve. One of Charlie's increasingly central characteristics — his ability to endure pain and grief without letting it destroy him — is revealed in this final scene. A social outsider, Charlie nevertheless does not let disappointments destroy his affirmation for life.

However different from the final scene of *The Gold Rush*, this conclusion does resemble the ending of that film in its hints of self-referentiality. Viewed from the perspective of Chaplin's unhappy second marriage, the angry divorce proceedings, and other problems that confronted Chaplin as he was working on the film (among them the pressure to follow *The Gold Rush* with another worthy of his reputation), Charlie's act of crumpling up and discarding the star suggests that Chaplin himself was at times doubtful that the pressures of stardom were healthy for him or his art. The ending of *The Circus* thus employs self-referentiality much as the ending of *The Gold Rush* does.[4]

The Circus is also self-referential in the sense of alluding to one's autobiography. Chaplin explores the contradictions of his own being in ways that recall *A Woman of Paris*. A number of people who knew Chaplin in the mid 1920s have noted how variable his moods were. Tully, in his *Pictorial Review* articles, for example, wrote that Chaplin had "moods that change like early March weather in his native England."[5] Lita Grey stressed the doubleness of the Charles Spencer Chaplin she knew: "I saw him in every conceivable mood, from the peak of elation to the nadir of prolonged depression. I was witness to his compassion and his cruelty, to his explosive rages and about-face kindness, to his wisdom and his ignorance, to his limitless ability to love and his incredible insensitivities."[6]

Doubleness in *The Circus* is expressed primarily through Charlie and the ringmaster, Chaplin's shadow self. Charlie expresses the joyous, resilient, amusing, compassionate side of Chaplin. We have already seen Chaplin's compassion for the poor and down and out expressed in *My Trip Abroad*. Tully also recalls that when he was "a hungry writer with more ambition than capacity," Chaplin gave him a hundred dollars that had helped him a great deal.[7] Though self-sacrifice was not a new trait of Charlie's in *The Circus*, his sacrifice of his own love for Merna's happiness, a decision that dooms him to a loneliness that Chaplin himself had experienced, was an act crucial to Charlie's character and crucial, too, one could argue, to Chaplin's best self-image.

If this image of a charitable, compassionate, self-sacrificing Charlie was not new, what *was* relatively new in *The Circus* was Chaplin's willingness to confront the harsher side of his being. As one critic has shrewdly noted, the ringmaster in *The Circus* is the first in a long line of shadow selves that appear in later Chaplin films. Allan Garcia played the ringmaster, who resembles a number of other Chaplin characters, including the millionaire in *City Lights* and the factory owner in *Modern Times* (the latter also played by Garcia). The ringmaster's costume in *The Circus*, which consists of a top hat, riding boots, jodhpurs, and a whip, is similar to the costumes worn by the Hynkel character in *The Great Dictator* and by Calvero when he does his "flea act" in *Limelight*. And the ringmaster's cruelty is not unlike the darker side of Monsieur Verdoux in the film of that title.[8]

The ringmaster is like Chaplin both professionally and personally. Professionally, his comic enterprise, the circus, functions as a metaphor for another comic enterprise, the movie studio concerned with making chaplinesque comedies. Many accounts of Chaplin on the set stress his complete control and his desire for perfection; in Tully's words, "Never did a despot dominate a country as Chaplin rules his studio."[9] Like Chaplin, the ringmaster is a demanding perfectionist: In the tryout he is constantly directing his clowns. In fact, his first line in the film, spoken to Merna — "you missed the hoop again" — mirrors Chaplin's tendency to control his set completely and to make sure a shot was perfect before moving on.

But the ringmaster also resembles Chaplin's darker personal side. The character denies his daughter food because she fails to perform up to his expectations. Later in the film he physically abuses her, and he summarily fires a group of men working under him when they seek higher pay. Although we only have Lita Grey's version of their marriage and divorce, if her account is at all accurate, Chaplin was at times incredibly cruel to his second wife from the day they were married — or perhaps even from the day he learned she was pregnant. Although the ringmaster does reluctantly approve of his daughter's marriage ex post facto — perhaps an acknowledgement by Chaplin that his own darker side could be brightened — he exhibits a human cruelty that Chaplin seemed to be discovering both in himself and in others as he struggled through some of his difficulties in the mid-1920s. This would become an increasing concern as he observed the human sufferings of the Depression and World War II.

These autobiographical links were not frequently drawn by critics of *The Circus* in 1928. However, Tully's charges about Chaplin's moodiness and despotism and more generally circulating stories about Chaplin's perfectionism did have some effect on his star image. Comments like Tully's transferred a potentially noxious germ to the body of Chaplin's star image, but for the time, at least, the illness remained latent. Not until the 1940s did the germ, in combination with others, come to infect the entire star image. On the other hand, the stories of Chaplin's perfectionism could be, and in the 1920s were, read more positively, as the true indication of Chaplin's demanding genius. As long as the resulting films were satisfying to audiences, his high standards were generally considered a positive quality.

How did *The Circus* fare with the critics and the public? *The Circus* did very well with both groups. Surveying the reviews, *Literary Digest* gathered the impression that Chaplin's "critical admirers are killing the fatted calf to celebrate his return to his own field of pure clowning."[10.] Critic Robert Sherwood had high praise for Chaplin: "Chaplin doesn't have to play *Hamlet*. He doesn't have to play any part created by any other genius from Shakespeare down." Countering those who thought Chaplin should abandon Charlie for more serious subjects, Sherwood, echoing comments by Seldes earlier in the decade, wrote that Charlie "is just as important, just as true, as all the melancholy princes who ever discovered that there is something rotten in Denmark."[11] To Alexander Bakshy, writing in the *Nation*, Chaplin was "again at his very best" in *The Circus*, and Young, in spite of some reservations about Chaplin's makeup and the handling of pathos in the film, also found the film a triumph.[12]

The critical reception of the film suggests that the expectations Chaplin had raised through his previous films were well satisfied by *The Circus*. More and more, it seemed that Chaplin was forming his own genre. Or, to put it another way, he was establishing an aesthetic contact with his audience, promising them a consistent central character, a romance tinged with pathos, inventive humor, and some serious themes or concerns (often, like many Hollywood films, based on moral contrasts rooted in individual characters) underlying the work. In exchange, viewers offered their dollars for tickets and their critical adulation. To them, Chaplin satisfied his end of the aesthetic contract in *The Circus*.

The film also did well at the box office, nearly as well as *The Gold Rush*. The United Artists balance sheets of domestic film rentals through the end of 1931 show that *The Gold Rush* had accumulated $2.15 million in rentals, while *The Circus* had garnered $1.82 million.[13] For some reason, Chaplin later did not remember *The Circus* as very successful, perhaps because he associated the making of it with an unpleasant period of his life. His attitude is suggested by the fact that he did not revive the film until 1969 (*The Gold Rush* was revived much earlier, in 1942) and that he mentions it only once in his autobiography, and then only in the context of his mother's final illness (MA, p. 288). It is too bad that *The Circus* has faded from public consciousness, for it is a fascinating film that shows Chaplin dealing successfully with interesting thematic material. It is also historically significant as the last film Chaplin had the luxury of making in the silent era.

NOTES

1 *New York Times* 29 November 1925, sec. 7, p. 5.
2 Quoted in *Literary Digest* 96 (24 March 1928): 41.
3 *New Republic* 38 (8 February 1928); reprinted in Kauffmann, *American Film Criticism*, pp. 201-4.

4 Kerr, *Silent Clowns*, pp. 339-43, argues in considerable detail that *The Circus* is "a comedy about the consciousness of being funny." See Smith, *Chaplin*, pp. 79-84, both on that notion and on more autobiographical issues, to which my discussion is indebted. Though both give fruitful readings of the film, I believe both undervalue it.

5 Tully, *Pictorial Review*, January 1927, p. 8.

6 Grey, *My Life with Chaplin*, p. 323.

7 Tully, *Pictorial Review*, January 1927, p. 8.

8 See Smith, *Chaplin*, pp. 82-83.

9 Tully, *Pictorial Review*, February 1928, p. 75.

10 "Bonnie Prince Charlie of the Custard Pies," *Literary Digest* 96 (24 March 1928): 36.

11 "Bonnie Prince Charlie," p. 42.

12 Bakshy's review, which appeared in the *Nation* on 29 February 1928, and Young's, which appeared in the *New Republic* on 8 February 1928, both are reprinted in Kauffmann, *American Film Criticism*, pp. 200-204.

13 O'Brien file, box 209, files 1-2, UAC. Since both films were through their initial release by this time, these figures provide a relatively accurate comparison.

[Professor Maland has told the present author that Graham Petrie's article (see next page) encouraged him to write his book on Chaplin's star image.]

GRAHAM PETRIE
So Much and Yet So Little:
A Survey of Books on Chaplin

Here we have a rare case of a film professor who is also a passionate, knowledgeable, and demanding critic of existing film books. His item-by-item analysis of books about Charlie Chaplin is a model of critical directness and informational simplicity, telling us what we need to know and asking why we are not better served. His examination of the overblown rhetoric and factual bloopers of the Robert Payne book is particularly satisfying and long overdue. In the course of his survey of various critics and historians he provides us with a great deal of information about the ways Chaplin has spoken to us.

Petrie teaches English and film at McMaster University in Hamilton, Ontario. His main question is for contemporary writers and teachers in film studies: Why have you not dealt with Chaplin, who is clearly a major figure, as you have with many lesser directors who present fewer problems? It is possible, we might suggest, that the theorists are not up to it, or at least haven't the relevant tools. It is also possible that the earlier writers have been correct in placing Chaplin simply in a tradition of message-givers rather than cinematic stylists.

This article appeared in an early number of the Quarterly Review of Film Studies *(November 1977), which was originally founded for the purpose of doing extended bibliographical studies on particular areas of interest to film scholars. Petrie also wrote a valuable critique of the auteur theory, "Alternatives to Auteurs," in* Film Quarterly, *Spring 1973.*

I.

Anyone attempting to read through even a fraction of the vast amount of material on Chaplin quickly becomes afflicted with a sense of *déja vu*. It is not just that the books endlessly repeat exactly the same biographical information; even the attempts at critical judgment and analysis are often virtually indistinguishable. Here, for example, are four different critics writing about a scene from *The Pawnshop*.

Deservedly the most famous passage in *The Pawnshop* is the alarm-clock scene. The ailing timepiece is brought in. Charlie puts a stethoscope to it, taps it like a doctor examining a lung, raps it as if testing porcelain, snaps his thumb on the bell, starts drilling with an auger, opens it with a can-opener, takes a significant sniff at its insides, then, with the telephone mouthpiece in his eye like a jeweler's magnifying glass, he examines it, oils it, uses dental forceps for some necessary extraction, taps it with a plumber's hammer, listens for noise, then pulls out the spring, measures it like a ribbon,

snips off lengths with a plier, then empties the remaining contents on
the counter, where he stops the worm-like wriggling of the springs by
squirts of oil. Finally sweeping the debris into the puzzled customer's
hat, he solemnly shakes his head. (The scene is photographed in two
long takes of several hundred feet each, separated by a two-foot flash
of the customer's face.) (Huff, 75)[1] . . .

And the metaphor itself can become notoriously unstable, changing
its terms without warning. There is a justly celebrated sequence in
The Pawnshop — composed of the two longest sustained "takes"
Chaplin had yet permitted himself — in which he is asked by a
customer to examine a clock. What will Charlie give him for it?
Charlie must test the reliability of the clock. He applies a stethoscope
to it, turning it into a sick baby. Failing to get to its insides with an
auger, he turns it into a can of tuna fish and cuts away its lid with an
opener. It does not have a very hopeful odor. The insides are attacked
with a jeweler's eyeglass; it is delicate Swiss-work now. But its teeth
are bad and a dentist's forceps must be applied. Defective plumbing
too; a hammer will help. Its inner mechanisms begin to uncoil. He
measures and snips them off like yardgoods. When its minor parts
begin to squiggle about on the counter like larvae, he uses an oil can
as an exterminator. He gathers the parts together into the man's hat
and gives them back. No deal. A clock — unlikely object — can be a
baby, a can of fish, an open mouth, a bolt of cotton — *anything.*
Chaplin has gone beyond mere look-alikes. The identity of an object
lies only in the attitude one takes toward it. The man of all attitudes
makes the universe his helpless plaything. (Kerr, 92).

[Petrie includes extended descriptions of the same scene by Robert
Payne and, in French, Jean Mitry.]

Although there are different degrees of elaboration involved
in the descriptions and some — Mitry and Kerr — are more
sharply and vividly written than others, none of these passages
goes much beyond an attempt to recreate verbally the images
available to us on the screen, together with their more obvious
implications. It is interesting that there is no disagreement whatever among the critics: all see exactly the same things (though
sometimes in a slightly different order) and their interpretations
of the visual metaphors are virtually identical.

Such unanimity is remarkable in film criticism and it raises
several, potentially disturbing, questions about the nature of
Chaplin's art. If four of the most influential interpreters of
Chaplin, writing over a period of a quarter of a century, can do
no more than provide four virtually interchangeable analyses of
one of the most famous sequences in his work, what does this tell
us about the work itself? Can it be that Chaplin has reached a
level of such universal simplicity and transparency, that he

speaks so directly and clearly to his audience, that there is nothing left for the critic to do but humbly to record his impressions of the film? This seems to have been the prevalent opinion between 1920 and 1940, when comment on Chaplin was almost universally rhapsodic and notoriously unconcerned with any attempt at what we would now regard as technical analysis.

A more sophisticated and also more prosaic generation of critics seems, however, to have drawn the obverse conclusion to this: if criticism of Chaplin's films lacks subtlety, ambiguity, depth, rigor, it is simply because the films themselves lack these and provide no opportunity for the kinds of criticism in fashion today. The critic is better advised to turn his attention to comedians like Keaton and Tati, where he can allow his taste for discussions of cinematic space, camera placement, narrative strategies, relationship between audience and image, and almost anything else, to run riot. Chaplin, by comparison, seems flat and one-dimensional; one offers an obligatory bow to his "greatness" and hurries on to more complex matters.

The contemporary shift in taste away from Chaplin and towards Keaton is, of course, a matter of common record (though it may be a question of critical rather than popular reaction, and Chaplin's overall popularity seems undiminished). Some critics have attempted to account for this and Gerald Mast suggests that the following factors may have contributed to the reaction against Chaplin: a new sensitivity to the many flaws in his films; Chaplin's own personality, especially as it emerges from his autobiography; the fact that the major films, by Chaplin's own choice, were largely out of circulation for almost thirty years; and a new attitude towards cinema and the status of film itself. David Robinson also comments on the "positive antagonism" often expressed towards Chaplin and he too attributes this to his personality, with its combination of arrogance and vanity, and to a reaction against the simplistic philosophy that seems to emerge from the films. To these I would add what I might term "professional jealousy" on the part of film critics: in the 1920s and 1930s anyone — poet, painter, novelist, scientist, playwright, philosopher, politician — felt free to comment on Chaplin's art. For many of these admirers, this was usually couched in terms such as, "I am not a great filmgoer — indeed, I despise the cinema — but in my opinion, Chaplin . . ." It is not perhaps surprising that a new generation of film critics, jealous of its hard-won standing in the world of the arts, should turn against a filmmaker admired by people who had no real interest in the cinema as such, and seek to erect its own hierarchy based on more purely cinematic criteria.

II.

The major books on Chaplin tend to be either biographical, with a minimum of critical commentary, or attempts to combine biography with critical analysis. For most critics the analysis rarely goes beyond this kind of retelling of the story evident in the extracts already quoted combined, if the critic wishes to be particularly profound, with comments on the "essence," "nature" or "essential validity" of the Chaplin persona. Nowhere in these books can one find a detailed analysis of the structure or technique of any major film or even of an important sequence within such a film. There is no serious dissection of Chaplin's camera style, editing, use of sound or music, or of the narrative or image patterns to be found within his work. There are no chapters headed, "Visual Distancing in Chaplin," "The Articulation of Color in *The Countess From Hong Kong*," or "*Modern Times* as a Brechtian Film."[2] Chaplin brings out the philosopher, the psychologist, and the sociologist in film critics, but he seems to have little to offer anyone even remotely interested in the current directions being taken by film theory.

The obvious answer to this might be that Chaplin is not in any sense a conscious film artist and thus there is no point in trying to approach him as though he were. His camera style and lighting are routinely described as "primitive"; his editing appears to be purely functional; his features, especially *City Lights* and *Modern Times*, are said to consist of a series of episodes that have little organic unity and could well be transferred from film to film without making too much difference; his music (laboriously composed by a process of whistling and humming to increasingly distraught arrangers) is tuneful and banal. Chaplin himself gives little comfort to those who would attempt to apply a sophisticated theory of cinema to his work. Though he seems to have thought seriously about the nature of comedy and the mechanics of building a comic sequence, his autobiography contains no more than ten pages (271-81) that could be said to discuss film technique and little more emerges from this than the observations that he prefers "simplicity of approach," sees the camera's main function as "facilitating choreography for the actor's movements," feels that "the camera should not obtrude," and prefers "subtlety and restraint in acting." Although some critics devote a good deal of space to his working methods, they almost mean by this his habit of shooting an inordinately vast amount of film from which bits and pieces were painstakingly extracted (by Chaplin himself) to produce the finished work. Camera angles are almost always straight-on close-up or medium long-shot, and rumors persist that, throughout his career, Chaplin never fully grasped the fact that a mere change of camera lens could alter the whole spatial relationship between subject and camera.

And yet. And yet. How could someone so woefully ignorant of the very basics of his medium produce some of the greatest films (not novels or plays or music hall turns but *films*) ever made? Will none of the critics tell us that?

III.

Most, unfortunately, seem to be blissfully unaware that such a question might need to be posed or answered. I will pass quickly over those works that are purely biographical[3] as the basic facts of Chaplin's career are by now fairly well established. The standard biography in English is still that of Theodore Huff, first published in 1951, but there are numerous other works of varying degrees of quality and accuracy. One of the earliest, by William Dodgson Bowman, which first appeared in 1931, has recently been reprinted; it has essentially been superseded by later works and is interesting mainly for its valiant attempts to defend Chaplin from charges of sexual impropriety. Gerith Von Ulm's "intimate biography" of Chaplin, based on conversations with his chauffeur Kono and published in 1940 is, if anything, even more defensive of Chaplin and manages to put a positive interpretation even on some of his more unforgivable actions — such as his breaking his promise to visit the children at the London orphanage where he had spent part of his childhood, during his second European tour. Like Bowman's book, this is often highly inaccurate in its accounts of the films themselves. Von Ulm claims, for example, that *In the Park* was the first film directed by Chaplin, and seems to believe that *The Idle Class* was never completed.

The Little Fellow, by David Cotes and Thelma Niklaus, contains little that cannot be found in the earlier books, though it too sports its own inaccuracies, such as the statement that Chaplin "banished" Edna Purviance after *A Woman of Paris* and would have nothing further to do with her. Robert Payne's *The Great God Pan* (1952) will be discussed more fully in a later section but draws heavily on Huff for its biographical details. More recent books, like Denis Gifford's *Chaplin* (1974) are essentially picture books with interspersed text, though Gifford writes well on Chaplin's early life; and Roger Manvell's *Chaplin* (1974) though rarely particularly original or profound, is a reliable condensation of the available material.

Works by members of the Chaplin family themselves are also fairly numerous. Chaplin's own *Autobiography* (1964), as reviewers unanimously complained, tells us little about his art and, after a promising section on his childhood, degenerates into a catalogue of famous names and a refusal even to discuss his marital problems. Lita Grey Chaplin's *My Life with Chaplin* (1966) is — considering the hostile treatment she has received from almost all the Chaplin biographers — surprisingly unvindictive and remarkably generous in its appraisal of Chaplin's artistic abilities. She informs us there that her original name was Lillita, not the supposed "Lolita" that psychologically inclined critics have seized on so eagerly; Charles Chaplin Jr. confirms this and gives a generally sympathetic account of both his parents, together with some interesting firsthand information about the shooting of some of his father's films.

In French, the main biography is probably that of Georges Sadoul (1957), though readers who come to it after Huff's book in particular will find in it little that is new. The director Robert Florey produced one of the earliest of the French biographies, in 1927, a short and largely anecdotal work, and Pierre Leprohon's *Charles Chaplin* (1946) and Maurice Bessy's *Charles Chaplin* (1972) round out the other major French work in this area. Like Sadoul's, each is sound enough and no doubt readable enough, and one's judgment will be based solely on which one happens to encounter first: the dozen or so available biographies on Chaplin inevitably repeat and rework the same basic information and, by the time one reaches the twelfth, there is a definite sense that saturation point has been reached and there is absolutely no call for further biographies of Chaplin until a writer of sheer genius can come along to make us look at the familiar evidence in a totally original light.

Few of these books offer anything of significance in terms of understanding of the films; most follow a standard formula of tracing the major stages of Chaplin's career (Keystone, Essanay, Mutual, First National, later features), attempting to isolate the characteristic features of each period and describing some of the major films. Most concentrate on the Chaplin persona and its significance, rather than on the structure of style of the films themselves, and many seem to be based on vague and often inaccurate memories of films seen many years previously — even Georges Sadoul makes the elementary mistake of placing the Thanksgiving Dinner and the "chicken" sequences of *The Gold Rush* within the *final* scenes in the cabin rather than in the first half of the film (Sadoul, 105-6).

Before moving on to fuller discussion of some of the books that *do* contribute to an understanding of Chaplin's art, it is worth grouping here some of the books and essays that offer minor, though sometimes significant, comments on this. The tone of Chaplin criticism in the 1940s and 1950s was probably set by James Agee in his famous essay, "Comedy's Greatest Era," though it is worth noting that, even at the time this first appeared, the major films were already out of general circulation and the early shorts were to be seen largely in mutilated, reedited versions, with allegedly humorous sound effects and music added. Agee had thus to be taken largely on trust and, in a brief three or four pages, he provides an impressive summary of received pre-1950 opinion on Chaplin: "The Tramp is centrally representative of humanity, as many-sided and as mysterious as Hamlet, and it seems unlikely that any dancer or actor can ever have excelled him in eloquence, variety or poignancy of motion" (Agee, 9). The ending of *City Lights*, he goes on to say, is "the greatest piece of acting and the highest moment in movies" (10). Such statements are likely to embarrass rather than convince a modern critic. Yet, even with new versions of the films available to work from, no defender of Chaplin has managed to come up with anything much better than a restatement, and watering down, of Agee's eulogy and method of approach.

Raymond Durgnat, who devotes a few pages to Chaplin in *The Crazy Mirror*, puts a good deal of emphasis on the elements of cruelty, sadism, and lack of scruples in the Chaplin figure that counterbalance the pathos and loneliness. *The Gold Rush* is about alienation and physical survival; *Modern Times* expresses sheer anarchy of spirit. Isabel Quigley, like many other critics, finds the essence of Chaplin in his gift for metaphor, his ability to transform and recreate everyday objects. Donald McCaffrey appears as the spokesman for the contemporary antagonism to Chaplin: his films are over-rated (though *The Gold Rush* has some merits), structurally flawed, crude, trite, and banal. Such hostility is perhaps understandable, however, if placed in the context of such simple-minded pro-Chaplin criticism as this, from John Montgomery, on *City Lights*: "The boxing match, one of the funniest sequences ever filmed, is timed with masterly precision. It would be impossible to see it without laughing." (105).

A more recent tendency has been towards the creation of an accurate descriptive filmography of Chaplin's work that would provide a reliable basis on which future critics could build their assessments. This is particularly important with the early shorts, which exist often under several different titles and in versions that may have very little relationship to the form in which they originally appeared. The most massive and detailed of these is Jean Mitry's *Tout Chaplin* (1972) — though Mitry confesses (6) that he is working in some cases on memories of viewings that took place many years ago. The book also claims to provide the most accurate list of credits yet supplied for Chaplin's work. Uno Asplund's *Chaplin's Films* (1973) is more modest in scope but similar in intent and, between them, the two books should make the kind of blunders that exist in almost all the biographies totally inexcusable in the future.

There seem to be two extremes, then, which writers on Chaplin seem to adopt: the purely factual and the purely impressionistic. The former gives us dates, facts, places, the actual content of the films laid out in meticulous sequences; the latter praises (or, more rarely, condemns) Chaplin in flights of ecstatic prose that seldom descend to the level of accurate examination of the images and their arrangement. The impressionistic tendency arrived full blown as early as 1922 with Louis Delluc's *Charlie Chaplin*, where Charlot is hailed as "the artist and the work of art at the same time" (14), a creator who has painted, modelled and sculpted his own body; and a film like *The Bank* is described in these terms: "Tragedy changes its style. And if, from Prometheus, stealer of fire from heaven, Marcel L'Herbier has made Monsieur Prevoyan, banker, then here is Orestes, with his manifold torments, become a little man-of-all-jobs in a paradoxical bank. Charlie, broom in hand, is heartbreaking. And there is nothing funnier, is there?" (74).

IV.

One might reasonably expect the full length critical works at least to mediate between these two extremes and to find a way of writing about Chaplin that is neither imprecise and misleading nor purely descriptive. Yet almost all the major critics have settled for a pattern that combines the weaknesses, rather than the strengths, of both approaches: there is rarely anything more than an attempt at an "imaginative recreation" of the experience of the films by means of words — the process illustrated in my opening four quotations — where the critic attempts to comment and describe simultaneously. This procedure may have been defensible in the 1940s and 1950s, when even the major features were largely inaccessible to the general public; there is little excuse for it nowadays, however, when they are once again easily available.

The dangers of this method can be illustrated by what is easily the worst — and unfortunately one of the most widely read — of the books on Chaplin, Robert Payne's *The Great God Pan* (1952, and reprinted in paperback as *Charlie Chaplin*). Payne first of all attempts to put Chaplin in a dual tradition of religious and comic figures that stretches back to the Greeks and takes in (to quote a few names at random) Navajo ceremonies, Kierkegaard, Kafka, Kleist, Punch, Grimaldi, Dan Leno, and Dickens. As Payne nowhere deigns to provide references or sources, it is difficult to judge the accuracy of what he is telling us about, for example, Greek religious ceremonies. But when one encounters a sentence like the following: "Now listen to poor mad Miss Flite as she contends with the unpaid rent and the avarice of lawyers in *Dombey and Sons*" (131) which manages at one stroke to transfer the character from *Bleak House* and to misquote the title of the novel in which she is alleged to appear, then I, for one, am not going to believe a word he tells me about activities in the Roman circus that are far more difficult to check and verify than the works of Dickens.

This, however, is not the worst Payne has to offer. As his book proceeds, he starts to come to grips with the films, employing an overblown, pseudopoetic prose that is intended to make us reexperience the films while reading about them. And here is what he has to tell us about a classic sequence from *The Gold Rush*:

> When we see Charlie again he is out on a foraging expedition and both his feet are wrapped in rags. Another shoe is cooking. Empty-handed, Charlie returns to the hut and prepares dinner. In the middle of the dinner Big Jim goes hideously mad, and imagines that Charlie is a plump chicken. Then the nightmare begins. Nothing like this nightmare was ever to occur to Charlie again; nothing like it had ever happened before. Big Jim is out to murder. He will take the neck of the chicken, lay it on the table and cut off the protesting head, and Charlie looks at him with immense sadness and pity, almost prepared to offer himself as a sacrifice. They chase each other around the room, and suddenly Charlie becomes the chicken, and the frightened chicken is standing on the table: all Mack Swain has to do is to wring its neck. But Charlie escapes his fate by the use of a transformation scene: he changes from a chicken back to a man again, and Mack Swain is sufficiently aware of the change to pause for a moment — no more than a moment. When he looks for the chicken again, it is fluttering in panic round the room. Mack Swain chases it round the room and out into the snowfields, seizes a gun, fires at it, and we see the flapping wings, but suddenly they are Charlie's arms. The scene is played in an unrelenting effect of tragedy. Mack Swain becoming Mephistopheles with a spurt of powder and a column of blue flame. (Payne, 199-200)

It is difficult to know where to begin when commenting on this farrago of total nonsense, for virtually none of this happens on the screen in anything resembling the manner in which Payne describes it. To begin with, Charlie never actually cooks his second boot; he merely offers it to the starving Big Jim, who shudders and refuses it. When the first transformation takes place Jim merely stares in amazement, there is no chase at this point, and at no stage in the whole sequence does Charlie-as-chicken take refuge on the table. Charlie changes back, Jim rubs his eyes, says, "I thought you was a chicken." Charlie glances at him warily and thoughtfully puts the carving knife out of Jim's reach. He changes again — after a long pause and not "no more than a moment" — and this time there *is* a chase, though it is only once around the room and Jim seizes his gun inside the room and not outside in the snowfields. Jim has no chance actually to fire the gun before the chicken becomes Charlie once again. Payne thus misrepresents every detail of the sequence — its events, its rhythm, its mood, its effect — and this is no isolated incident within his book as a whole. It is riddled with this kind of misinformation — we are solemnly told about a sequence in *Modern Times*, for example, when Charlie "dives across a road on skates and plunges recklessly towards destruction" (235). Payne's book is a disgrace and it is a sad comment on the state of Chaplin criticism that it remains in print as one of the standard accounts of his life and art.

Although all the other books to be mentioned are immeasurably superior to Payne's, they all share his disinclination to look sharply enough at the actual images of the films themselves; it is almost as if, having accepted as a working premise the belief that Chaplin had no specifically cinematic talent, they feel obliged (or free) to write about his work from a purely mythic, psychological, philosophical, or sociological viewpoint, using the bare narrative of the films as a point of reference. Theodore Huff's book, for example, is much stronger as a biography than it is a work of criticism: he traces with some care the development from the crude, often cruel comedy of the Keystone films, through the subtler pantomimes and satire of the Essanay series, to the perfection of comic technique and character evident in the Mutuals, but the accounts of specific films are confined to descriptions of the story and brief evaluative comments. Like Delluc, he sees *A Dog's Life* as Chaplin's first true masterpiece and, like most pre-1960 critics, he writes with great enthusiasm about the legendary *A Woman of Paris*, which is the only film to receive anything approaching a technical or stylistic analysis. *City Lights* is presented as perhaps Chaplin's greatest film and Huff gives quite a careful account of the way in which the music is employed within the film. *Monsieur Verdoux* is attacked for its abandonment of the Charlie persona and for its structural weaknesses and technical inadequacies.

One might expect Parker Tyler's *Chaplin: Last of the Clowns*, which appeared in 1948, three years before Huff's book, to offer something more idiosyncratic at least but, though it contains some valuable insights, this is not one of Tyler's better books, and it is disappointingly slight overall. Tyler suggests that Chaplin mingles "the aplomb of an adult with the awkwardness of a child" (p. 35), discusses his problems with women, his personal sexuality and frustrations, and sees the major films, with their recurring themes of doubles, amnesia, dreams, and mistaken identity, as projections of Chaplin's own conflicts. Interesting as these observations are, they are not followed through in sufficient detail, though there is still certainly scope for a later critic to pick up on them and develop them. The book concludes with an essay on *Monsieur Verdoux*, which Tyler views as the deliberate murder of one of Chaplin's artistic ego pairs by the other.

This idea is also important in Andre Bazin's *Charlie Chaplin* (1972), a collection of all Bazin's essays and reviews of Chaplin's work, some of them already well-known and previously published in *What is Cinema?* Inevitably, the book is fragmentary and repetitious, and Bazin's constant search is for the mythic significance of the Chaplin persona rather than for a detailed examination of the films themselves. *The Great Dictator* and *Monsieur Verdoux* offer the greatest scope for this kind of approach and a large proportion of the book is devoted to these two films: in the former, Bazin delights in the coincidence that allowed Hitler's "appropriation" of Charlie's moustache to open the way to Chaplin's annihilation of him; with the latter, he concentrates on the opposition between the Charlie persona and Verdoux and concludes that the significance of the film resides in the fact that society kills Charlie in the final sequences at the same time that it executes Verdoux.[4] *Verdoux* matters, Bazin adds, not because of its style and structure (which are weak), but because it provides a symbolic revelation of Chaplin's feelings about women. *Limelight* too has to be taken on trust: it is important because it is by Chaplin and for what it reveals about him, though Bazin attempts to boost this argument towards the end of the essay with some cloudy speculations about the manner in which Chaplin's archaic style makes other films seem conventional and trite. A similar approach is taken to *A King in New York*, where Bazin confesses that script and ideas are worthless unless placed within the context of Chaplin's personal universe and achievement. The last essay in the book, on *A Countess From Hong Kong*, is written by Eric Rohmer, who begins by promising an approach through technique for a change, rather than through myth, but little more emerges than some comparisons of the film with 1930s Hollywood comedy and the observations that Sophia Loren is deliberately given some of "Charlie's" characteristics.

Marcel Martin's *Charlie Chaplin* (1966) and Jean Mitry's *Charlot et la "fabulation" chaplinesque* (1957) are probably the two most valuable of the French critical works, and the former at least attempts an approach by means of motifs instead of the conventional chronological survey. Martin begins with some highly dubious speculations on Chaplin's supposed Jewish origins and his links with Jewish folk art and traditions; and he also attempts a defense of Chaplin's filmic techniques, arguing that silence, the static camera, and close-ups are essential to his art. Later chapters deal with the various paradoxes evident in the films (the sexual ambiguities, the childlike qualities and yet Chaplin's own dislike of children, the ruthlessness and cunning that are often employed even against other victims), and with a consideration of the treatment of such themes as work, objects, money, war, religion, and politics. Martin, like Tyler and Bazin, is fascinated by the Charlie/Chaplin duality and agrees with them that the latter finally takes over and eliminates the former. He concludes by mentioning the three basic critical approaches that can be taken to Chaplin's work: the aesthetic/cinematic, the historical/sociological, and the psychological/mythological. His own work, though he does not of course put it this way himself, is stronger on the second and third of these elements than on the first, but in this respect it merely conforms to the pattern which we have observed throughout this essay.

Mitry's book is also mythic/psychological/sociological, but it brings together and examines these elements more fully than any of the others mentioned so far. Like Huff, Mitry traces the development of the screen character: the Keystone figure is cruel, vain, cunning, instinctive and only slowly acquires a soul; he is rejected by society rather than opposed to it, though he is already conscious of his own spiritual superiority. He combines a will-to-power and a desire to submit, to be loved; and he possesses in double focus a need to transcend his self and an urge towards imposition of self. The Essanay films have both a primarily balletic structure and a greater depth of humanity: "le ballet devient la traduction dansée et mimée d'un véritable mouvement interne, l'objectivation lyrique d'un ètat d'âme" (p. 63). After *The Kid*, this is brought into closer conjunction with an investigation of the conditions obtaining in the real world: the short films create their own world centered round Charlie, while the later ones show an interaction with a real, complex society. Charlie constantly encounters the resistance of objects, which he masters by transforming them; he conquers the world by reshaping it for his own purposes. On a spiritual level, he refuses likewise to accept society's fixed scale of values and sees behind this to a higher reality. Charlie represents the Absolute, whose actions transcend and make absurd the conventions and rules which control others and to which they tamely or blindly submit. In the early films, social comment was expressed through sarcasm and caricature: institutions, authority, class distinctions, and moral principles were all ridiculed. Later on, there is a greater bitterness and loneliness, the focus shifts towards Charlie's struggle for survival. Chaplin is constantly concerned with the contrast between the surface condition of his characters and their true essence. In the last films (at the time of writing), *Monsieur Verdoux* and *Limelight*, the message becomes too verbal. It is crude and vulgarized. If Charlie is a mythic figure, Mitry concludes, he is nevertheless firmly based in the reality of Chaplin's early experiences and settings.

Mitry leaves little more that can be said about these aspects of Chaplin's work and his own later *Tout Chaplin* (1972), in its critical aspects at least, is little more than an extension and elaboration of these observations. As with the biographies, one is tempted to suggest a moratorium on critical comments on the Charlie persona and its mythological, philosophical, psychological, and sociological implications, and recommend an attempt to find an approach to Chaplin's films that would justify considering him as a great *filmmaker* or would at least explain the paradox of how someone who was an incompetent filmmaker came to make so many indisputably great films. Some recent critics, such as Gerald Mast and Raymond Durgnat, have thrown out the suggestion that Chaplin's methods might be compared to Brecht's, but neither made much attempt to follow this up. Perhaps we could, in all seriousness, welcome an essay on *Modern Times* (or *City Lights* or *The Gold Rush*) as a Brechtian film. There is surely also scope for some kind of semiological analysis of the interchangeability of objects and signs in Chaplin's work, and of the way in which, in *Modern Times*, a red flag on a truck can "mean" one thing, while the same red flag picked up and waved by a passer-by "means" something else.[5] And surely something could be done with narrative structure, camera placement, and editing that is at least less perfunctory than almost everything that has been written on these subjects by Chaplin's critics so far.[6]

The two most recent analyses of Chaplin by American critics, the sections by Gerald Mast in *The Comic Mind* (1973) and Walter Kerr in *The Silent Clowns* (1975), do not take us very far in any of these directions, though each is acceptable enough in terms of the standard approaches. Mast follows the traditional sequence of Keystone/Essanay/Mutual/First National, making the by now expected distinctions between each stage. In the major films, the themes are those of duality: instinct versus masquerade, nature versus artifice, essence versus form. The structure of *The Gold Rush* is based on the needs for food, money, shelter, and love. The sound tracks of *City Lights* and *The Great Dictator* are subtle and complex; *Modern Times* and *Monsieur Verdoux* display a sharp sense of irony and cynicism, though in the latter this collapses towards the end.

Walter Kerr *writes* better about Chaplin than almost any other English language critic, and he is clearly aware of the need to try to say something new about the films. His solution comes in the form of a variation of the standard observations, however, rather than in the imposition of a wholly new orientation. Like Mitry, he finds that Chaplin succeeds by readjusting the universe to suit his own convenience. There is a logic and seriousness behind the gags, he takes his comedy seriously. The character's chief fascination lies in his ability to become, or to do, anything he decides he wants to do; he can become anyone. But this contains the implication that he therefore has no real identity of his own and must always return to nothingness after each transformation. His dancing facade allows him detachment from action as well as participation in it: it shields him against the world's instabilities. Kerr's treatment of the features follows the familiar pattern of "imaginative recreation" combined with an evaluative summing up of the success or failure of each film: *The Circus*, for example, is flawed by its premise that Charlie can be funny by accident, without realizing it. *City Lights*, which Kerr greatly admires, is "an utterly stable film about total instability" (p. 352). *Modern Times*, the last of the films that Kerr discusses, investigates and rejects the idea that Charlie can ever find a "home."

Good as it is, Kerr's book (which is not, of course, solely about Chaplin) exemplifies both sides of the strange and almost baffling paradox that Chaplin's work presents: for all that has been written about it and for all the acclaim that it has achieved, there is no one critical book, either in English, or in French, that can be unreservedly recommended as an exploration of all facets of his achievement; there is likewise nothing that concentrates, with total commitment and seriousness, on the films as films and not as excuses for talking about something else. Of what other director of equal stature can as much, and yet as little, have been said?

NOTES

1 References are to books listed in the bibliography at the end of this essay.

2 These titles are adapted from those to be found in Vol. 1, no. 3 of the new periodical *Wide Angle*.

3 The books to be discussed are the main critical works in English and French, together with the most important of the essays to be found in books on film comedy in general.

4 David Cotes, whose previous comments on the films have been at best perfunctory, suddenly rises, in pp. 120-122 of *The Little Fellow*, to a subtle analysis of *Monsieur Verdoux* which comes to conclusions almost identical to those of Bazin. Although Bazin's comments appeared first (in 1947 and 1948), the resemblance appears to be purely coincidental.

5 It is, of course, a gray flag on the screen. Perhaps Chaplin is more aware of visual paradoxes, of the manner in which an audience "reads" a visual image than we give him credit for being.

6 We could also do with an analysis of *A Woman of Paris*, seen from the viewpoint of the 1970s, and of the differences between Chaplin as director only, and Chaplin as both director and actor.

BIBLIOGRAPHY

Agee, James. "Comedy's Greatest Era." in *Agee on Film, Vol. 1* (New York: McDowell, Obolensky, 1968).

Amengual, Barthelemy. *Charlie Chaplin* (Lyon: Premier Plan, 1963).

Asplund, Uno. *Chaplin's Films* (Newton Abbot: David and Charles, 1973).

Bazin, A. and E. Rohmer. *Charlie Chaplin* (Paris: Ed. du Cerf, 1972).

Bessy, Maurice and Robin Livio. *Charles Chaplin* (Paris: Ed. Denoel, 1972).

Bowman, Wm. Dodgson. *Charlie Chaplin: His Life and Art* (New York: Haskell House, 1974). Reprint of 1931 edition.

Chaplin, Charles. *My Autobiography* (London: The Bodley Head, 1964).

Chaplin, Charles Jr. (with N. and M. Rau). *My Father, Charlie Chaplin* (New York: Random House, 1960).

Chaplin, Lita Grey. *My Life with Chaplin* (New York: B. Geis, 1966).

Cotes, Peter and Thelma Niklaus. *The Little Fellow: the Life and Work of Charles Spencer Chaplin* (London: Paul Elek, 1951).

Delluc, Louis. *Charlie Chaplin* (London: John Lane the Bodley Head, 1922).

Durgnat, Raymond. *The Crazy Mirror: Hollywood Comedy and the American Image* (London: Faber & Faber, 1969).

Florey, Robert. *Charlie Chaplin* (Paris: Les Publications Jean-Pascal, 1927).

Gifford, Denis. *Chaplin* (New York: Doubleday, 1974).

Huff, Theodore. *Charlie Chaplin* (New York: Henry Schuman, 1951).

Kerr, Walter. *The Silent Clowns* (New York: Knopf, 1975).

Leprohon, Pierre. *Charles Chaplin* (Paris: Ed. Jacques Melot, 1946).

Manvell, Roger. *Chaplin* (Boston: Little, Brown, 1974).

Martin, Marcel. *Charlie Chaplin* (Paris: Ed. Seghers, 1966).

Mast, Gerald. *The Comic Mind: Comedy and the Movies* (Indianapolis: Bobbs Merrill, 1973).

McCaffrey, Donald W. *4 Great Comedians* (London: A. Zwemmer, 1968).

McDonald, Gerald D., et al. *The Films of Charlie Chaplin* (New York: Bonanza Books, 1965).

Minney, R.J. *Chaplin: the Immortal Tramp* (London: George Newnes, 1954).

Mitry, Jean. *Charlot et la "fabulation" chaplinesque* (Paris: Ed. Universitaires, 1957).

Mitry, Jean. *Tout Chaplin* (Paris: Ed. Seghers, 1972).

Montgomery, John. *Comedy Films 1894-1954* (London: George Allen & Unwin, 1954).

Payne, Robert. *The Great God Pan* (New York: Hermitage House, 1952). Reprinted in paperback as *Charlie Chaplin*.

Quigley, Isabel. *Charlie Chaplin: The Early Comedies* (London: Studio Vista, 1968).

Robinson, David. *The Great Funnies: A History of Film Comedy* (London: Studio Vista, 1969).

Sadoul, Georges. *Vie de Charlot* (Paris: Les Editeurs Francais Rèunis, 1957).

Soupault, Philippa. *Charlot* (Paris: Librairie Plon, 1931). A novel based on episodes from Chaplin's films that offers many insights into the "Charlie" persona.

Tyler, Parker. *Chaplin: Last of the Clowns* (New York: Vanguard Press, 1948).

Von Ulm, Gerith. *Charlie Chaplin: King of Tragedy* (Caldwell, Idaho: Caxton Printers Ltd., 1940).

MICHAEL ROEMER
Chaplin: Charles and Charlie

Rich in allusion, thoughtful in comparative descriptions, this is a particularly valuable essay on the ideas and emotions expressed in Chaplin's films. It deserves the attention of film students and critics as a model of content, style, and structure. It appeared in the Yale Review, *December 1974.*

Professor Roemer teaches in the department of art history at Yale University. His article on "The Surfaces of Reality" in Film *Quarterly, Fall 1964 (reprinted in Richard Dyer MacCann,* Film: A Montage of Theories, *NY, Dutton, 1966) is still one of the important statements of American film theory. His 1974 feature film,* Nothing But a Man *(co-written with Bob Young), was a study of African-American life in the South, and he has made a number of documentaries. Born in Berlin and raised in England during World War II, Roemer directed a feature-length impressionistic salute to the silent film era while a student at Harvard.*

Danger, tension, suffering, disaster, Roemer says, are always threatening the childlike Charlie, yet he "threads his way through" with extraordinary grace and energy, managing, as most of us do, to "balance and survive." He is asexual, at least since the Keystone days; he is reverent toward women and can be hurt only by them; he is unpredictable in everything else; he is constantly on the move and surrounded by violence; yet his comedy always takes precedence over pathos; he is not a tragic figure, but always theatrical and sometimes fantastic; his world seems real to us because it is subjective from a child's point of view.

A year after Chaplin was born, his parents separated. At the age of five, he appeared on stage in place of his mother, a vaude-ville singer who was losing her voice. He sang, danced, and picked up the coins that the audience threw at him.

When Hanna Chaplin could no longer support her children, she moved into the Lambeth workhouse. Chaplin and his half-brother Sidney, were sent to a Dickensian orphanage, where children were flogged. A brief family reunion did occur, but then Hanna Chaplin went mad and had to be confined to an asylum. Her sons were sent to another orphanage, even more frightful than the first.

When Chaplin was seven, a court forced his father to take care of the boys. For several months they lived with him and a woman called Louise. Both adults drank heavily and fought constantly. Louise, who had a child of her own, resented the boys, and frequently locked them out of the house. As soon as their mother was better, they rejoined her. Chaplin found a job with a troupe of clog dancers and performed in London and the provinces for a year. Then he developed asthma and had to be sent home. With his mother, he spent a strange summer at the fashionable house of a friend, who had left the stage to become the mistress of a wealthy old colonel.

In 1899, Chaplin's father died of dropsy and alcoholism. His friends had had to get him drunk so they could take him to the hospital. Sidney went off to sea, and Chaplin — now nine — talked his way into a series of odd jobs. He worked for a chandler, in a printing shop, as a glassblower, old-clothes salesman, and as a page boy in the home of a rich doctor. He taught dancing and tried making toy boats. Often he was fired the day he was hired. One evening he came home and found that his mother was mad again. She was returned to the asylum. Terrified of being sent back to the orphanage, Chaplin spent his days roaming the street.

He tried finding work as an actor. In 1901, at the age of twelve, he landed his first part in a play. During the next four years, he played drama and comedy in London and the provinces. While his life with a theatrical company was far from sheltered or secure, the days of sheer physical want were over. When he was seventeen, Sidney — himself an actor now — found him a job with Fred Karno, the most successful impresario of music hall in England. Chaplin quickly established himself as a gifted and popular comedian. On a company tour of the United States he was spotted by Mack Sennett, who hired him for the movies.

If his early life resembles the dark trial that begins so many fairy tales, his good fortune from this point forward seems like a magic reversal. In the years 1914-1917, he turned out sixty-two short films, writing and directing all but the first few. His work was so phenomenally successful that in 1916 he signed a contract for $670,000 a year, plus a bonus of $150,000. By the time he was twenty-six, he had become the most popular entertainer in the world.

Most people are emotionally destroyed by a childhood like Chaplin's, even if they survive it physically. They are permanently robbed of a whole range of feelings, and their existence seems to depend on locking their early experience into a walled-off chamber of the heart. Providentially for Chaplin and for us, he had early access to the theatre, which thrives on extremes and in which the excesses of his childhood could find expression. By virtue of his extraordinary gifts and the happy circumstance that brought him to the silent cinema, his childhood — instead of being forever buried — became instead the source material of his work.

Chaplin has said, "All my pictures depend on the idea of getting me into trouble." In the first films Chaplin made for Mack Sennett, Charlie's troubles are still minor and mostly of his own making. But soon the pressures take on a palpable, physical urgency and the situations confronting him take an ominous turn. By the time of the Mutual and First National films — *Easy Street, The Adventurer, The Immigrant, A Dog's Life,* and *Shoulder Arms* — Charlie is in constant danger, forever on the run from cops, prison guards, enemy soldiers, or some huge bully. The wellspring of his farce is violence, hunger, fear, greed, need, desolation, mistrust, despair, suicide, and drugs. A catastrophic imagination is at work. "Almost everyone frightens me," Chaplin once told Lita Grey. Everyone and everything — for Charlie lives in perpetual jeopardy of being beaten, imprisoned, wiped out. Nothing less than his survival is at stake.

The basic comic situations in *The Gold Rush* are built on hunger and cannibalism. Charlie is threatened with death by starvation or cold, with getting eaten or shot. The comic here is deeply rooted in the terrifying. The shoe-eating sequence was inspired by a documentary account of the Donner Pass crossing: some of the settlers ate their dead and others their moccasins. Chaplin's version of the great Yukon gold rush is a story of dire need. Greed for gold may motivate Big Jim and Black Larson, but Charlie himself is simply trying to survive. He has stumbled into the white wilderness without design or ambition; *his* needs are far more primary than gold: he is looking for food, shelter, warmth, and human affection.

Chaplin's films thrive on physical tension. The cabin in *The Gold Rush* teeters on the edge of an abyss; Charlie and Jim cling by their fingernails to the steeply slanted, ice-covered floor, and every time Charlie coughs they drop closer to disaster. In *The Circus*, he is caged with a sleeping lion who threatens to wake up at the slightest noise, and besieged by a troupe of monkeys when he tries to balance on a high wire. In *Modern Times*, he skirts destruction by roller-skating blindfold along a sheer drop. And in *The Great Dictator* an enormous artillery shell keeps pointing itself at the little barber and a live grenade gets lost inside his bulky uniform.

Many scenes are structured by mounting tension, with disaster threatening till the very end. In the restaurant of *The Immigrant*, a starved Charlie orders food that he plans to pay for with a found coin. When another customer is brutally beaten and kicked because he is ten cents short, Charlie anxiously feels for the coin in his pocket; it's gone. Panicked, he spies another coin on the floor and manages to get hold of it, but the villainous-looking waiter twists it in his teeth and tosses it back onto the table: counterfeit! Charlie desperately plays for time but muffs an opportunity to extricate himself and doesn't escape until the last moment.

Even when the issue isn't survival, things are touch-and-go. In *The Circus*, Charlie unwittingly takes away the chair of the evil ringmaster and lands him on the floor. A moment later, he removes the chair a second time — and just barely manages to slip it back under the ringmaster's bottom. A continuous sequence of kinetic effects like this keeps us in a state of physical tension that explodes into laughter whenever the danger is averted.

Chaplin steers much closer to the dark and dangerous edge of existence than most comedians. There are people who respond so strongly to the tension and danger in his work that they can't laugh. But though his comedies are fed by dark waters, Charlie's survival is assured from the start; his annihilation is constantly threatened but never — in the silent films — carried out. Survival is guaranteed by his very continuity as a character from one picture to the next. He is as indestructible as the heroic creatures of our animated cartoons, who reconstitute themselves miraculously after orgies of destruction. Charlie may not get the girl at the end and the last shot often finds him walking alone into the horizon. But he *is* walking or running — and not so much into the horizon as into the next film. In Charlie's world, to survive is to win. Cast perpetually into jobs for which he is unfit — as a boxer, a singing waiter, a policeman, or a trapeze artist — he inevitably finds some ingenious and unorthodox way out. Even in his romances there are occasional victories — in *Easy Street, The Pawnshop, The Immigrant, The Gold Rush,* and *Modern Times*.

One of the chief pleasures of watching him lies in the extraordinary skill with which he extricates himself from every predicament. His physical agility borders on the magical. He is infinitely resourceful, and can transform an ordinary object into a weapon or means of escape. He is forever surprising us: we think he is going to throw a punch but he delivers a kick instead — or sits suddenly in his opponent's lap. Energized by fear, he never stops moving. His physical agility is supported by stupendous energy and other unique gifts. Like a great dancer, athlete, or magician, he seems to defy man's physical limits. Watching him is exhilarating: he appears to defy the physical laws that the universe has imposed on the rest of us. In his greatest moments, action resolves into dance, and movement is so harmonized that it comes close to music. As he threads his way through disaster after disaster, Charlie is graceful in the oldest and deepest sense of the word: full of grace, blessed, a darling of the gods.

With notable critical consistency, Charlie has been called a representative of the common man. Chaplin himself has described him as the Little Fellow, beset by misfortunes and dreaming of some simple happiness that is forever out of reach. But as we watch these films — or, rather, live through them — something more is at work than our identification with Charlie as a universal underdog. The secret of his appeal and power is that he draws, in a most direct way, on our deep and universal experience of childhood. For this little fellow is just that — a child — and what we so continually recognize in his films are the feelings and experiences we had as children.

Charlie is frail and small — most often the smallest figure on the set. He has trouble walking, keeps falling down and tripping over his own foot. His clothes don't fit: his trousers and shoes are too large. Like a child, he is forever trying to make friends with those who are bigger and stronger. He pats Big Jim in his fur coat as though he were a large, tamable beast. He will jump into someone's lap to ingratiate himself, stop him from hitting, or to express his affectionate delight. He plays dead. He holds Limburger cheese with one hand and his nose with the other. He is perpetually playful and quick to turn any situation into a game. Even when he kisses another man, we're not shocked or surprised, for we respond to him as to a child. His reactions are those of a child. In *The Gold Rush*, Georgia accepts his invitation for New Year's eve; as soon as she leaves the cabin, he goes berserk with joy, jumps up onto the bed, swings on the rafters, punches open a bag of flour, rips up his pillow, and sits on the floor in a cabin afloat with feathers.

Food, a central concern of childhood, is surely the most common ingredient in Chaplin's gags: Charlie at the dinner table of the rich; Charlie eating watermelon, Charlie eating soup on a rolling ship; the Kid cooking for Charlie; Charlie eating a candle or a child's hot dog; Charlie the baker, and countless variations on Charlie the waiter. Few films are without their food scene, and most of them — including the food-fight between Hynkel and Napoloni at the buffet table — have a primary, elemental intensity that takes us right back to childhood. In contrast, Chaplin's drunk acts, though extraordinary in their inventiveness and grace, seem like variations on a music-hall routine. Alcohol never achieves the compulsive reality of food.

Of course, Charlie isn't the only child. Big Jim in his peaked cap that makes him look like an out-sized goblin, the huge round clown in *The Circus*, even the millionaire in *City Lights*, all act and think like children. "You're my best friend! . . . Come on, we'll have a party!" They squabble and fight like children. In *The Pawnshop*, Charlie and his fellow clerk pounce on each other the moment the storekeeper leaves, and go into an elaborate charade of work as soon as he returns. When Edna surprises them in the midst of battle, Charlie flings himself on the floor and goes into a heart-breaking crying act to answer her maternal pity.

They treat each other like children. When Charlie has cooked the shoe, in *The Gold Rush*, he helps himself to the uppers and serves him the ugly-looking sole, spiked with long nails. But Jim simply switches plates, and since he is stronger that settles the issue.

Other comedians also draw in some measure on the reality of childhood. Laurel and Hardy behave like overage boys: Ollie looks like a baby, Stan has a crying act, and when there is no outsider to unite them, they invariably turn on each other. The Marx Brothers, like naughty boys, neglect all order and authority and thrive on anarchy and destruction; they don't just deflate the pompous and fraudulent but gleefully attack everything and anything. As Groucho puts it: "Whatever it is, I'm against it."

But in Chaplin's work the experience of childhood is evoked on the broadest and deepest level. Most children are spared the extremes of Chaplin's early years, yet they too are familiar with danger and fear. Like Charlie, they often find themselves in situations over which they have no control. Like Charlie, they're at the mercy of those who are bigger and stronger, and their days are full of dramatic physical confrontations. Haunted by a fear of failure, they dream of sudden power and glory, a dream that for Charlie often becomes fictive reality. Such dreams are not idle wish-fulfillment, for they touch on our secret strength and resilience: they help us to balance and survive. Like the novels of Dickens, the films of Chaplin transmute extreme hardship into laughter and fictively redeem a threatened and anguished childhood in which many of us recognize our own.

Nowhere is Charlie more explicitly a child than with women. In the early Keystone shorts, he was still a distinctly sexual creature, enmeshed in plots of classical farce — mixed-up bedrooms, philandering husbands, and cheating wives. As late as *The Count*, there is a magnificent scene in which he is brought to the verge of ecstasy by a curvaceous vamp: he works out his sexual frenzy on a buffet table instead of her — plunging his cane into a fried chicken, chopping up a huge cream cake, and finally wrecking every dish in sight.

But, as his work developed, Chaplin turned away from traditional farce and Charlie loses his sexuality. He becomes younger and more innocent — a shy and gallant figure, who races to the rescue whenever the villain makes his indecent advances. This Charlie is capable at most of a chaste and embarrassed kiss on the cheek. The women, too, lose their sexuality. Mabel Normand, in the Keystone films, still has an air of naughtiness. But her place is soon taken by Edna, Georgia, Merna, Virginia, and Paulette, who are children at heart if not in body and play with Charlie in utter innocence. In *The Circus*, Merna is sent to bed without supper by her cruel father; Charlie sneaks food to her and, when she stuffs herself greedily, he gives her a lesson in table manners. In *Modern Times*, he shares a shack with the Waif but sleeps in the doghouse; and in *The Great Dictator* the little barber is so unaware of Paulette as a woman that he lathers her face with shaving cream instead of doing her hair.

Charlie's approach to women is utterly consistent and predictable, but in everything else he displays a protean inconsistency. He is infinitely changeable and can accommodate every kind of contradiction: he scraps like a street urchin one moment and displays perfect drawing-room manners in the next; he waddles like a toddler yet possesses uncanny physical skill; he can shift from rank stupidity to suavest sophistication. In *The Adventurer*, he tries to make a woman more comfortable by shoving a pillow under her wooden stretcher, then brilliantly outwits a whole pack of pursuers. In *Modern Times*, he can't serve a meal without spilling the food but performs an enchanting love song in a mixture of fake Romance languages.

Because he is a child at heart, Charlie has no self-limiting consistency or "integrity," and is still wide open to the polarities of human nature. His behavior veers mercurially. Like Punch, he can play any number of roles without rupturing his elastic identity; he is equally real as a vagabond, sophisticated drunk, innocent lover, or rich swell. In several films he takes two parts: he can even play a woman without ceasing to be Charlie. Beside him, Keaton, Lloyd, Fields, and even the Marx Brothers are models of consistency.

Like the Karamazovs, Charlie has a broad soul. Mack Sennett first cast him as a villain and, though he soon became purer and more innocent, he retained much of his original craftiness. He even remained capable, until much later, of deliberate and unwarranted cruelty. Walt Disney is said to have detested the character, and surely Mickey Mouse is Charlie's antithesis — a child without darkness and impurity, without breadth or depth.

Protean inconsistency is fascinating in fiction, but makes for anarchy in life. Real children are obliged to grow up — define and limit themselves, become integrated, specialized, and predictable. They learn to suppress their contradictions and try to become reliable citizens who won't spring too many surprises on their fellow men. But Charlie is fiction and can remain a child. He continues to act out the impulses the rest of us have learned to repress. His films, like so much of the theatre, live out the hidden and forbidden, the spontaneous and violent. Everyone in the film can respond directly and immediately; no one stays neutral or cool, and action leads to liberating reactions without inhibition or delay. Theatre has always thrived on characters who react strongly and express themselves openly. Oedipus, Lear, and Mother Courage don't hide what they feel; like Charlie, they are caught in situations that won't permit them to stay neutral. In tragedy, as in slapstick farce, feelings are translated into direct action.

All slapstick is inherently violent, but the violence is seldom personal. Mack Sennett's films are packed with pratfalls, chases, and wrecks, but the characters don't often attack each other except with pies. When Laurel and Hardy have a score to settle with someone, they turn on his home or car, and even the Marx Brothers don't often resort to bodily aggression.

In Chaplin's shorts, however, violence is emphatically personal. Blows, beatings, and kicks govern most relationships. Charlie himself is no kindlier than the rest: he treats people the way they treat him — brutally. His cane is primarily a slap-stick, a weapon more lethal than Punch's, for it has a sharp point at one end and a useful hook at the other. In *The Kid*, he bashes a bully on the head with a brick till he has him staggering, then administers a few lighter blows to finish him off. No one is safe from violence in Charlie's world.

In the films of Keaton, the hero is often alone. There is a sense of space around him, and his problem may be a runaway train, an abandoned ocean liner, or a rushing river. But Charlie moves through a crowded social scene. Like Keaton and Lloyd, he has trouble with objects, but his real problem is other people. Personal violence in his films is developed to the highest level of sophistication, for without that defense, he would perish.

Of course we get the satisfaction of hitting without the painful consequences. Even the most ferocious blows fail to injure, let alone kill. Though the big bully in *Easy Street* is struck on the head by a cast-iron stove which Charlie drops from an upstairs window, he turns up in the following scene in the best of health.

Aggression and violence may be deeply rooted in Chaplin's past, but his films transmute them into farce.

The constant movement in Chaplin's work produces a strong kinetic effect in us — a muscular empathy that may well be the most direct response film can elicit. His work, moreover, is rich in sensory detail that arouses our physical participation.

In *The Adventurer*, a scoop of ice cream slips into Charlie's pants, slides down his trouser leg, drops through the balcony grating to the floor below, lands on the bare back of a stately dowager, and disappears inside her dress. In *The Count*, Charlie and Eric Campbell engage in a kicking duel on the dance floor and maneuver their unsuspecting partners around like shields; the soft, billowing posteriors of the women are in constant danger of being kicked and create a very palpable, fleshy sense of participation.

When Keaton, in *The Navigator*, is trapped under water, the effect is largely graphic. But the water in the dugout of *Shoulder Arms* is sensory and wet; everything is soggy and submerged in it: Charlie lies down on his flooded bunk, fluffs out his soaked pillow, rests his head on it, and covers himself with a dripping blanket.

There is, of course, something primary and even primitive at work here. When we grow up, most of us lose touch with our senses; we no longer use our skin but cover and neutralize it. The pristine experience of what things feel like is lost to us; we increasingly use our eyes and ears — abstracted and aphysical senses — and surrender our concrete, tactile relationship to the world; in effect, we give up one kind of experience for another. But Charlie continues to live in the sensory world that we have, for the most part, forgotten. Significantly, the one area in which adults develop some capacity for tactile sensation and response — their sexuality — is the one area in which Charlie remains aloof and aphysical.

In Chaplin's work we never feel the absence of speech, as we so often do in silent films. Charlie's silence is not imposed on him by a limited technology; it is his natural state. Unlike the pantomime of most silent screen actors, who were forced to render complex adult responses in gestures that were often reductive and oversimplified, Charlie's mime is perfectly suited to express his true nature and experience. It constitutes an original, proverbial language.

Chaplin's encounter with the silent cinema was a happy coincidence that fostered and developed his extraordinary gifts. On the vaudeville circuit he had performed largely in sketches that depended on the spoken word, and had he continued on stage he would never have confined himself to pantomime though it was his forte. But in front of the camera, speech was useless, and everything had to be transformed into gesture and movement — a limitation that may well have pushed him into exploring and mining the rich resources of his own childhood.

Much has been made of Charlie's pathos and deep feeling. Perhaps too much. The shorts are existential farces without a moment's pause for feeling or thought. They are packed with violent action, but the emotions of violence — anger, rage, hurt, and anguish — are never rendered. All scenes involving sentiment are passed over very quickly. In *The Immigrant*, the death of Edna's mother is accorded only the briefest mention while every gag is given loving and extended attention. Occasionally, there is a trace of feeling: Charlie loses the girl in *The Bank* and *The Tramp*, and a torrential downpour lends the end of *The Immigrant* a faintly melancholy air. But by and large the characters are no more vulnerable to feeling than the wooden figures in a puppet show.

Chaplin himself says of the early Charlie: "His brain was seldom active then — only his instincts, which were concerned with the basic essentials: food, warmth and shelter. But with each succeeding comedy the tramp was growing more complex. Sentiment was beginning to percolate through the character. " In the shorts, Charlie's survival is so insistently at stake that there is room only for his immediate, physical reactions. But in the features the physical pressure on him lets up and he can, for the first time, afford the luxury of feeling.

Chaplin was clearly interested in letting Charlie develop into a more complex figure, capable of feeling. But he was well aware that sentiment presents a serious threat to comedy, especially to slapstick farce. The problem is apparent in his first long film, *The Kid*. Here he is working with a highly charged, emotional subject, the relationship between Charlie and an abandoned child. But though the story has poignant reference to Chaplin's own childhood, the situations are almost entirely transformed by laughter.

When Charlie first finds himself stuck with the unwanted infant, he tries to get rid of it. No sentiment here: he even considers dropping it down a sewer. Though he grows fond of the Kid, their relationship continues to unfold in a sequence of gags. Throughout the film, the awful threats of separation and loss are undercut by passages of brilliant comedy. Feelings serve as the subsoil of the farce — its point of departure. They inspire the comic situations much as the threat of physical annihilation inspired the shorts. They create tension by posing a threat of suffering — a threat that is never fulfilled, just as Charlie in *The Gold Rush* teeters on the abyss without ever falling into it. Suffering is consistently short-circuited for, like danger and disaster, it is funny only as long as it is averted. We are spared the hurt and find ourselves laughing with relief.

In *The Kid*, as in so many of the films, even the corrosive anguish of poverty is sublimated into farce. A graphically rendered flophouse becomes a scene of such deft comic invention, we quite forget that fear and desperation are the source of our laughter. Even poverty can be funny as long as we're not emotionally involved.

Chaplin observed that his mixture of "raw slapstick and sentiment . . . was something of an innovation" — an innovation that works only when sentiment is contradicted by laughter. Wherever pure feelings appear in the films, they threaten the very reality and texture of farce.

Most comedy denies the reality of feeling, for feelings open us to empathy and suffering. Comedy is often unfeeling to the point of derision and cruelty. It holds nothing sacred and takes an unempathetic, alienated view of the world. Nietzsche says: "A joke is an epigram on the death of a feeling." And Parker Tyler quotes Chaplin's comment that "comedy is life viewed from a distance." For distance — in time or space — has a distinctly cooling effect: the closer we are to an event, the more it involves us; the further we are away, the less we feel it. Significantly, there are few close-ups in Chaplin's films — and surely the most memorable is the last shot of *City Lights*, in which the mask of Charlie's face is broken apart by deep and uncontradicted feeling.

In Charlie's world, pure feeling is focused almost entirely on women. In the shorts, women had been part of the comic scene and occupied no special, elevated position; they could even be villains, a monstrous wife stalks Charlie throughout *Pay Day*, and in the alternate end to *The Vagabond* he is saved from drowning by a woman so ugly, he takes one look at her and jumps right back into the water. But starting with *The Kid*, Chaplin's heroines are no longer part of the comedy. Once they become the object of Charlie's feelings, they stop being funny.

The women he worships don't often take Charlie seriously, for he is childlike, naive, and far too romantic. They feel protective about him at best and naturally reject him for men who are more adult. Their rejection crushes Charlie; it is the one experience he can't seem to handle, for he opens his heart to them as he does to no one else. When his best friend, the millionaire in *City Lights*, refuses to recognize him and throws him out of the house, Charlie bounces right back into action. Men have no power to wound him, but women can sap his energy and reduce him to helpless hurt.

The word "tragic" has been used extensively and rather too easily in descriptions of Chaplin's work. We are certainly touched by Charlie, by his loneliness and disappointment. But to speak of tragedy here is careless and sentimental, for Charlie's pathos springs almost entirely from his blighted romances, and his feelings for women are too much like puppy love to evoke our deepest response. Chaplin mined his dark childhood for some of the most beautiful comedies of our time, and this in itself may have denied him access to tragedy. For surely the tragic is found in the very realm of feeling and suffering, of disaster and death, that his films so skillfully avoid and subvert. Disaster and suffering may be the springboard of Chaplin's farce, but Charlie himself is no tragic figure. He has the dark eyes and the quick, uncertain smile of our common diaspora, but his genius is that of the eternal survivor.

From the start, Chaplin's style was intensely theatrical. His silent films, particularly the shorts, are surreal pirouettes in which everything is pushed to the limit. There are no normal people or ordinary events: every moment is heightened and intensified, every action accelerated. Nothing happens at a natural pace; the end of one motion is already the beginning of another, and incident follows incident without break or pause. The screen is a whirl of activity in which a great deal happens at once: Charlie courts Edna even as he is engaged in a kicking contest with Eric Campbell.

The acting is as pushed and unrealistic as the action. Chaplin's performance is a rapid sequence of shifts and transformations that violate every rule of naturalistic acting. To evade the huge masseur in *The Cure*, Charlie becomes in rapid succession a ballet dancer, wrestler, and bullfighter. In *The Pawnshop*, he examines a defunct alarm clock as if he were a doctor listening to its heart, opens it with a can-opener, shakes it as though it were a cocktail, extracts a spring as if it were a bad tooth, peers at it through a jeweler's glass, and finally squirts the whole sorry mess with oil. Allusions, quotations, and metaphors follow each other in free, playful succession; the style has the range and flexibility of Elizabethan blank verse.

The theatricality of the films easily accommodates dreams and fantasies. When, in *The Kid*, Charlie has his vision of Paradise, the ghetto street is simply decorated with flowers and the slum-dwellers — dressed in nightgowns and white wigs — swoop around the set on wires. When hunger drives Big Jim to hallucination, Charlie turns into a chicken right in front of us. There is no attempt at a realistic illusion, for his disguise is a moth-eaten costume — a theatrical effect that beautifully points up Charlie's dilemma: Jim sees him as a huge chicken but he is clearly human to the rest of us.

The staging and camera work are derived from the theater. Space is treated two-dimensionally: sets and action are photographed from a single vantage point — most often from the center of the missing fourth wall; there are few reverse shots and we never see one character from the point of view of another. The camera seldom moves. In *The Gold Rush* there is just one dolly shot — with Charlie and Jim strolling down the ship's deck like royalty, attended by their retinue of flunkies. But the very limitations of the camera-work — its flat, restricted point of view — are perfectly expressive of Charlie's experience. Like a child, he is preoccupied with *what* is happening — with effects, not causes. He deals with things as they come upon the stage of his awareness and doesn't look into the wings for their origin. Esthetically, his restricted vision is not simply a limitation: it permits Chaplin to leave out what he doesn't want us to see. Most filmmakers, even those who are suspicious of montage, depend on editing to condense their action and to eliminate whatever is obvious or time-consuming. But Chaplin, working in a theatrical tradition, can edit the *action* instead of the film — just as he would on stage.

All of the great comedians of the American screen — Chaplin, the Marx Brothers, Fields, Laurel and Hardy, Lloyd, and even Keaton — worked in a flagrantly theatrical style. Their films thrive on the very stylization, excess, and exaggeration that we tend to think of as uncinematic.

In a persuasively "real" medium like film, comedy may well have to stress its own unreality more emphatically than it does on stage. For once we *believe* in something, we're apt to lend it our feelings; if we were to believe in the aggression and cruelty of American comedy, they would horrify us instead of making us laugh. Since film, with its persuasive reality, has immediate access to our feelings, comedy may well have to disrupt our emotional involvement by insisting on its own unreality.

But Chaplin's work, unlike most screen comedies, confronts us with an apparent contradiction. For though his style is patently theatrical, he continually uses the persuasive reality of the medium to anchor his stories firmly in the physical world. Indeed, much of his comedy *depends* on the physical credibility of his scenes. The teetering cabin in *The Gold Rush* might well have been built on stage — but the abyss under the cabin could only have been suggested and would never have had the urgent immediacy it has on the screen. In the theater, the antics of the men would have been charming and funny, but there would have been none of the danger, tension, or kinetic involvement that are so essential to Chaplin's work.

Unlike the farce of Mack Sennett or the Marx Brothers, Chaplin's farce has a startling authenticity that seems to belie his theatrical style. In part this no doubt derives from the way in which Charlie's world coincides perfectly with the visible, physical realm that the medium renders so persuasively. He is in constant motion and expresses himself wholly in physical terms. Moreover, his films are a mosaic of precisely observed detail that the camera reports with stunning fidelity.

The most preposterous farcical events occur in utterly realistic settings and are substantiated with painstaking detail. In *One A.M.*, while Charlie wrestles with the Murphy bed, one of its legs comes down inside his top hat. A few minutes earlier, if we're very watchful, we can just barely catch Chaplin placing the hat in the required position on the floor; it is done as casually in the course of a drunken stumble that, unless we're actually looking for it, we remain unaware of it till the moment it is spiked by the bed.

Some of these preposterous moments are authenticated by Chaplin's mimetic genius. When Charlie eats the shoe, we feel the grease on his fingers; when he swallows a penny-whistle, his hand moves to his chest in a gesture so frail and pained, we respond to every burp; and when his uncanny gift for observation and mimicry turn Charlie's face and two dinner rolls into a ballerina, we seem to share in the transformative magic of art itself; we're enchanted and persuaded by the reality of the unreal.

Though Chaplin said that "comedy is life viewed from a distance," he continually pulls us into the action. This effort to *involve* us is crucial to his work, for his comedy thrives on tension — building on our involvement till it erupts in laughter. Yet surely his concern with authenticity was no mere attempt to snare us into theatrical participation. Surely the source of his work was so central to his existence and the stories it thrust upon him so utterly "real" that he was compelled to report them with utmost "reality." The films may be entertainment for us, but for Chaplin they were the transformation of a central existential experience.

Perhaps Charlie's world seems real to us in spite of its theatricality because childhood authenticates even the most extreme moments. To a child, life is intensely theatrical, full of surprises, excesses, and dramatic confrontations. Moreover, Chaplin used the imaginative freedom of the theater to render the *subjective* component of our experience — which the naturalistic cinema has so largely had to neglect and ignore. When Charlie turns into a thinly disguised chicken, the very theatricality of the moment gives us a sense of how he feels: he is trapped inside the clumsy costume just as he is in Jim's hallucination, and flaps his wings in a futile effort to escape. Far from undermining reality, the theatrical here gives us access to Charlie's subjective experience and so endows the scene with palpable reality.

Proust said: "We must never be afraid to go too far, for truth lies beyond." Perhaps even the camera must find an essential part of its truth "beyond" — in the subjective experience of reality that has ever been the source and province of art. This poses a serious problem for a medium so committed to the visible and material world. But surely no esthetic reality is long viable that cannot accommodate the invisible and subjective along with the visible and objective world. Carl Dreyer spoke regretfully of "the fence with which naturalism has surrounded the medium." It isn't a fence that ever contained Chaplin, for he drew his work from the reality of childhood, which is far too inclusive to be rendered by a narrow naturalism.

Childhood authenticates his films from within and validates the broad range of his style. Perhaps his use of the medium is ultimately so rich and effective because he could give — as only childhood can — to the invisible and subjective the concrete imminence of fact. In childhood, as in Charlie's world, there is no hard, defining line between inner and outer experience; to children and Charlie, both are equally real — the imagined and the actual, the tangible and the fantastic, the visible and invisible, "fiction" and "fact."

Charlie
Chaplin
in *The
Circus*

Buster
Keaton,
*Steamboat
Bill, Jr.*

Buster Keaton
Drawing by John Tibbetts

Chapter 3

Keaton

One of the first things I noticed was that
whenever I smiled or let the audience
suspect how much I was enjoying myself
they didn't seem to laugh as much as usual.
— *Buster Keaton.*[1]

The Great Stone Face: Buster Keaton, film maker and comedian. He wrote, produced, directed, and acted in ten feature-length comedies within five years in the 1920s. He was also in 124 other films, short and long, over a 50-year period, right up to his death in 1966.

Keaton loved the camera and the projector, as he loved all kinds of machinery, and he certainly gave his cameraman a workout. He made the camera follow him riding a motorcycle, propelled by a cyclone, hanging over a waterfall, driving a locomotive, rolling down a hill with a hundred rocks, and repairing an ocean liner underwater. More than Chaplin, he liked to show the audience, as he said, "the real thing: real trains, horses and wagons, snowstorms, floods."

More conscious of such cinematic possibilities than Chaplin was, he still tended in much the same way to combine realism with theatrical scope, stressing the full view of the action and the actor, rather than tricky angles or editing. Before Andre

1 Keaton (with Charles Samuels), *My Wonderful World of Slapstick* (1960), p. 13.

Bazin ever theorized about it, Buster Keaton was doing long takes in whatever depth was possible with early film stock. And if there was danger, Buster wanted it all in the same shot with himself, so that no one could say he was faking it. Keaton was one of the great stunt men in motion picture history.

Chaplin smiled now and then, especially when he went into his little dance and tried to please some huge bully. Keaton didn't smile. His eyes, though, his shoulders, his whole body — all five feet five of him in motion — were uniquely expressive.

A greater difference between Chaplin and Keaton was the difference in characterization. In the first place, the Keaton roles ranged more widely than the class-conscious tramp persona. Buster could be rich, middle-class or poor. He was likely to have a definite, hardworking job: a projectionist in *Sherlock Jr.*, a railroad engineer in *The General*, a broker in *Seven Chances*, a cowboy in *Go West*, or at least a clear family connection, as in *Our Hospitality, The Navigator, Steamboat Bill Jr.*

Charlie's jobs were rare, unsteady, and on the shady side. His advantages were gained mostly by luck or deviousness. In *The Kid*, Chaplin's first attempt at a feature, Jackie Coogan breaks windows so that Charlie can come around and re-install them. In *The Gold Rush*, the snow he shovels lands next door, ready for him to collect a bigger fee.

What Keaton accomplishes, he does by doggedly working at it. Keaton himself said: "Here's the difference between Charlie and me. . . . If he saw a suit in the window and wanted it, Charlie would search his pockets, find a dime, shrug and move on. He'd hope to be lucky, or steal the money if there's no other way. . . . My little man would never steal, but figure out how he could earn the money to buy the suit."[2] There is a momentary exception in *City Lights* (1931), when Chaplin first gets serious about trying to earn money to help a blind girl. In the end he has to steal it and run.

Buster Keaton is the small-town American, trusting, optimistic, not class-conscious. He is subject to all kinds of weird happenings, because that's part of the comedy business. But in the long run this rugged individualist is inventive, hardworking, happy, and free, and he gets his just rewards. The failure-becoming-success theme of most of his features represented a continuing advertisement for the American way of

2   Keaton, p. 126.

life, whether he intended that or not. Harold Lloyd's get-ahead themes were more overt, more self-conscious, and at the same time leaned toward the parody of the Fairbanks comedies. Keaton's search for self-fulfillment was more personal, more earnest, more dutiful.

His early life had a lot to do with Keaton's outlook. He was a performer from childhood, like Chaplin, but the conditions were far different. He and his parents and two younger children were a close and happy family for his first twenty years. His father had met his mother while playing in her father's medicine show, and Buster was born on tour, in Piqua, a tiny town between Yates Center and Iola, in southeastern Kansas.

His very earliest stunt was observed by the famous magician, Harry Houdini, a member of their vaudeville company. Six-month-old Joseph rolled down a flight of stairs at a theatrical boarding house and came up laughing. For this exploit Houdini and Joseph Senior nicknamed him "Buster." Keaton also claimed he was twisted out of the house and down the street by a cyclone when he was three. After that he was taken under protective custody — on stage. They bearded and wigged him like his father, who took to throwing him around like a football and billed him as "the Human Mop."

"All little boys like to be roughhoused by their fathers," he wrote in his autobiography. However true that general statement might be, he professed that he always thought himself "fabulously lucky" and that "my parents were my first bit of great luck. I cannot recall one argument that they had about money or anything else during the years I was growing up." Also he was treated "as an adult and a full-fledged performer" from the time he was ten.[3]

He did not, however, let the audience know he was enjoying his rough treatment on stage. He took care to look "miserable, humiliated, hounded, and haunted," because that was what brought the laughs. He also learned not to yell in pain immediately after a swift kick but to give a very slow delayed reaction (five full seconds), as if it took that long for the sensation to reach his brain. The audience howled, and he realized that what they liked was "the Slow Thinker."[4]

3   Keaton, p. 13-14.
4   Rudi Blesh, *Keaton* (1966), p. 44.

Some people thought such a durable target must be a midget. Others were just as convinced he should be in school. Social uplift groups kept the family act out of New York City for two years running. He was not well adapted to school, tending to make audience-pleasing jokes in answer to the teacher's questions. He had to learn reading at home and on the road and never added up one full year of public school classes.

One of the routines Buster went through with his father as he grew older was a surreal representation of the origin of all wars. As he swept a table top with a broom, he would pick up an imaginary object and move it to a different spot. Joe Senior, interrupted in his declamation of some poem or song, would go over and replace the thing where it was before. Buster would take it away again, Joe grabbing it and putting it back. Soon they were "fighting wildly, blasting, kicking, punching, and throwing one another across the table and all over the stage."[5]

More mysterious in origin and appeal was Myra Keaton's saxophone scene. During her sirupy-sad performance Buster stretched a basketball to the end of a long elastic rope and let it go, bashing Joe's head into the mirror while he was shaving with a straight razor.

Such prodigies of anger, danger, and suspense were great crowd-pleasers along the national vaudeville circuits. They also got Buster Keaton thoroughly in trim for the thrills and surprises that later sold tickets for him in movie houses.

There were many happy tours, many pleasant family summers on Lake Muskegon in Michigan. But eventually there was trouble. The familiar occupational disease of show business — alcoholism — caught up with Joe Keaton senior. Mrs. Keaton determined to break up the act in 1917, and Buster got a job on his own with a new musical revue on Broadway for $250 a week — clear indication of his own personal fame at 22.

Then, before he could start, he visited the set of a Fatty Arbuckle film production on East 48th Street. That was the beginning of a new life. He was invited to "do a bit" in the two-reeler starting that day, *The Butcher Boy* (1917). He was to come in the door, looking back, then turn and (as Arbuckle said) "it will be there." The brown paper bag filled with flour

5   Keaton, p. 34.

was propelled by Arbuckle with such force, Keaton reported, that "it put my feet where my head had been."

Buster turned down the $250 for a chance to work in a new medium — $40 a week to start. He worked with Arbuckle from 1917 to 1919, with eleven months out for service overseas in World War I. Then Joseph Schenck, who had been handling the finances for the Arbuckle films, decided to let young Keaton produce a series of his own pictures. It was a handshake deal. Schenck was to distribute, Keaton to co-direct, co-write, and star at $1000 a week plus 25 percent of the profits.

There were nineteen two-reelers in the next two years, including *One Week, The Goat, The Boat, Cops, The Blacksmith, Balloonatics*. Starting in 1923, Keaton made two feature films a year. They cost about $200,000 apiece and brought in an average of $2,000,000: good business for Joe Schenck. He left Buster free to work as he pleased, but he kept ownership of the films.

Keaton's way of working tells something about his easy relationship with the American audience. When his off-the-cuff directing (assisted by Eddie Cline) ran his unscripted continuity into problems, he did not walk off the set and disappear, as Chaplin did so often. He simply called for a couple of innings of baseball. This healthy diversion seemed to soothe the subconscious and bring forth the idea for the gag or the transition that was needed. It was said that he queried all applicants for employment as to what position they might play: Clyde Bruckman was hired as "outfielder and writer."[6]

Keaton determined that his features, unlike some of his shorts, must be plotted carefully and be basically believable: no fantastic events like climbing inside the hood of a car or unloading a dozen Keystone cops from one vehicle. Yet mere description of the happenings in these movies may miss the accumulation of absurdities that so unobtrusively develop along the way.

The features are full of action and transportation, combined with mechanical expertise which is not always apparent on the screen. They are also supplied with elaborate threats which Keaton knew would please the audience. These are well characterized by William O. Huie Jr. as "near-miss gags." The railroad train that almost cuts him down (in *Sherlock Jr.*)

6   Blesh, p. 148.

and the cannon that faces him on his own railroad flatcar (in *The General*) but fires at his enemy instead thanks to a curve in the track — these are comedy constructs comparable to our experiences of movie cartoons. Keaton becomes for a moment like a two-dimensional character who recovers immediately from total destruction. Holding to his realism, Keaton still keeps for us the build-up and the thrill, but at the last minute saves himself from extinction.[7]

In *The Three Ages* (1923) — a plain parody of Griffith's four ages in *Intolerance* — Keaton and Wallace Beery compete for the hand of a fair lady in various slapstick styles and costumes congruent with the stone age, the Roman empire, and the modern era. Keaton gets to launch himself in a catapult, pole-vault with a spear, and crash through a series of awnings. He also executes a ride on a dinosaur by means of — yes — cartoon animation.

Sherlock Jr. (1924) is a treasure-house of ingenuity and wild action. Tricked by a rival, Buster momentarily has to give up his girl. But as he naps in his projection booth, he dreams of entering the very movie he is screening. He thus becomes a great detective and tracks down his rival (also now in the movie) after an unbelievable chase. At one point he's sitting on the handlebars of a motorcycle and doesn't know the driver has fallen off.

In *The Navigator* (1924) Buster is rejected again. Naturally he finds himself on an objective correlative for his state of mind: a deserted ocean liner, drifting out to sea. The ship is not totally empty, it turns out, since his desired girl friend is somehow there too. They keep hearing things but don't see each other until the morning after they arrive. They don't meet until they circumnavigate the ship a few times — a nicely nonviolent double chase as hilarious as any ever seen on the screen. Then they settle down and figure out how to eat with the oversize utensils available in the ship's kitchen. They are attacked by primitive islanders, but eventually rescued.

In *Seven Chances* (1925) Buster has to be married before seven in the evening on his birthday or else lose an inheritance. After several haughty turn-downs, starting with his best girl, a well-meaning friend helps him by putting an ad in the paper, mentioning the inheritance. Buster waits at the

7   William O. Huie Jr., "Buster Keaton and the Near-Miss Gag," unpublished paper (c. 1985).

church. He's tired. He lies down in the front pew and goes to sleep. In back of him the church fills up gradually, then faster and faster, with hundreds of prospective brides. He wakes up, stands, turns around, stops, stares, and — the Slow Thinker again — starts running, followed immediately by all those women. At the end he is accepted, just in time, by his own true love.

What Keaton deeply felt about women seems uncertain and murky today. His deteriorating first marriage may be reflected in the considerable misogyny of *Seven Chances*. In other stories, the leading ladies tend also to be a tough sell for his proposals or worse: incompetent, foolish, and unable to understand or give credit to the hero. Perhaps it is worth noting that none of these actresses in real life ever had the proficiency to become stars in their own right.

Still, the brave deeds in his pictures are interpreted by J.P. Lebel as "valorous love," deeds of a knight-errant performed to win the approval of women. "When he must court her on a sofa with flowers (*The Navigator*) or with bonbons (*Sherlock Jr.*) . . . he's a dismal flop. But when he must work wonders to woo and win her, then he is in his element. Only put him in a storm-tossed ship and you'll see if he knows how to woo a woman or not." Andrew Sarris, more skeptical, allows him no more than "the girl as a convention" although "perceiving the beauty of women through all their idiocies and irritations."[8]

Daniel Moews, in a book-length close analysis, claims that in all of Keaton's independent features starting with *Our Hospitality* in 1923, the action is basically the same. Buster is a loser who gets to be a winner. He starts by being inept or amateurish — an adolescent term of trial — then undergoes a more or less magical sleep, and wakes up strong, inventive, experienced, and ready to defeat the odds. Only incidentally does he win the girl.[9]

His fans may not like to think so, but Keaton does seem to stick to that upbeat formula, without repeating gags or situ-

8   J.P. Lebel, *Buster Keaton* (1967), p. 92. Andrew Sarris, *The American Cinema* (1968), pp. 62, 63.

9   Daniel Moews, *Keaton: The Silent Features Close-Up* (1977). As for the attempts of Blesh, Gerald Mast, and others to assimilate Keaton to a tradition of pessimism because he ends *Cops* with a tombstone, *Daydreams* with a paddlewheel treadmill, and *The General* with a train wreck—well, most critics just don't realize how hard it is to find endings for comedy films.

ations. He transmutes from drudge to daredevil in *Sherlock Jr.* while he's napping in the booth. He also sleeps in *The Navigator* and in *Seven Chances.*

There is another night's rest in *Go West* (1925). Before that, Buster is definitely not at home on the range. He doesn't know what to do about milking a cow, although he does make friends with her (a rare example of Chaplin-style pathos in a Keaton film). He follows along when the cattle are shipped to Los Angeles. The train is ambushed. He is left absolutely alone as the cattle cars roar along into the city, but he manages to stop it and in a superhuman, tumultuous finale, guides the cows through town to the stockyards.

In *The General* (1926) he is an expert to start with, as a locomotive engineer. But (Moews points out) he has to become an expert soldier to win the hand of his lady love. So he goes behind the lines to rescue his very own engine in this Civil War story. In *Steamboat Bill Jr.* (1927), he has to win his father's respect as well as the hand of the girl, and also survive a cyclone. Sleeping occurs in both of these pictures, and he certainly comes out a winner. During the cyclone there is a terrible moment when the whole front face of a house falls on him as he stands — and we see him emerge through a window. He told an interviewer, "You don't do those things twice."

We have said that Keaton's early life was happy and that his comedy is basically robust and cheerful. Probably there's a connection between the two. But later on, the house did fall on him in real life, and his inexperience with evil and trouble made it hard to cope.

In the first place, he trusted his brother-in-law, the veteran producer Joe Schenck, to take care of his business affairs. But in 1928 Joe advised him to give up his independence and go to work at M-G-M. It took away his creative freedom and after two more pictures he began to suffer both personally and professionally. Before long he was taking big cuts in salary to keep working as actor or adviser on comedies at various Hollywood studios. He did stay busy (unlike D.W. Griffith) but the declining years were bitter and degrading.

About the same time, his home life collapsed around him. His marriage in 1921 to Natalie Talmadge (whose sister Norma had married Schenck) started well and it lasted ten years. But he was appalled at his wife's financial demands and her jealousy of the women in his movies. As they moved from one house to another seeking grandeur and giving lavish parties, he took to drinking. Finally there was a divorce, taking much of his property and income and separating him from his two sons. He went through various hells: physical stupor, pain of withdrawal, loss of memory. Eventually his remarkable physical resilience and desire to live pulled him out of it. His mother was still living and was sometimes able to give him care.

One day in 1938 when he and his mother and some cronies were playing one of those marathon bridge games that helped him (like baseball) to focus and have fun, he met a 19-year-old girl who also loved to play bridge. Eleanor Norris liked this weary, humorous old man who was so interesting and so kind to her. After a long acquaintance, she encouraged him to marry her and stayed with him till the end. No longer an adolescent, it seemed he had once more, in his own life, been severely tested and had overcome the odds.

Before the end, there was a burst of appreciation. Keaton was invited to make two short films at the Canadian Film Board and to do a long scene with Chaplin in *Limelight*. He profited financially from a rather poor film biography of himself. He found steady activity in early live television (including commercials). He was feted and applauded at the London National Film Theater, at the Venice Film Festival, and did a turn in the great indoor circus in Paris. And most important of all, copies of all his best features were found and saved.

BUSTER KEATON
The Human Mop

From Keaton's autobiography, My Wonderful World of Slapstick, *we have chosen two early passages. First, a description of the rough treatment Keaton enjoyed as a child in the family's vaudeville act. Second, his baptism of fire as a walk-on in a short film comedy starring Fatty Arbuckle.*

He claims he enjoyed being battered and bruised as a part of the show, because it meant he was accepted as "an adult and a full-fledged performer." His childhood memories are thus centered around the presence and the love of both of his parents, a sharp contrast with the Chaplin history. At the time when he had to pull free of the family and was about to go on his own in New York, he was introduced to the movies. He not only saw film as the medium of the future, but as a medium without limitations.

Here are pages 12-14, 34, and 90-94 from Keaton's own story, written with Charles Samuels, published by Doubleday in 1960.

If I say I "officially joined" my folks' act in 1899 it is because my father always insisted that I'd been trying to get into the family act unofficially — meaning unasked, unwanted and unbilled — practically from the day I was born.

Having no baby sitter, my mother parked me in the till of a wardrobe trunk while she worked on the stage with Pop. According to him, the moment I could crawl I headed for the footlights. "And when Buster learned to walk," he always proudly explained to all who were interested and many who weren't, "there was no holding him. He would jump up and down in the wings, make plenty of noise, and get in everyone's way. It seemed easier to let him come out with us on the stage where we could keep an eye on him.

"At first I told him not to move. He was to lean against the side wall and stay there. But one day I got the idea of dressing him up like myself as a stage Irishman with a fright wig, slugger whiskers, fancy vest, and over-size pants. Soon he was imitating everything I did, and getting laughs. . . ."

Even in my early days our turn established a reputation for being the roughest in vaudeville. This was the result of a series of interesting experiments Pop made with me. He began these by carrying me out on the stage and dropping me on the floor. Next he started wiping up the floor with me. When I gave no sign of minding this he began throwing me through the scenery, out into the wings, and dropping me down on the bass drum in the orchestra pit.

The people out front were amazed because I did not cry. There was nothing mysterious about this. I did not cry because I wasn't hurt. All little boys like to be roughhoused by their fathers. They are also natural tumblers and acrobats. Because I was also a born hambone, I ignored any bumps or bruises I may have got at first on hearing audiences gasp, laugh, and applaud. There is one more thing: little kids when they fall haven't very far to go. I suppose a psychologist would call it a case of self-hypnosis.

Before I was much bigger than a gumdrop I was being featured in our act, The Three Keatons, as "The Human Mop." One of the first things I noticed was that whenever I smiled or let the audience suspect how much I was enjoying myself they didn't seem to laugh as much as usual.

I guess people just never do expect any human mop, dishrag, beanbag, or football to be pleased by what is being done to him. At any rate it was on purpose that I started looking miserable, humiliated, hounded, and haunted, bedeviled, bewildered, and at my wit's end. Some other comedians can get away with laughing at their own gags. Not me. The public just will not stand for it. And that is all right with me. All of my life I have been happiest when the folks watching me said to each other, "Look at the poor dope, wilya?"

Because of the way I looked on the stage and screen the public naturally assumed that I felt hopeless and unloved in my personal life. Nothing could be farther from the fact. As long back as I can remember I have considered myself a fabulously lucky man. From the beginning I was surrounded by interesting people who loved fun and knew how to create it. I've had few dull moments and not too many sad and defeated ones.

In saying this I am by no means overlooking the rough and rocky years I've lived through. But I was not brought up thinking life would be easy. I always expected to work hard for my money and to get nothing I did not earn. And the bad years, it seems to me, were so few that only a dyed-in-the-wool grouch who enjoys feeling sorry for himself would complain of them.

My parents were my first bit of great luck. I cannot recall one argument that they had about money or anything else during the years I was growing up. Yet both were rugged individualists. I was their partner, however, as well as their child. And from the time I was ten both they and the other actors on the bill treated me not as a little boy, but as an adult and a full-fledged performer. Isn't that what most children want: to be accepted, to be allowed to share in their parents' concerns and problems? It is difficult, of course, for a man of my age to say with certainty what he felt and thought and wanted as a little kid. But it seems to me that I enjoyed both the freedom and privileges of childhood, certainly most of them, and also the thrill of being treated as full grown years before other boys and girls. . . .

Meanwhile, as I grew older, our act became progressively rougher. For one thing, we never bothered to do the same routines twice in a row. We found it much more fun to surprise one another by pulling any crazy, wild stunt that came into our heads.

The act started with Pop coming out alone and announcing that he would recite. Sometimes, he said he would sing a beautiful song. He had hardly started on "Maud Muller" or "Where Is My Wandering Boy Tonight?" when I'd come out and fastidiously select one of the thirteen or fourteen old brooms that were on the end of the battered kitchen table we used in our act.

Ignoring him, I would carefully sweep off the table, then appear to see something that wasn't there. Picking up this imaginary object with my cupped hand, I examined it and then put it down on another part of the table. This distressed Pop. Stopping his singing or reciting, he moved the invisible thing back to the place where I'd picked it up. I'd move it to where I wanted it, he'd move it back. That went on with our rage mounting until we were fighting wildly, blasting, kicking, punching, and throwing one another across the table and all over the stage.

But our most popular fighting routine was one in which I whaled away at him with a broom while he retaliated by skidding his hand off my forehead. We started with tiny taps exchanged in fun. These were followed by harder blows, then slams to which we gave our all. In the middle of this fight the orchestra leader, reacting as though all this had never happened before, got to his feet, tapped his baton, and had the orchestra start playing "The Anvil Chorus," to which we kept time by hitting one another.

In another routine we used the house set. Every vaudeville theatre also had one of these which represented usually a room in a farmhouse. Mom came out in front of this and played the saxophone. She continued this, ignoring the chaos which erupted behind and all around her. As she played on, Pop hung a mirror on the corner of the house set, lathered his face, and started to shave himself with a straight, old-fashioned razor. I tied a long, thick rubber rope on a hook above the mirror. This was attached to a basketball, which I carried to the opposite corner of the stage. With each step I took, the audience screamed, expecting the rubber rope to break and snap against his head.

When the rubber rope was stretched as tautly as possible, I let it go. As Pop was shaving his throat with his old-fashioned open razor, the basketball would sock him on the head and push his lathered face into the mirror. With the audience shrieking, Mom placidly continued playing her saxophone.

In 1910 when Annette Kellerman, the Australian aquatic star, created a sensation with her one-piece suit, we got Mom to put on one under a breakaway dress. She wore a big picture hat with the outfit. For a finish Pop pulled a string that stripped off the dress, leaving Mom playing the saxophone in a tight-fitting bathing suit and that large, dressy hat. . . .

On reaching New York in February 1917, I had gone straight to the office of Max Hart, New York's most influential theatrical agent. I told him I had broken up the family act and wanted to work on my own for a while.

"I'll get you all the work you want," Hart told me. He immediately put on his hat and took me to the Shubert Brothers' office which was just down the street. They were casting the new edition of their annual revue, *The Passing Show*, which was then one of the best showcases for actors on Broadway. . . .

The Passing Show usually played in New York for six months, then went on the road for the remainder of the year. My salary was set at $250 a week for New York and $300 on tour. A few days later I got a script of the revue.

But just a day or two before rehearsals were to start, I ran into Lou Anger, a Dutch comedian, who had worked on vaudeville bills with us many times. Anger was with Roscoe (Fatty) Arbuckle, the screen comedian. As he introduced us, he explained that Arbuckle had just broken away from Mack Sennett to make two-reel comedies of his own. Joe Schenck was producing them, and Anger had quit vaudeville to be Joe's studio manager.

I had seen some of Arbuckle's work in Sennett comedies and greatly admired him. He said he'd caught our act many times and always liked it.

"Have you ever been in a movie, Buster?" he asked.

When I told him I hadn't, Roscoe said, "Why don't you come over to the Colony Studios tomorrow morning? I'm starting a new picture there. You could try doing a bit in it. You might enjoy working in pictures."

"I'd like to try it," I told him.

The Colony Studios were housed in a big loft building on East 48th Street. When I got there the whole place was humming with activity. Besides the Arbuckle company, Norma Talmadge's own company, her sister Constance's and a couple of others were making romantic dramas in other parts of the studio. This seemed wonderful to me. It was like being in a great entertainment factory where different shows were being manufactured at the same time.

The two-reeler Roscoe was starting that day was *The Butcher Boy*. The scene was a country store, and my role was that of an innocent stranger who comes wandering in just as he and Al St. John start to heave bags of flour at one another. Like Arbuckle, St. John had been one of Sennett's Keystone Cops.

Roscoe had brown paper bags filled with flour, tied up and ready for use. He lost no time in putting me to work. "As you come in the store," he explained, "I will be throwing some of these bags at St. John. He will duck and you will get one right in the face." It seemed like nothing at all after the punishment I'd been taking from Pop all of these years.

"Now," Arbuckle said, "it is awfully hard not to flinch when you are expecting to get hit with something like that. So as you come in the door, look back. When I say 'Turn!', you turn, and it will be there."

It was.

Arbuckle, who weighed 280 pounds, had established himself as a master custard-pie thrower while with Mack Sennett. I found out that day that he also could put his whole heart and every ounce of his weight into throwing a flour bag with devastating accuracy. There was enough force in that thing to upend me completely. It put my feet where my head had been, and with no cooperation from me whatever. Enough flour went up my nostrils and into my mouth to make one of mother's old-fashioned cakes. Because I was new to the business, I was politely picked up and dusted off. But it was fifteen minutes before I could breathe freely again.

The plot called for me to buy a quarter's worth of molasses. I had brought along a tin pail for the molasses. But after it was ladled out I discovered that I had dropped the quarter into the molasses. Roscoe, Al St. John, and myself all took turns at trying to get the quarter. The three of us were smeared with molasses from head to foot before we were finished. That same day I was also called upon to be bitten by a dog. Between one thing and another, I would say that my long career as a human mop proved most useful from the start of my work as a movie actor. And everything about the new business I found exciting and fascinating.

Incidentally, I've been told that my first scene in *The Butcher Boy* is still the only movie-comedy scene ever made with a newcomer that was photographed only once. In other words my film debut was made without a single retake.

Roscoe — none of us who knew him personally ever called him Fatty — took the camera apart for me so I would understand how it worked and what it could do. He showed me how film was developed, cut, and then spliced together. But the greatest thing to me about picturemaking was the way it automatically did away with the physical limitations of the theatre. On the stage, even one as immense as the New York Hippodrome stage, one could show only so much.

The camera had no such limitations. The whole world was its stage. If you wanted cities, deserts, the Atlantic Ocean, Persia, or the Rocky Mountains for your scenery and background, you merely took your camera to them.

In the theatre you had to create an illusion of being on a ship, a railroad train, or an airplane. The camera allowed you to show your audience the real thing: real trains, horses and wagons, snowstorms, floods. Nothing you could stand on, feel, or see was beyond the range of the camera.

The same was true of the movie makers' use of light. They had not yet learned how to use mechanical light as effectively as they did a little later. Even so, they were making the *sun* work for them on their open stages on the roofs and in their studios which had large skylights. The sun gave them their back-lighting and cross-lights, and they increased this with reflectors. In the theatre only artificial lights could be used. These produced only effects, could only create and increase an illusion or highlight in a particular spot on the stage. And this, everybody in pictures agreed, was merely the beginning!

From the first day on I hadn't a doubt that I was going to love working in the movies. I did not even ask what I'd be paid to work in Arbuckle's slapstick comedies.

I didn't much care.

Men who know a good deal about financial matters have often told me I am stupid in my handling of money. I would not say they are wrong. But even though I've spent my whole life in the most insecure of professions, money somehow has never seemed important to me.

I am not unaware that one can be extremely uncomfortable without money enough for good food, shelter, and decent clothing. But from my babyhood on The Three Keatons always had enough — and a little more — for whatever they wanted. We even managed to stash away quite a bit in the bank against the proverbial rainy day.

It seems to me that if you are a good craftsman your principal concern should be to keep working. If you manage to do that your employers will have to pay you sooner or later exactly what you are worth. How can they avoid it?

I say all of this, but I must admit being quite surprised to find just forty dollars in my pay envelope at the end of my first week as a movie actor. When I asked Lou Anger about it, he said that was all his budget permitted him to pay me. Six weeks later I was increased to $75 and not long after that to $125 a week.

Max Hart, like any other theatrical agent, was not a man to underestimate the importance of a big pay check. But when I told him I wanted to withdraw from my $250 a week job in *The Passing Show* to act in the movies for forty dollars he said I was doing a very wise thing.

"Learn everything you can about that business, Buster," he said, "the hell with the money. Movies are the coming thing, believe me."

DAVID ROBINSON
Three Keaton Shorts

For most of the years since his death, Keaton's short films have been hard to find. Here are descriptions of three of them by the noted motion picture critic of the London Times. *Robinson has recently published a major biography of Chaplin, based on access to the family's documents and files. But he has also been for years a devoted Keaton fan. The following extracts are from his book,* Buster Keaton *(Bloomington, Indiana University Press, 1969) pp. 52-63.*

The Goat was the first of a remarkable succession of five shorts, each made within a month and yet each one comparable in polish and accomplishment with his mature features. Keaton's usual co-director throughout the period of the two- and three-reelers was Eddie Cline. For *The Goat*, as for *The Blacksmith* the following year, Keaton worked instead with Mal St Clair, who had just left Sennett, differences of opinion between producer and director having come to a head, it seems, over a Ben Turpin film, *Bright Eyes*. The co-director was evidently simply one of the total creative team. Eddie Cline always gave full creative credit to Keaton; and Keaton recalled in relation to his codirectors: "Well, when we started making our own pictures we worked so different than a dramatic company and we knew what we had in our mind and a director would only help confuse you. And any time I'm out in front of the camera working if there was any technical flaws I only had to look at the cameraman and he'd tell me or one of the writers standing off the side or even the prop man sometimes says, 'You can do that better.' So, all right, let's try it again. So that's all there was to that."

The Goat is distinguished (and it is impossible to say whether this was due in any way to the influence of St Clair) by its extreme complexity, the way in which gags are interwoven throughout the film. Near the start of the picture, for instance, there is a wonderful scene in which Buster (more of a simpleton here than usual) stares with rubber-neck curiosity through the bars of a police-station window. Wily Deadshot Dan, who is inside having his identity picture taken, bends down out of range of the camera lens and triggers the camera so that it is Buster, behind bars, who is photographed, after which Dan makes his escape. It is only in the second part of the film that this gag is taken up again, as the 'Wanted' posters identifying Buster as Dan begin to appear in the streets. At first bewildered, then terrified by this unexpected notoriety, Buster eventually turns it to his advantage by using Dan's lethal reputation to frighten off a troublesome taxi-driver. There are other examples of this delayed gag development. Buster decoys a gang of policemen who are pursuing him into a pantechnicon and shuts them in just as it moves off. Much later in the film, when we have forgotten the gag, the pantechnicon suddenly reappears, backs on to Buster, and the police all tumble out to resume the chase.

Between times he has gallantly knocked down a man whom he discovers insulting a pretty girl. Later, when he finds himself a wanted man, he supposes (as a one-shot flashback reveals) that he must have killed the man. The sudden appearance of the white and ghost-like figure of a man whom we have already seen in altercation with a plasterer, confirms his fears. Running off, Buster lands straight in the arms of a detective, who gives chase. Later, having eluded his pursuer, he meets the girl again. She takes him home to supper. When her father comes home, he turns out to be the same detective and the chase begins all over again. This structural intricacy, added to the tragic singleness of the theme — the totally innocent Buster becomes constantly more deeply embroiled with the police as the chase becomes more desperate — makes *The Goat* one of the most densely textured of all Keaton's films.

Gag inventions proliferate: Buster absent-mindedly standing behind two tailors' dummies under the impression that they are at the end of the free bread-line; leaping on to the spare tyre on the back of a car just as it is moving away only to find that the tyre is quite detached, a garage advertisement; hiding on the back of a clay model of an equestrian statue, which gradually sinks at the knees under his weight as it (and he) is publicly unveiled; luring the detective under a cart of logs, then collapsing the load on top of him, adding one extra small chip of wood for luck. For good measure there is one of the best train gags. Pursued by the police, Buster jumps on the back of a train; but as it moves away it slips its couplings, leaving Buster's part stationary and him looking foolish as he makes insolent gestures at the police. Suddenly recognizing his predicament, he runs off after the train. He gets on the back of the train, runs through it, out on to the roof and slips the hind part of the train just as the police run through it. Iris out and in. From the far distance the train runs towards the camera. As it comes closer and into full close-up, we see that Buster is sitting on the cow-catcher. He walks off nonchalantly as the driver scratches his head on finding his train is mislaid.

After *The Goat*, Keaton's whole professional and private life underwent complete revolution. This was the last film he released through Metro. The Keaton Company bought the Lillian Way Studios and, still with Joseph Schenck as producer, began to release through First National as the Comique Film Company, and from mid 1922 as Buster Keaton Productions Inc. In late March or April 1921 Keaton broke his ankle on an escalator which was one of the elaborate props of his own devising for *The Electric House*. This accident resulted in a prolonged rest which seems, on the evidence of the brilliant run of work which followed it, to have been refreshing. It also necessitated the release of *The High Sign*, which Keaton had until now managed to suppress. During this period, too, Keaton contracted the marriage with Natalie Talmadge (sister-in-law of Joseph Schenck who had married the actress Norma Talmadge) which was to prove so unhappy and destructive to him, but which at the time seemed idyllic. The accident also persuaded Keaton to hire a regular special effects man; and the resourceful and inventive Fred Gabourie was to prove a valuable collaborator. . . .

The Boat can rank with the great feature-length comedies. It has the same kind of comic substance as *The Navigator*. Its hero is the quintessential Keaton, small, brave, indomitable, though catastrophe follows catastrophe with terrible inevitability, facing each misfortune with a great, still, sad stare and a resource which still remains equal to the next one.

The film begins with one of Keaton's favourite surprises. "Eight bells and all's not well": we find the hero in a storm-tossed boat . . . then discover that the boat is on dry land, and that it is rocked not by the sea but by one of Buster's small, unsmiling, bothersome sons. "All finished and ready for launching." Buster has built the boat in the cellar, but the exit door is too low. Undeterred, he removes a few bricks from the top of the openings and hitches the family Ford to tow it out. But he has not noticed that the boat is too wide as well as too high; and as it comes through the doorway it dislodges the foundations of the house, which collapses entirely. Buster, his wife and their sons regard the destruction with faces as inscrutable as that of Garbo at the end of *Queen Christina*. Buster inspects the debris. The lifeboat is wrecked, so he loads up the bath.

"There's more than one way to launch a boat." Buster is towing the boat into position on the slipway when his attention is momentarily distracted (one of the children has got caught up somewhere). He drives straight over the dock edge. He gets out before the machine finally tips over: then peers curiously as it sinks in the harbour.

The boat, "The Damfino", is finally ready for launching. The skipper stands proudly on the deck. His wife tries to break a bottle of Cola on the stern, but the bottle stays intact while the stern is dented. Buster obligingly leans over the side and smashes the bottle with a hammer before preparing for one of the greatest single Keaton images. Proud and erect he stands on the prow of the boat as it goes slowly down the slipway — and down . . . and down . . . until the water comes up to Buster's neck and his head suddenly swivels round in helpless bewilderment.

But "You can't keep a good boat down." "The Damfino" is at last seaworthy and ready for its odyssey of disaster. Buster puts the funnel down on top of one of the children, then, recognising the cries from within, picks it up, neatly ejecting the child into the water. Then he has to go in after the child. He forgets to untie the boat and carries off the mooring-post together with a fisherman who happens to be sitting on top of it. He is crowned by a funnel, for he has fixed up all the deck gear like a ship in a bottle so that it can all be collapsed in order to go under low bridges; and has another ducking. He casts the anchor; which promptly floats to the surface. "Ten seconds later . . ." says a title mad enough for *L'Age d'Or*.

After lunch — a touching family affair with Buster and the boys in complicity not to let on to mother that her pancakes are too tough to eat — the troubles start again. Buster nails a picture to the cabin wall, and springs a leak. One of the pancakes comes in handy to patch it. The boat is practically capsized by a sporty passing motor launch. They all go to bed (the children in night-shirts and their little Buster hats), but Buster has difficulties with his bunk. Then he is washed out of bed by a sudden assault of water through the porthole.

A storm rises. Buster gamely tackles it with, successively, a candle, an umbrella and a telescope; but they are all washed overboard; and he follows them. He radios the coastguards for help; but when in reply to their request for identification, he replies "Damfino," they curtly reply: "Neither do I," and shut down on him.

The boat is turned over and over. The leak bursts open again, and despite Buster's ingenious efforts to drain the water out of new holes which he bores in the floor, it sinks. The family are set adrift in the bath, leaving Buster to go down gallantly with his ship. When his little hat floats by, they bow their heads . . . until Buster rises up underneath the hat, which he is actually still wearing. The family are reunited in the bath. One of the children asks for a drink of water, and Buster obligingly gets it out of the bath tap. While the parents are trying to summon help, the smaller child playfully pulls the plug out of the bath and throws it away.

As they sink, Buster encloses them in an embrace, and closes his eyes. A moment later he opens them again as the bath touches bottom. Hand in hand the little family get out of the bath and walk off into the darkness. They turn for a moment. "Where are we?" Buster mouths, "Damfino" . . . and they vanish into the night.

No Keaton film previous to *The Boat* was quite so sustained in its melancholy; or provided such continuous laughter.

The Boat had somewhat taxed the ingenuity of Keaton's new special effects man. Keaton recalled to Rudi Blesh that Gabourie had made two boats, one to float and one to sink, but that they persistently performed each other's functions.

The astonishing thing about the whole series of nineteen shorts released between September 1920 and March 1923 is their variety. Keaton never repeats a gag or a story structure. Every film seems to be an experiment towards the mature work of the features. . . .

The astonishing run of successes reached its climax and its end in *Cops*. The working-out of this film has the inevitability of tragedy; and the melancholy underlying *The Goat* and *The Boat* is here more than ever pronounced. Buster's "working man, and honest" is thrust by fate and in perfect, ignorant innocence, into the role of a criminal; and in this role he is forced into opposition with the entire New York police force. The ending is very peculiar, and much nearer tragedy than farce.

The film opens with a Keaton surprise. We see him disconsolate behind bars. The camera moves back to take in a larger view, and we see that he is in fact gazing through the girl friend's garden gate. A series of confusions with a taxi and an aggressive fat policeman leave him the surprised possessor of the policeman's wallet (and already, in consequence, a criminal). He falls victim to a con-man who, on the pretext that his wife and children are starving, sells the soft-hearted Buster the contents of someone else's home. The true owner is a policeman who is actually moving house, so that when Buster starts to load his goods into a horse-cart he has just bought, the man is not surprised, taking him for the removal man. Buster himself is a little taken aback when the stranger helps him load. His trip through the town, negotiating busy urban traffic with a horse which is deaf as well as unwilling, proves to be the usual Keaton confrontation of disaster and resourcefulness.

All at once he finds himself at the head of the annual New York police parade. He is only momentarily surprised by the cheering which he graciously acknowledges as if it were meant for him. Suddenly (a direct reference to the 1919 Wall Street outrage and all the other post-war bomb scares) anarchists on the roof of a building throw down a bomb, which lands on the seat beside him. Absently he lights a cigarette from its burning fuse, and throws the thing over the side. It explodes, wrecking the parade and panicking the crowd. The whole of the police force is now in pursuit of Buster; a wild chase sequence ends with him using a ladder to catapult himself to safety over the heads of the police who have surrounded him.

The concluding sequence begins with a shot of an empty street — a strange perspective view like a Palladian stage setting, seen through a great archway. Keaton comes into view round the corner; and a moment later, after him, a huge army of policemen. They all move forward and disappear out of the bottom of the frame, to reappear a moment later and retrace their steps, the police still in pursuit of the little lone figure. They follow him into a doorway. The camera draws back: it is the police station. The

doors close behind them. A moment or two later a figure in police uniform stealthily comes out of the door, shutting it and
locking it behind him. It is, of course, Buster. The girl — the one
from the garden of the beginning of the film whom we sub-
sequently saw sitting beside the mayor in the reviewing stand —
passes by. She cuts him. He unlocks the door and goes back into
the police station. "The End" title is written on a gravestone, on
which is perched Buster's flat hat.

Following on the high comedy of the cart-ride through the
town — Buster striding the back of the piled-up cart like the captain on the bridge of a ship; or rigging up a telephone to commu-
nicate with the deaf horse; or fixing up a system of mechanical
hand signals (which naturally punch a policeman) after his pro-
truding hand has been bitten by a passing dog — the strange and
surrealist melancholy of the end is as mysterious as it is haunting.

TIMOTHY W. JOHNSON
Sherlock, Jr.

This inventive movie is not only a kind of double detective story. It also has in it one of the most hair-raising rides in any silent film and a couple of sequences in which the movie mixes up its "real life" story and the way film works. Johnson is one of the younger scholars given the task of writing new reviews of major films in the three-volume series edited by Frank N. Magill, called Magill's Survey of Cinema: Silent Films *(Englewood Cliffs, N.J., Salem Press, 1982).*

Released: 1924
Production: Joseph M. Schenck for Buster Keaton Productions
Direction: Buster Keaton
Screenplay: Clyde Bruckman, Jean C. Havez, and Joseph A. Mitchell
Cinematography: Elgin Lessley and Byron Houck
Editing: Buster Keaton (uncredited)
Length: 5 reels/4,065 feet

Principal characters:

The boy/Sherlock, Jr.	Buster Keaton
The girl	Kathryn McGuire
Her father	Joe Keaton
The sheik/villain	Ward Crane
The butler/handyman	Erwin Connelly

Buster Keaton's *Sherlock, Jr.* is a film about film, about reality and illusion, about dreams and fantasies. Containing another film within itself as well as perhaps a dozen instances of one character being transformed into another, through cinematic devices or through disguises, *Sherlock, Jr.* is so technically impressive that film craftsmen of the time went to see it repeatedly to marvel at its effects and to attempt to understand how they were done. In this film, Keaton drew upon both his early background in vaudeville and his quite rapid mastery of the effects and artistry of motion pictures to create a film which is impressive on many different levels. Keaton himself directed the film, but he may have worked with Roscoe "Fatty" Arbuckle on some of the early sequences, although the latter is uncredited.

Sherlock, Jr. both begins and ends in a small-town film theater and concentrates upon the real and fantasized adventures of a character designated simply as "a boy" (Buster Keaton). Indeed, most of the characters in the film are not given names but are merely identified by such descriptions as "the girl," "the girl's father," and "the sheik."

After the opening sequence which establishes that the boy works in the theater and is "studying to be a detective," the story begins with the boy's visit to the girl (Kathryn McGuire) at her house. He presents her with a box of chocolates, but he is soon outmatched by his rival, the sheik (Ward Crane), who appears with a larger box of candy. Then the girl's father (Joe Keaton, Buster's father) announces that someone has stolen his watch. The audience knows that the sheik has stolen the watch and pawned it to buy the large box of candy, but the boy does not. He promptly decides to solve the case himself and, after consulting his book on how to be a detective, he begins searching everyone. His search reveals nothing, but when the father searches the boy, he finds a pawn ticket for the watch. The ticket was, of course, planted on him by the sheik, but the damning evidence causes the father to order the boy out of the house, and the sheik's success is complete.

The boy does not give up trying to solve the case, but after a fruitless (but decidedly eventful) attempt to find out something by following the sheik, he returns to the theater for his job as projectionist. The film he begins projecting is entitled *Hearts and Pearls* or *The Lounge Lizard's Lost Love*. The boy then quickly falls asleep and begins to dream. It is at this point that *Sherlock, Jr.* opens into another dimension: a dimension in which the character in *Sherlock, Jr.* becomes entangled with those in *Hearts and Pearls*. A transparent figure of the boy separates itself from the sleeping boy and looks at the film being projected in the theater. Soon, he sees that the people in his life have become characters in *Hearts and Pearls*, and that the sheik is the villain of the film and is threatening the girl. He runs down the aisle of the theater, now no longer transparent, and attempts to save her by jumping into the picture on the screen. The villain, however, throws him back out of the film. He then reenters the film and stays there, but he is not completely allowed into the world of the film. For example, when he sits down on a garden bench, the film cuts to a city scene and the disappearance of the bench causes him to fall down in the street. As the film changes to other settings, he continues to have trouble with the abrupt transitions; a dive into the ocean, for example, becoming a dive into a snowbank.

Finally, though, the boy becomes completely integrated into the film within the film. In *Hearts and Pearls*, the characters are members of the fashionable upper class, and there is a theft, but it is the theft of a pearl necklace by the sheik/villain and his accomplice the butler (Erwin Connelly, who plays the father's handyman in the other story). The boy's importance is also increased considerably in the transition from one story to the other. After the father makes a telephone call, the sheik exclaims, "We are lost! He is sending for the world's greatest detective — Sherlock, Jr.!" Presently Keaton enters as Sherlock, Jr., elegantly dressed and completely confident. He skillfully eludes the traps the villains have set for him — an exploding billiard ball, a booby-trapped chair, and a poisoned drink. Then, just as he did in the other story, he follows the sheik to try to solve the crime. At first, this shadowing echoes that of the other story, but it then continues into a wildly exciting and diversified chase in which Sherlock receives essential help from his assistant Gillette (played by the same man who plays the theater manager in the other story), who uses several disguises to fool the villain.

Sherlock retrieves the pearls from a group of villains and rescues the girl from the butler, finally ending up in an automobile that is sinking in a river. As he begins to swim, viewers are returned to the original story and see Keaton as the boy waking up in the theater projection booth. The girl, who had gone to the pawn shop and found out that it was the sheik who pawned the watch, comes to see him. "Father sent me to tell you that we've made a terrible mistake," she says. The boy does not know how to respond until he looks down at the screen and sees the conclusion of *Hearts and Pearls*. The man in that film kisses the woman's hand; the boy then kisses the girl's hand. The man gives the woman a ring; the boy does the same. The onscreen couple embrace; the boy kisses the girl rather tentatively. Then the other film has a fade out and fade in to the couple sitting side by side, with two babies on the man's lap; the boy turns, scratches his head, and *Sherlock, Jr.* ends.

Thus, there are many levels in *Sherlock, Jr.* and much interaction between "real" life and cinema, as well as some parodies of conventions of the cinema and of specific films and types of films. For example, Daniel Moews — in his excellent study of Keaton — suggests that *Hearts and Pearls* is a parody of Cecil B. De Mille's films about the very rich as well as of John Barrymore's *Sherlock Holmes* (1922), and that the girl's resemblance to Mary Pickford is a comment on the many people who used film stars as their models. In any case, the last scene is certainly an explicit treatment of the theme of the influence of film on its audience, a topic that is still discussed and debated today.

In addition to the witty treatment of the nature of cinema, including effects and implied commentary that have not been surpassed in the succeeding decades, *Sherlock, Jr.* has many delightful and impressive scenes that need little or no help from the camera. For example, to escape the villains in one instance, Keaton dives through a window that he has previously prepared. As he jumps through the window, he also jumps into a woman's dress and emerges on the other side disguised as a woman. This is shown in one shot so that the audience can see that no camera trickery was used. Soon after that scene, Keaton is still pursued. He sees an old woman selling ties from a case suspended from a strap around her neck. Keaton heads straight for the case and jumps through it and seemingly through the body of the old woman. (The supposed woman is actually the detective's assistant, who has cleverly arranged himself and a dummy lower body and a trap door to make possible the escape.) Keaton also rides on the handlebars of a motorcycle that has lost its driver. These stunts were not without their dangers. In one of them, Keaton fractured his neck, but he continued working and only learned the seriousness of the injury when he was X-rayed many years later. All in all, *Sherlock, Jr.* is a continually surprising and exciting film that is amazing and enjoyable throughout as well as being thought-provoking.

BUSTER KEATON
Filming *Seven Chances* and *Steamboat Bill Jr.*

Keaton always enjoyed explaining his technical exploits. Here he shares the dangers he went through on two of his later independent productions. He was interviewed at a film festival by James Blue, an American documentary film maker, and John Gillett, a historian on the staff of the British Film Institute. The extracts are from "Keaton at Venice," Sight and Sound, Winter 1965-66, p. 28.

J.G.: *By the time you came to the features, the action was no longer just the basis for the gags but thoroughly integrated with them. Do you consistently look for a gag that will help to advance the action?*

Take one from a picture that I am about to re-release, *The Seven Chances.* I am running away from a batch of women who are chasing me. A friend has put it in the paper that I'll marry anybody so long as I can be married by five o'clock — it has to do with inheriting an estate or whatever. So all the women in the world show up to get married. They chase me out of the church, and so on. I went down to the dunes just off the Pacific Ocean out at Los Angeles, and I accidentally dislodged a boulder in coming down. All I had set up for the scene was a camera panning with me as I came over the skyline and was chased down into the valley. But I dislodged this rock, and it in turn dislodged two others, and they chased me down the hill.

That's all there was: just three rocks. But the audience at the preview sat up in their seats and expected more. So we went right back and ordered 1,500 rocks built, from bowling alley size up to boulders eight feet in diameter. Then we went out to the Ridge Route, which is in the High Sierras, to a burnt mountain steeper than a forty-five degree angle. A couple of truckloads of men took those rocks up and planted them; and then I went up to the top, and came down with the rocks. That gag gave me the whole final chase, and it was an accident in the first place.

J.G.: The great thing about that chase is that a lot of it is shot from a long way away, so that you get the effect of the tiny figure with the rocks all round. You often seem to prefer to work within a rather large shot, rather than using a lot of close-ups.

When I've got a gag that spreads out, I hate to jump a camera into close-ups. So I do everything in the world I can to hold it in that long-shot and keep the action rolling. When I do use cuts I still won't go right into a close-up: I'll just go in maybe to a full figure, but that's about as close as I'll come. Close-ups are too jarring on the screen, and this type of cut can stop an audience from laughing.

If I were going to show you this hotel lobby where we are now, for instance, I'd go back and show you the whole lobby on that first shot, and then move in closer. But the main thing is that I want you to be familiar with the atmosphere, so that you know what my location is and where I am. From then on I never have to go back to the long shot again unless I get into action where I am going to cover space in a hurry.

J.G.: Could you tell us something about Steamboat Bill Jr., *with the big cyclone at the end when you get the impression that the whole set is being systematically destroyed? It must have been one of the most elaborate of all your films to stage.*

The original story I had was about the Mississippi, but we actually used the Sacramento River in California, some six hundred miles north of Los Angeles. We went up there and built that street front, three blocks of it, and built the piers and so on. We found the river boats right there in Sacramento: one was brand new, and we were able to age the other one up to make it look as though it was ready to fall apart. My producer on that film was Joe Schenck, who at that time was producing Norma Talmadge, Constance Talmadge and myself, and who later became president of United Artists. Then later on 20th Century-Fox was Joe Schenck, and his brother Nicholas Schenck was head man of Metro-Goldwyn-Mayer. Schenck was supposed to be my producer but he never knew when or what I was shooting. He just turned me loose.

Well, the publicity man on *Steamboat Bill* goes to Schenck and he says: "He can't do a flood sequence because we have floods every year and too many people are lost. It's too painful to get laughs with." So Schenck told me, "You can't do a flood." I said, "That's funny, since it seems to me that Chaplin during World War One made a picture called *Shoulder Arms*, which was the biggest money-maker he'd made at that time. You can't get a bigger disaster than that, and yet he made his biggest laughing picture out of it." He said, " Oh, that's different." I don't know why it was different. I asked if it was all right to make it a cyclone, and he agreed that was better. Now he didn't know it, but there are four times more people killed in the United States by hurricanes and cyclones than by floods. But it was all right as long as he didn't find that out, and so I went ahead with my technical man and did the cyclone.

J.G.: *How about the technical side? The marvelous shot, for instance, of the front of the building falling on you, so that you are standing in the window as it hits the ground. What were the problems in staging that scene?*

First I had them build the framework of this building and make sure that the hinges were all firm and solid. It was a building with a tall V-shaped roof, so that we could make this window up in the roof exceptionally high. An average second story window would be about 12 feet, but we're up about 18 feet. Then you lay this framework down on the ground, and build the window round me. We built the window so that I had a clearance of two inches on each shoulder, and the top missed my head by two inches and the bottom my heels by two inches. We mark that ground out and drive big nails where my two heels are going to be. Then you put that house back up in position while they finish building it. They put the front on, painted it, and made the jagged edge where it tore away from the main building; and then we went in and fixed the interiors so that you're looking at a house that the front has blown off. Then we put up our wind machines with the big Liberty motors. We had six of them and they are pretty powerful; they could lift a truck right off the road.

Now we had to make sure that we were getting our foreground and background wind effect, but that no current ever hit the front of that building when it started to fall, because if the wind warps her she's not going to fall where we want her, and I'm standing right out in front. But it's a one-take scene and we got it that way. You don't do those things twice.

PENELOPE HOUSTON
American and Free

Another prominent British Keaton fan wrote a retrospective piece about him, "The Great Blank Page," in Sight and Sound, *Spring 1968. This extract appeared on pages 63 and 67.*

Sight and Sound, *the film quarterly published by the British Film Institute, is in terms of length of life, breadth of coverage, and quality of writing, a contender for the title of most notable film magazine of all time. Ms. Houston was its editor for thirty-five years.*

. . . In the years between *The Boat* (1921) and *Steamboat Bill Jr.* (1927) there were a lot of Keatons.

He had two spectacular advantages: his timeless American face, which means that in a costume picture (even in the absurd hearthrug and fur boots of *The Three Ages*) he never seems any more ridiculous than he intends to; and his chameleon classlessness. His indolent millionaires (in *Battling Butler* and *The Navigator*) or his pushing young men from Main Street (*Three Ages, Seven Chances*) never look as though they were making off in some richer boy's clothes. Chaplin's comic personality started from English class-consciousness; Keaton's was American and free. In disguise — at the beginning of *Steamboat Bill Jr.*, when he turns up in moustache and beret — he could look curiously seedy, like a weasel made up as a hairdresser's assistant. It is a great moment, made much of, when the moustache comes off and the Keaton face emerges: the great blank page, on which he could write every process of thought. . . .

At the opening of *Steamboat Bill*, the camera moves classically across a wide riverside scene, checking for a moment to watch a man watching the water, and so giving the audience a point of perspective. Buster is the college-boy son of the old riverboat captain, a long-lost child whose return is eagerly awaited. The reunion is a crushing disappointment to both sides, and in the first scenes father takes command — dragging his distressingly prim and silly son off to the barber and the hat-shop and crushing his offending ukulele underfoot. The hat-changing scene is of course classic: the face stern and wild under an avalanche of Stetsons of bowlers of panamas, while the eyes keep sliding off towards the awful checked cap he has set his mind on.

From the moment when Buster meets the girl, the daughter of his father's rich rival, the relationship switches. The father's pathetic old family feud bores Buster: he is playing at being a naval officer, marching grandly, if unsteadily, around the old boat. His now fond father does small, kindly, protective things, like wiping the engine grease off his jacket or giving him a chew of tobacco — Buster keels right over from the impact of this offering. The sea-faring disguise, which obviously gives its wearer much fatuous pleasure, is short-lived. When Buster decides that he must at least make a grown-up effort to get his father out of jail, he is wearing plainer clothes, topped by a mournful upside-down umbrella. And now, with the work of establishing character completed, the wilder comedy can edge its way in; as it does in the jail-break scene, which finds Buster tenderly clutching a hollow loaf into which he has packed a whole set of escape tools.

Inevitably, the film moves into a climax of fantastic movement, with the hurricane replacing the chase. Buildings topple; the roof comes off a hospital, revealing Buster in bed with an ice-pack on his head; there's a surrealistic shot of the neat hospital bed sliding through a stable, past surprised horses. Like a man trying to fight a moving staircase, he slips and slithers in a sea of mud; suddenly he's in a theatre trying to take a dive through the backcloth; then heroically still under the falling house. The turning point in any Keaton climax comes when something triggers all his maniacal energy and resourcefulness into action. He rescues the girl, then drops her when he sees his father in his now floating prison. She essays a faint, but sits up abruptly when dropped: Keaton heroines need to keep their heads.

Steamboat Bill contains practically every element of Keaton comedy: the physical helplessness, transformed to perfect coordination when his mind is set on some practical purpose, such as a rescue; the self-contained one-shot joke, or the chain-reaction joke, like the scene at the station when father and son are both peering warily at any number of unlikely men wearing white carnations; the machine joke, when he runs up an elaborate set of ropes and pulleys to equip the boat for rescue. It also finds Keaton in one of his happiest settings, the Mark Twain country where the spruce steamer and the rusty paddleboat glower at each other across the water.

This was the last of the independent comedies; he joined M-G-M, made *The Cameraman,* and found himself in a studio world where "You had to requisition a toothpick in triplicate." If one follows Rudi Blesh's biography, Thalberg's beautifully polished studio machine was the real destructive force in Keaton's career. And the more one sees of the great comedies, the more one realises how essentially Keaton needed the freedom not to create gags, but to create worlds. The wistful cow-puncher, mounting his horse by rope ladder; the college boy doing an immense run-up to the high jump, only to have the bar topple off as he gets there; the snappish young businessman snatching back his tip from the hatcheck girl; the running figure on top of the train, all owe part of their comic truth to their settings. Arbuckle understood his partner when he said that Buster "lived in the camera."

J.P. LEBEL
Valorous Love

> *Keaton is "a courtly lover . . . a gallant knight." The feats he performs "to win, protect or save his lady constitute the principal dramatic springboard of almost all his films." So does Lebel label the motivation of the hero, whatever his job or status, in the Keaton feature films. But this also involves the drive to "surpass himself," which is the motivation (or plot mechanism) Daniel Moews prefers to ascribe to him.*
>
> *Lebel seeks a pattern in the ten features of the 1920s but is more willing to emphasize the differences among the films, and his use of language is intuitive and enjoyable. His book,* Buster Keaton *(A.S.Barnes & Co.) was published in 1967. Our extract is from pages 92-98.*

. . . Just as it has been said that Keaton has no intention of addressing a "message of general interest,"[1] it has been said that Keaton "doesn't love." "If he is amorous in all his films, his love is tepid and comes more of habit than conviction."[2]

Such critics are confusing *love* with *sentimentality.* For indeed, when it comes to billing and cooing, Keaton certainly does show little conviction. He loses his footing in sentimentality and drowns in rose water.

Keaton, for whom the woman serves as an impetus to show what he can do, to surpass himself, and therefore to show that he loves, is ill at ease when it comes to wooing a girl in a normal fashion. When he must win her with well-phrased compliments and facile gallantry (*The Cameraman, College, Sherlock Junior, Seven Chances, The Navigator*) he always loses out to others. When he must court her on a sofa with flowers (*The Navigator*) or with simple declarations and customary gallantries (*The Cameraman, College*, the portrait in *The General*, etc.) he's a dismal flop. But when he must work wonders to woo and win her, *then* he is in his element. Only put him in a storm-tossed ship and you'll see if he knows how to woo a woman or not.

In *The Navigator*, he is — beneath his seemingly cold exterior — taken by so great an exaltation for the girl he loves, that he seeks the grandiose. He would fly through space to get to her, but is reduced to crossing the street in his huge limousine, performing a graceful but limited U-turn which seems to call for wider flights. (Here, too, it's the form Keaton's act, his gag, takes — its positioning in space — which gives us its meaning, a meaning more significant than the act itself.)[3]

In the same token, when he must declare his love to a girl on a garden swing, according to the rules, he flounders; but when he must woo her while striving to hold himself up before a table which is sinking in the earth (*Battling Butler*), he does so marvelously.

Similarly, he is at a disadvantage when it comes to "taking out" the girl he loves (*The Cameraman*). At the swimming pool he more or less manages to make a good impression; he is, after all, in his element there, and can shine. But when it comes to making small talk and driving her home, Keaton finds himself in the dickey seat, in the rain, while his rival scores points.

Keaton is not "tepid." Quite the contrary. It's just that he dislikes cramped banality; he spices things. When, in *Sherlock Junior*, he overturns the box of chocolates to show the price, this is not an intentionally provocative act. But he is like a child, proud and happy to show the value of the beautiful gift he has given. For Keaton the gesture does not count so much as the intensity of the gesture, and in this case the intensity of the gesture is given by the price sticker.

Let this act help him to break the bonds of cramped banality and Keaton will be completely prepared to give himself over to traditional billing and cooing.

As, for instance, the two-year kiss which ends *The Paleface*. Two years is a long time for a kiss to last; but above all, one has the impression that Keaton sustained it for two years because the position in which he found himself with the young Indian maiden was of such visual beauty, was so perfectly placed in space, that two years seemed a suitable duration for it.

Keaton is ever ready to "call on" the girl he loves, to throw his love-sick heart at her feet, if to do so he must make a mockery of distance and present himself before her at the end of an incredible run, hardly breathless, excusing himself for being slightly late, although she has just finished asking him to come on the telephone (*The Cameraman*).

It is therefore unfair to say that Keaton does not love. Considering the prodigies he performs for the sake of women, it's hard not to call the feeling that inspires these prodigies love. As a matter of fact, Keaton is the only comic hero who succeeds in giving real scope to his love. Alone in the comic cinema where sexuality plays almost no role to speak of and where most manifestations of love are reduced to feeble attempts at sentimental billing and cooing, Keaton stands out not as a platonic but rather as a courtly lover.

Indeed, apart from occasional mishaps with some diabolical Venus, Keaton is a gallant knight. No one would dream of denying this; the remarkable feats that he performs to win, protect or save his lady, constitute the principal dramatic springboard of almost all his films.

Unlike Chaplin who, if he doesn't win his lady's heart by outwitting the villain or by a stroke of luck, is loved for his weakness itself, Keaton wins *his* lady's heart by his very real triumph. It is his force and his courage which overcomes his timidity and assures Keaton his greatest success.

At the end of the Roman episode of *The Three Ages*, Keaton, a leaping, flying Douglas Fairbanks-type avenger, tears his lady from the clutches of the "villains" and metes them out a severe but well-merited punishment.

Love brings out Keaton's matchless ingenuity and indefatigable energy, makes him perform marvellous visual and physical feats and become a veritable hero (*The General*).

Love enables Keaton to bring a liner gone berserk under control (*The Navigator*).

Love makes him master of a tempest and enables him to save a ship, its owner and his daughter from the storm (*Steamboat Bill Junior*).

Love makes him play the indomitable detective (*Sherlock Junior*).

Love makes him the most fantastic news reporter ever seen, makes him direct a street battle and save his girl from the diabolical machinations of a maddened outboard motorboat and a certain death by drowning (*The Cameraman*).

Love enables him to save his girl, at the last moment, from the crashing falls of a mute Niagara (*Our Hospitality*).

Love makes him break more sports records than any athlete has ever broken (*College*).

And so on.

When we say that love makes Keaton perform the countless incredible feats that lard his films and show him in all his visual beauty, we do not mean to say that love is necessarily, in its crudest form, the direct cause of what drives him to perform these feats. Another cause that is not love may put him in a position to perform them (in *The Navigator*, it is chance). But inasmuch as these deeds are always what makes the girl (who has hitherto usually repulsed his advances) recompense him, love profoundly determines Keaton's actions in the second stage.

The feats performed by Keaton when in love owe nothing to chance. He alone is responsible for them. In *College*, for instance, sheer strength of will, fed by love, permits him to lead his sculling team to victory, to achieve the final turnabout, effect his astounding hurdle race and become the best athlete in the college. And this is what differentiates him from all other comics.

The finest example of Keaton's manner of surpassing himself for the sake of love is obviously the one already given in *Battling Butler*, when, first a toy in the violent and expert hands of the professional boxer, Keaton manages to turn the situation about and knock the boxer out, purely by calling up his own untapped forces. The slow development of the change in Keaton, *all of which takes place before our eyes*, is properly admirable. In a similar situation, Chaplin would have slipped a horseshoe into his boxing glove, or clumsily bumped up against something which would cause a heavy weight to fall on his adversary's head.

For Keaton the woman is obviously therefore a sort of catalyst, *an opportunity for him to surpass himself*. It is the woman who reveals him to himself, who enables him to effect the remarkable physical, athletic, dynamic, choreographic, and visual self-accomplishment we spoke of earlier in this book, all of which is the sign of a sort of moral ascendancy.

Inasmuch as love makes him surpass himself and forget himself, makes him open to the world and produces in him a self-accomplishment on a higher level, love for Keaton has Eluardian overtones, the only difference being that for Eluard, love is a question of reciprocal self-surpassing, and love opens a man to others.

In Keaton's films, as has often been stressed, love is not usually a reciprocal matter. Women often display a certain indifference towards him (for which reason he is led to surpass himself). Nor are they always and immediately grateful for what he does for them; at times, in fact, relations between Keaton and his girls are rather strained. The girl in *The Navigator* shows a certain ungraciousness; she even does him some nasty turns, as, for instance, when she obliges him to put on a diving suit and repair the propeller. When Annabelle's foot gets caught in a trap in *The General*, Keaton gets it out; but in so doing his own foot, as well as a hand, gets caught in it; the furious girl is completely indifferent to poor Keaton's plight.

But the girl he chooses always ends by loving him. Keaton is not "unlucky in love." It may take time to make the girl love him, and she may love him less passionately than he loves her, but she will love him eventually nevertheless.

The trials he imposes on himself to "merit" his lady are of the same nature as those imposed on knights in the time of courtly love. Keaton, too, engages in tournaments to win his lady, but his tournaments are of a slightly special nature, for in them he jousts with the whole world.

But the gallant knight, having won his lady's heart at last, can allow himself to indulge in billing and cooing. Knights, even fearless fighting knights, are adept at turning pretty phrases. But to turn these phrases without first fighting for the right to turn them is meaningless for Keaton. Because he has been accepted by the girl does not mean that he can sink back into a dull routine. In *Battling Butler*, only after Keaton has wed Sally O'Neill does he really surpass himself. Besides which, and unlike the knights of old, Keaton does not really consider the woman to be his goal, to be an end in herself; the woman is above all a means for him to surpass himself.

Surpassing himself constitutes the very *form* his love takes. His proving himself is homage to the lady. Displaying his possibilities is not merely the means to win the lady's favours; the display itself is the very incarnation of his love.

Many have held that Keaton, contrary to appearances, does not love women because they introduce disorder into his ordered universe. This false supposition rests on a false appreciation of the very nature of Keaton's character. If Keaton puts the world in order, this is not because he's seeking bourgeois comfort; he is not the mythical incarnation of the little tinkerer who always gets by. Such a conception requires that Keaton be an inhibited little person closed in on himself. But the ultimate goal of his activity is not to secure for himself a tranquil corner of the universe, well protected against the unforeseen; and to want to see his actions as such is to want to see in him a stoic experiencing life fatalistically as he struggles to survive.

Now, we have seen that Keaton is concentration open to the world. The "poetic" way he handles objects bears witness to that. His very readiness to throw himself into the most dangerous adventures for the sake of a woman is only one more indication of his openness to receive and accept all that calls to him.

And love, which gives him the opportunity to accomplish himself supremely, shows us again how open he is to the world. At the end of *The Cameraman* we see Keaton, led along by the girl he has won at last and with whom he shall at last taste happiness (thereby fulfilling the logic of his love) accept the cheers of a crowd, cheers intended for Lindbergh but which Keaton has earned as much as the aviator, if not more.

And thus we see that Keaton's luck in love, far from cutting him off from the world, shows how capable he is of assimilating and openly responding to the call of life and of doing so masterfully.

NOTES

1 Always as a reaction to that literature consecrated to Chaplin, and which would strive to place Keaton in the realm of pure comedy.
2 J.P. Coursodon, op. cit., *Cinema* 58, no. 30, p. 34.
3 This proves that in the end Keaton is never satisfied with comfort. He may be used to it, but he never makes a value of it. When everything seems too comfortable at the start, he puts all sorts of obstacles in his way (as, for instance, the first part of *The Navigator* or the first part of *Battling Butler* when, as the son of an upper-class family, Keaton finds himself in the grip of an ultra-perfected camping equipment). Only later will he have to fend for himself and utilise a maximum of energy and ingenuity (the fight in *Battling Butler*, the domestication scene in *The Navigator*). Keaton does not succeed on his social position but on his personal merits, which have nothing to do with any kind of domesticity.

DANIEL MOEWS
The Youthful Hero

Here the emphasis is on the "leap from failure to success" in all the Keaton films; only secondarily is romance involved. Moews' book is an admirable, not to say intimidating, close analysis of a film maker generally agreed to have done his best work as an intuitive and independent artist. But if the psychology of Keaton heroes does seem to repeat itself over and over, his fans may want to say in reply (as in fact Moews does himself): Very well, but the ten movies he made in the 1920s are nevertheless uniquely valuable—every one.

This is most of pages 2 to 17 from Keaton: The Silent Features Close Up *(Berkeley, University of California Press, 1977), which then goes on to give us even more of a devoted and detailed study of Keaton's films: a full chapter on each of them.*

The Keaton hero is almost always a young hero, initially presented as untried, unformed, and decidedly callow. In *Sherlock Junior* and in *Steamboat Bill Jr.*, the juvenile status proclaimed in the titles is emphasized in the eponymous leading characters. In *Sherlock Junior* and *College*, the hero is even labeled "the boy," though in the first film there are some parodic complications in the use of the word. In *The Navigator* and *Battling Butler*, if the hero seems a little older, he is initially shown as childishly spoiled and inexperienced; and in the second film his parents deliberately send him off on a camping trip in the hope "it will make a man" of him. Even in *Seven Chances*, where the hero is a mature and sophisticated twenty-seven, when a title describes him as a partner in a law firm, he is predictably a junior partner. Only in *The General* is the hero initially given completely adult status, though even there his name, Johnnie Gray, follows a diminutive pattern set in *Our Hospitality* and *Seven Chances* by Willie McKay and Jimmie Shannon, all apt appellations for characters played by the diminutive Keaton, whose small size often makes him resemble some strange adult child. And though he is an adult, Johnnie's character includes a major adolescent quality, one common to all Keaton's heroes, that of change.

Basic to the Keaton heroes is a psychological dynamic of essentially adolescent transformation. They always make some traditional move from youth to maturity, from being a novice in life to being an expert. They invariably begin as despised raw rookies and wind up as seasoned and respected pros. And as they so change and succeed, there is concentrated in them much agreeable adolescent feeling, which is the primary source of the films' emotional appeal. The heroes are all charged with youthful supremacy, that state in which the young are continually conscious that they are growing up into something and continually hopeful that the something will turn out to be wonderful, heroic rather than commonplace. The transformations that dynamize the heroes, in fact, owe as much to the hopes of adolescent dreams as to the realities of adolescent achievements. The transformations are adroit and inviting mixtures: in substance they are often acceptably realistic, involving the sorts of improving changes actually realizable by the young and most common to them; but the accomplishment of the changes is always wonderfully fictitious, managed with a rapidity possible only in the realm of fantasy. By the end of the films, the improved heroes always shine with the realistic light of plausible youthful development. They also always glow with the pleasing but implausible aura of a very young man's desire for instantly and extravagantly achieved growth and glory.

The fantasy element is most evident in a formula central to the structure of the features: the Keaton hero must fall asleep halfway through his adventures. Following a prologue, which quickly establishes characters and situation, the main action of the films is neatly balanced about this sleep, an action that, with classical deference to the unity of time, usually occupies one day or, if the sleep is at night, two consecutive days. The sleep is generally elliptical, abbreviated into a few shots and a single title, and it is always pivotal to the action, marking a brief but decisive turning point for the hero. Waking, he will have undergone one of two possible kinds of change. In the six films where he is closest to being a conventional comic underdog, he will in the first half do no more than bumble and fail at something, and then in the second half, after he wakes, he will be astonishingly improved and will therefore astonishingly succeed. In three more complicated films, (*Seven Chances, Battling Butler,* and *The General*), he awakens first into a major role reversal, an unpleasant new identity, which absurdly causes him to be or do the opposite of what he was or did before, but in these films, too, he eventually improves and then succeeds where he earlier had failed.

In all nine films, though most noticeably in those moving simply and directly from failure to success, the sleep of the hero not only provides a natural and dramatic pause before the coming transformations, but also in a curious causal way seems responsible for them. Though other explanations are always offered, the sleep alone seems a sufficient and satisfactory reason for the changes the hero and his fortunes undergo. He has only to fall asleep to wake up to another and better or at least far different day, most often to a kind of waking dream of wish-fulfillment and success, occasionally first to a comic nightmare of exchanged identities and goals, though that, too, always turns into a dream of success and a triumphant assertion of his own heroic self. After the sleep, his subsequent adventures take place in a world of happily egoistic imagining, in what becomes a projected youthful reverie in which the winning of glory and the establishing of an admirable adult identity should be and always are quickly achieved — in less than a day. If the films look real, they seem dreamt. The recurring sleep does curiously bring about the changes in the second half in the sense that the films all develop as objective realizations of daydreams or occasionally incipient nightmares, developments that the hero, if he were an actual person, might easily have fantasized for himself as he rested. Even though the hero wakes up, the films invariably proceed as though he had not. They are or soon become dreams of glory, and to participate in them as a viewer is, as is the case with our own dreams of glory, a very cheerful, very inspiring, slightly escapist, and slightly transcendent experience.

The basic fantasy pattern of failing, sleeping, waking, and winning is best exemplified in *Steamboat Bill Jr.* After graduating from an effete Boston college, the hero returns to River Junction, a small southern town, where his father is owner and captain of an old paddlewheel boat. On the first of the film's two days, he quickly proves a major disappointment to Steamboat Bill Sr., presenting himself as a foppish and callow collegiate, an incompetent at all work on the boat, and the inappropriate wooer of a rival riverboat owner's daughter. Then night and sleep charitably end a day of multiplying failures, and in the morning a better day, at least for the hero, dawns. When a climactic cyclone strikes, he expertly maneuvers his father's boat, in contrast to the previous day's bungling, and one by one, in a comic apotheosis of the heroic, he rescues from the flooding river his girl, his father, her father, and even, in preparation for the happy ending, a priest.

Other films introduce variations in the pattern, though recognizably holding to it. In *Sherlock Junior*, the usually disguised fantasy and wish-fulfillment elements are made explicit. In the course of a morning the young hero, who is mistakenly accused by his girl's father of stealing a watch, tries and fails to solve the crime. In the afternoon, he falls asleep, and in this film he does not wake up. The dream of glory that follows is actually the hero's dream of glory, starring himself as the world's most famous and successful detective. In *The Navigator*, many nights' sleep are compressed into one. On the first day the hero and heroine find themselves alone on an otherwise empty ocean liner and drifting across the Pacific. Both of them are rich and foolish and unused to waiting on themselves, and the day's events are a comedy of bumbled efforts to secure food and shelter and of infantile frights over imagined terrors. In the last shot of the day, they uncomfortably sleep, sitting up side by side at a table, and then there is a fadeout to a title that begins "Weeks later . . ." This is immediately followed by the film's second and final day, in which they rise from the comfortable staterooms and, since the title's few seconds' duration has provided them with ample time to learn, credibly proceed to perform with incredible competence all the tasks they had so badly bungled the seeming though not actual day before. In a concluding chase and battle, they even adultly meet and conquer real and savage dangers, to replace the first day's Halloween frights, and the film is then happily over.

Seven Chances is one of the films in which the dream of glory begins as a nightmare. About noon on his twenty-seventh birthday, the hero learns that he must be married by seven P.M. that day in order to inherit a seven million dollar fortune, so all afternoon he actively seeks a wife, asking every woman he meets and being rejected by each of them. At five he goes to a church, where a friend has promised to secure him a bride if he still needs one by then, and there, exhausted by seventeen strenuous and unsuccessful proposals, he falls asleep. What the friend has done is to place a story in a newspaper describing the situation and suggesting that any girl who would like to marry a millionaire should come to the church in bridal attire and ready to wed. An uncomely throng of would-be brides respond, and when the hero wakes, he finds the church filled with them and himself surrounded. When he had proposed before, they all usurp the male's courtship role and propose now; and where he had single-mindedly sought a wife, he must now flee some seven hundred of them, as they chase him from the church, through the city, and into the hills. He does not stop running, in fact, for the entire second half of the film, though by the end, which is about one minute before seven, the nightmarish chase has turned into a triumphant trial of endurance, and having passed this test, the hero is rewarded with a wedding to the girl he loves.

Though *Battling Butler* doubles the format, being divided into two parts that each feature a transforming night's sleep, only one of the films, *College*, noticeably departs from the customary pattern of a unified period of one or two days centering on a restful pause that changes or refreshes. Nevertheless, even *College* contains a curious analogue. After spending much of his freshman year unsuccessfully trying out for various athletic teams, the hero has one last sporting chance. On the orders of a friendly dean, he is appointed coxswain of his college's rowing crew just before the big annual meet with another college. When the angry coach slips some sleeping powder into his cup of coffee, so that the former and better coxswain can replace him, it is the regular coxswain who accidentally drinks the drugged brew and passes out. At the hero's turning point, therefore, there is as always a sleep, though here it is that of a surrogate. With no other substitute available, the coach reluctantly sends the hero off with the crew, and while the coxswain snoozes, his formerly inept rival is transformed into an athletic wonder and a glory. Ably if somewhat eccentrically, he coaxes the rowers to victory, and afterward, in a running, leaping, throwing, tackling rescue sequence, he further succeeds at all the athletic events in which he previously had failed.

Even in *College*, though the hero stays awake, force of habit seems to have led the film makers to put someone else to sleep. The dream of glory that concludes the film requires a sleeping presence to inaugurate and sustain it. In *College* as in the other films, the incredible changes undergone by the hero after he or his substitute falls asleep seem right and reasonable because they are shaped to the demands of an emotional logic, that of dream or reverie or wish-fulfillment fantasy. Like much popular art, including many later Hollywood movies, the films mirror and manipulate their audience's emotional needs and fantasy life. They are every man's, at least every young man's, dream of instant success, in which reality always acquiesces to the heart's desires and what should be immediately is. A severely unimaginative realist might resist their appeal; most daydreamers would be quickly and cheerfully drawn into them. . . .

The pattern of work and learning, from the initial essaying to the final mastery of a new discipline, recurs in seven films. In these the hero is quickly involved in some programmed physical activity, an occupation or a sport or something that at least resembles them, where proficiency in handling professional tools or gear is required and professional routines or movements must be expertly executed. In *Go West*, a young eastern tenderfoot starts work as a cowboy herding cattle. Saddles, horses, lariats, guns, branding irons, holsters, spurs, and chaps constitute the inventory of a cowboy's equipment and working dress, and the routines involving these items, from saddling a horse to roping a steer to pulling a gun from a holster, are learned rather than natural activities. They are also activities that the farcically bumbling beginner of a hero must perform for what is obviously the first time in his life, without benefit of study or practice. As he goes through the required steps, his execution of them is either so miserably ineffectual that it leads quickly to failure or else so eccentrically and precariously performed that the resulting success is more a parody of achievement than an actual accomplishment.

In six other films, other professions with other routines employing other tools of the trade are featured. When the landlubber hero of *Steamboat Bill Jr.* is introduced to the engine room of his father's riverboat, he twice accidentally pushes the forward control lever, causing two collisions; on deck he is continually tripped up by guy wires and ropes and often nearly falls overboard. In *The Navigator*, having never labored in his idle life, the hero must suddenly perform all the work on an empty ocean liner, from making breakfast in the galley to sending up signal flags to repairing a propeller, in the last activity fully rigged out in an air-tight rubber suit, plentifully supplied with tools, and even advised by a small booklet entitled *Instructions for Deep Sea Divers*. In *Battling Butler* and *College*, in the latter once again armed with instruction books, the hero tries his inept hand at sports and athletics — hunting, fishing, professional boxing, baseball, and track (including most of the events of the decathlon) — and also in *College* manages to stumble through the dexterous routines of a soda jerk and a waiter. In *Sherlock Junior*, having been introduced with a magnifying glass, fake mustache, and yet another book of instructions, which he frequently consults, he labors at the tasks of a private detective, primarily at the art of secretly and surely following a suspect. Finally, in *The General*, he works for most of the film as a railroad engineer, though this time, in what is a unique variation on the formula, he is from the beginning an accomplished professional at his job. In two railroad chases and a concluding battle sequence, however, he conventionally first bungles and then masters the work routines of a soldier, which is what from the start he has desired to become.

Though work, expanding the term to include the labors of an athlete, is a topic not much explored in most of the arts, it is obviously basic to the art of Keaton. Work is for him a way of creating in silence a distinctive and highly individual hero, for while the Keaton character does not indiscriminately support the work ethic, usually limiting himself to jobs with a strong heroic potential and much youth appeal, he is likely to be identified by his career and its activities. He is a man employed, frequently a man in the easily identifiable uniform of his profession, even if there is a ludicrously visible gap between the knowledge the uniform proclaims and the ignorance of the young novice who wears it. . . .

. . . The nine Keaton films are all variations on a single ideal Keaton comedy, which contains in its structure several major experimental and emotional patterns most common to adolescence. The films all follow the emotional curve of wish-fulfillment fantasy — of failing, sleeping, and miraculously waking to a day of glory. In a highly compressed way, if we consider only the beginning and the end, they also utilize the pattern that most learning follows, from bumbled beginning at a new job or task to final proficient accomplishment. Similarly, there is in the films a pattern of identity development, of a transcendent move from a lesser to a higher level of being, in which potentialities of character are for the first time realized and expressed. This pattern is most evident in the progression from constrained and imposed gestures to unrestrained, self-willed, and self-proving actions.

The final form of youthful experience in the films, a last cheerful variation on the hero's instantaneous leap from failure to success, is that of frustratedly wooing and then happily winning a girl. Though such romance is always featured, however, its presentation is usually such as to make it subordinate to the patterns just summarized, an important but secondary emphasis in most films.

Though the Keaton hero invariably loves a heroine, she generally remains a somewhat distant and dramatically underdeveloped figure. She is used in a stylized and simplified way to provide a primary motivation for him, an initial impetus for his subsequent actions. Either she or her family or both will disapprove of him, and he therefore has to win her or their approval, which he accomplishes in a manner appropriate to an adolescent ego, by becoming a heroic hero in an adventurous fantasy, someone they will all have to admire, as in the end they always do. In seven of the nine films, when the heroine is kidnapped or threatened by death or by a chaste and comically underplayed sexual assault, he is even called upon to perform dangerous feats in her rescue, an ultimate means of securing her admiration and love without ever transferring the center of action and interest from himself. If the films are all love stories, the major focus still remains exclusively on the hero. The girl is apt to be reduced to a sketchy background figure, designed not to compete for attention with the hero but rather to serve simultaneously as a football-like prop to be carried by him across some athletic battlefield, as an

admiring cheerleader to look on and applaud while he victori-
ously shines, and as a coveted silver prize finally to be won. In
these respects, she seems to be only limitedly there, present
merely to fulfill the requirements of a love object as needed by an
immature and self-centered male. In the dream world of the
films, though the hero's feelings are often fiercely projected toward her, somehow they still remain egoistically within and actually fixed upon herself. To describe the same state of things
from a point outside rather than inside the films, in movies that
are vehicles for Keaton, the camera and consequently the audience are required to concentrate on only one person, the star. . . .
    The high priority placed on the hero, and the hero alone, par-
tially explains Keaton's often perfunctory depiction of romance.
A respect for comic decorum is a second reason, for in film any
realistic and extended presentation of love is apt to be too emotionally involving for an audience to find it funny. A historical
perspective on the transitional period in which Keaton worked
also reveals a third cause. While some silent films, like *Flaming
Youth* or *Our Dancing Daughters* or Clara Bow's *It, The Primrose
Path,* and mildly blasphemous *My Lady of Whims,* reflected a jazz
age emancipation that points to the present — a reflection, however, much more faint than the audience-luring titles would suggest — others, like the films of Griffith, Pickford, Chaplin, and
Keaton, are backward-looking, mirror what was still Victorian in
American culture, and seem in many ways more of the nineteenth century than our own. Youthful romance in a Keaton film
is therefore circumscribed by a Victorian attitude, the attitude of
a culture somewhat more restrained than ours, which stressed
love and sex as an adult privilege to be earned rather than an instant proof of adulthood to be enjoyed as soon as biology permits. Ideally, a young man of the respectable middle class was
expected to prove his adulthood in nonsexual areas before being
allowed the joys of love or its presumed equivalent, marriage. As
a potential suitor of a middle-class young lady, he was calvinisti-
cally required to prove his worth as a provider, as someone with
a job or a career who could properly maintain a wife, before he
would be accepted by her and her parents. Only after such proof
were an engagement, marriage, and the pleasures of marriage allowed. Generally depicted as a still untried youth who has not
yet fought the battle of life and in some way proved himself, the
Keaton hero as a late-Victorian survival must first do that before
he is allowed the joy of having his girl. And it is upon his first
victory, upon a proper Victorian young man's first demonstra-
tion of his adult worth in various nonsexual arenas (themselves

equally Victorian in their Alger-like concern with work and with self-improvement), that the films most intensively dwell, to the moderate exclusion and partial deferment of a love interest. Only at the end, at the puritanical threshold of adult love, is the virginal hero rewarded with an actual or promised wedding.

Although lingering Victorian attitudes about what activities of adolescence should or should not be encouraged on the screen have a sadly retardant effect on the Keaton hero's love life, they do not adversely affect the Keaton movies. The latter simply concentrate on what was allowed, and what they can do they do well. The conclusion to be drawn from this description of the narrative and character formulas in the films is that the major patterns of self-transcendent adolescent experience, which are stressed in plot and hero, are not only what the films most intensively dwell upon, but also what they most significantly and successfully are about.

Location shot of Buster Keaton
in *The Cameraman* (M-G-M),
Eddie Sedgwick directing.

Harry Langdon and Harold Lloyd
Drawings by John Tibbetts

Chapter 4

Lloyd and Langdon

The glasses would serve as my trade-mark
and at the same time suggest the character
— quiet, normal, boyish, clean, sympathetic,
not impossible to romance . . . . I would be an
average, recognizable American youth.
                              — Harold Lloyd.[1]
Langdon's comic characterization is unique.
It is that of one who is chronically,
pathologically semiconscious.   *— Joyce Rheuban.*[2]

As the silent screen made its way into history in the 1920s, the two great contemplative geniuses of comedy, Chaplin and Keaton, were joined by two widely divergent hardworking talents from Nebraska.

Harold Lloyd was the very epitome of energy, the all-American boy in action, finding fulfillment in overcoming his limitations and winning the approval of others — including the girl of his dreams. He accomplished this image by working with gags and danger, like Keaton, but also paying close attention, like Chaplin, to personality and philosophy. With eleven silent features in eight years in the 1920s he won more money at the boxoffice than any of his competitors.

1   Harold Lloyd (with Wesley Stout), *An American Comedy* (1928) p. 102.
2   Joyce Rheuban, *Harry Langdon* (1983) p. 15.

Harry Langdon, exactly opposite, was the sad incompetent clown, a lost soul perhaps from some European circus, slow-moving and slow-thinking, embarrassed, rejected, fumbling, confused by women, "unAmerican" from head to toe. He pursued this image of vacancy and vagueness while yearning to equal the intense pathos and demanding personality achieved by Chaplin; he showed only limited skill in developing extended gag sequences like Keaton. As long as the plots of his pictures turned his unfocused image around in the end, making him "the worm that turns," the 1920s audience accepted him. When he tried to be consistently slow, sad, and even tragic, the audience turned away.

"In New York even the owner of the smallest enterprise acts with alacrity."

So Charles Chaplin, Englishman, observed during his first visit to America. He noted the "fury of speed" it took to make a malted milk: vanilla flavoring, ice cream, malt, and milk were each popped into the container, shaken, and delivered "in less than a minute."[3]

Charlie later mixed a quick drink in his own Mutual film *The Rink* and briskly pulled apart a clock in *The Pawnshop*. But it remained for Harold Lloyd to express in full detail Chaplin's image of American alacrity — at a soda fountain. This took place in his last silent feature, *Speedy* (1928). And he was pretty much the same character who had announced hopefully three years earlier in *The Freshman* (1925): "I'm just a regular fellow. Step right up and call me Speedy."

In his feature films Lloyd, outfitted with horn-rimmed glasses and usually a business suit, established himself as the optimistic hardworking American get-ahead individualist. Of course there was exaggeration in his stories: "exaggeration is the breath of picture comedies."[4] He was always subject to

---

3   Charles Chaplin, *My Autobiography* (1964) p. 120.
4   Lloyd, p. 102. Much of my information on Harold Lloyd's life and films depends on several very good authors: Donald McCaffrey (*Four Great Comedians: Chaplin. Lloyd, Keaton, Langdon* 1968), Richard Schickel (*Harold Lloyd: The Shape of Laughter* 1974), Adam Reilly (*Harold Lloyd: The King of Daredevil Comedy* 1977), Tom Dardis (*Harold Lloyd: The Man on the Clock* 1983), and of course Lloyd himself (1928). None of them are responsible for my descriptions, evaluations, and opinions.

strange experiences which made him entertaining. But individual achievement and success were part of the American scene, and Lloyd himself had lived that success.

He did not learn success from his father. Darsie Lloyd had failed at a dozen jobs and enterprises in various Nebraska and Colorado towns. Son Harold was more conformist and congenial — not Huckleberry Finn, as he often said, but Tom Sawyer. He was constantly working outside of school, mowing lawns, working in a department store, delivering newspapers. He set up a number of self-help enterprises, including selling popcorn to people coming through on the train, and these were on average more enduring than those of his father. On one occasion when the family had to depart from Denver, two other boys were working for him on his newspaper route, and he sold the route for a profit.

Mrs. Lloyd was the kind who kept up on New York theater happenings and attended every traveling show that turned up in the vicinity. This passion for the drama was transmitted to her son. He was forever putting on magic shows or performing dialogue scenes of his own devising, with mute manikins or with friends. Yet the boy's attachment and affection leaned toward his easygoing father and Harold stayed with him when the parents separated.

Like Horatio Alger, he had his lucky moments. A chance conversation in front of a store window led to a friendship with John Lane Connor, who was playing in a local stock company and needed a place to stay. Young Harold immediately volunteered his mother, who was willing occasionally to be landlady and cook. He thereafter spent many hours at the theater, where Connor instructed him in acting and Harold returned the favor by giving his new friend pointers on make-up.[5]

Connor later moved to San Diego, and Harold's luck took him there as well. His father was involved in a traffic accident, and damages came to $3000. After the hospital expenses were paid, there was enough money to make a move, and the two adventurers tossed a coin. If it had come up heads, they would have gone to New York. But Harold won the toss and

5 Like Mary Pickford, whose father died when she was five, and Douglas Fairbanks, whose father decamped when he was five, Harold Lloyd was the beneficiary of boarding-house life, presided over occasionally by his mother. Mack Sennett's mother also had experience along this line.

chose the west coast. Soon he was working with Connor again as a dramatic coach and actor. Before long he discovered movies.

After a few parts with the Edison company on location in San Diego, he moved to Los Angeles. His skills in enterprise and competition, along with a bit of unfair advantage, got him into the Universal lot as an extra. He discovered that the man at the gate didn't check faces too carefully after lunch hour, and anyone wearing make-up got inside. Harold daubed his face, walked in after one o'clock, and started right away getting assignments and making friends.

One of the people he talked to was Hal Roach. Roach claimed he was some day going to get into production on his own and make Lloyd a comedy star. Sure enough, he came into some money, set up an office in a mansion near downtown Los Angeles, and became a producer. It was touch and go for a while, since neither of them had any training in movie comedy shorts. Chaplin, Keaton, and Langdon brought to their movie careers years of vaudeville experience. Roach had played only cowboys and Lloyd mostly dramatic roles. They had a lot to learn.

"Willie Work" didn't work, and "Lonesome Luke" was too obviously a Chaplin imitation. But in time the future all-American hero discovered "the glasses character." Suggested by a movie he saw about a peaceful parson who roused himself to beat up on the villain and rescue the girl, Harold's hero with the horn rims became popular in one- and two-reelers. By 1921, Lloyd and Roach edged toward features with the four-reel *A Sailor-Made Man. Grandma's Boy* came the next year and was a great success. Lloyd was the first of the leading silent comedians to make the firm choice to move into feature film making.

Chaplin worked within the ordinary laws of drama in his frequent confrontations with imposing personal villains, often played by grisly Goliaths like Eric Campbell or Mack Swain. Keaton's characteristic stance offered a kind of mysterious universality, a contrast between his imperturbable visage and awesome dangers like typhoons and masses of policemen. For Harold Lloyd there was a more frankly American atmosphere —fast, sometimes furious, genial, and always hopeful.

It was workmanlike comedy, full of surprises, gags, and thrills. He was eventually billed as "the king of daredevil comedy." Such a label failed to take into account some of his more thoughtful stories of character development and conflict. It tended to type him as the star of up-in-the-air danger pictures like *Safety Last* (1923), in which he appeared to climb the face of a tall building. Some of Lloyd's on-the-ground chases more truly entitled him to the thrill billing.

In *Girl Shy* (1924) it seems absolutely necessary for Harold to get to a church and stop a wedding, and his trajectory is embellished by the kinds of vehicles any American might find at hand: three different cars, a truck, a police car, a horse, a fire truck, a trolley car, a motorcycle. In *For Heaven's Sake* (1926), after being kidnapped by his rich friends to prevent his own wedding to a mission worker, he manages to escape and reach the altar after a wild ride on a double-deck bus. In *Speedy* (1928), he has to get a trolley car back to a starting line to prove it is still traffic-worthy and prevent the big monopoly from taking over: he borrows a pair of horses to haul it there just in time.

In *Why Worry?* (1923) and *Doctor Jack* (1922), on the other hand, he is occupied with showing that a hypochondriac can overcome fears of ill health. In *Grandma's Boy* (1922) he wants to prove that self-confidence can be learned, and in *The Kid Brother* (1927) he demonstrates that a puny third son can prove his manhood by his wits. In *The Freshman* (1925) he parodies excessive expectations from college friendships, and in *Safety Last* he is making sly fun of the upward drive for success.

It cannot properly be said that Lloyd's features of the 20s were all about getting ahead. They were usually about individual prowess tardily discovered, much like the Keaton pictures. He was often a cocky bumbler at first, rarely poor, and in three of his early films he was a wealthy idler. But the atmosphere of his movies was one of fast-rising expectations. They were of their time, and so was he. When depression struck in 1929, "Speedy" was subject to arrest.

Donald McCaffrey, the leading academic analyst of Lloyd, says "the key to understanding the comic character created by Lloyd lies in the leading figure's zeal. The enthusiasm of this character gives it distinction. . . . Some of the best comic moments of his films occur when Harold's zeal leads him into situations which backfire." In *Safety Last* and *The Freshman* "he attempts feats he is ill-equipped to handle. . . . In each case, however, the fault that gains laughter is also the virtue that wins the victory. Victory is achieved, it must be pointed out, with the assistance of luck."[6]

The coming of sound, of course, had a discouraging effect on everybody, especially Chaplin, who chose to defy it, and Keaton, who was overwhelmed by Jimmy Durante, Red Skelton, and the Marx Brothers in addition to being talked out of his independence at M-G-M. When Lloyd did a couple of sound pictures of his own it seemed as if he was talking too much. By the time *Movie Crazy* (1932) and *The Milky Way* (1936) came along he did get good reviews and boxoffice.

But hard work and even good scripts and good directors (Clyde Bruckman, Sam Taylor, Elliott Nugent, Leo McCarey) couldn't bring the optimistic aura of Lloyd and the bitterness/anarchy of W.C. Fields and the Marx brothers into any kind of acceptable balance for 1930s audiences. The depression meant the end of both Horatio Alger and Harold Lloyd.

It was ironic that a pampered son of a rich mother, a brilliant, intellectualized, Europe-oriented, dialogue-happy aficionado of comedy theory like Preston Sturges should have set himself to try to give Harold Lloyd — the middle-class apostle of self-help and good will — a new lease on life with *The Sin of Harold Diddlebock* (1947). Like so many of Sturges' comedies, it was a one-joke story: the hero of *The Freshman* is at the same job and the same desk twenty years later. He does not — repeat not — get ahead. After that there are gags about lions and circuses but no heart. And even though Howard Hughes undertook to recut it as *Mad Wednesday* (1950), Lloyd didn't have the heart to go on with new productions.

He was independently wealthy and he enjoyed being the proprietor of a very large mansion in Beverly Hills, with an extraordinary surrounding estate and gardens. He became a somewhat serious painter and photographer, active in charities and the chamber of commerce, and a devoted Shriner, ascending to the topmost national position of Imperial Potentate. Unlike Buster Keaton, he took no jobs as performer

6 McCaffrey, *Four Great Comedians* (1968) pp. 81-82. In all his features there is a happy ending for the hero: he moves up, makes friends, escapes danger, "gets the girl." There were three women: Bebe Daniels, who worked in many of the shorts, Mildred Davis, whom he married, and Jobyna Ralston, who played in six features.

or comedy adviser, although he tried producing a couple of films at RKO. Like D.W. Griffith, he simply had to wait for the end of his life.

As Harold Lloyd was the embodiment of alert American-style alacrity, Harry Langdon was the model of alien apathetic mediocrity.

Langdon's image was individualism in reverse, a hero in hiding, a tiptoe weakling in a state of permanent hesitation, a wan intruder on the American screen. To laugh at him was a kind of embarrassment, an open announcement of the old Aristotelian audience superiority — in this case so easy to claim it was shameful. The type would reappear in the sound era as an idiot child, played in various raucous ways by Jerry Lewis, and in the 1980s by the mechanical doll, Pee-Wee Herman.

Harry's parents were not quite so haplessly poor as Chaplin's: they had jobs in the Salvation Army. Harry himself, like Harold Lloyd, was ambitious. Born in 1884, nine years earlier than Lloyd, he also grew up in Nebraska and at the age of ten was on an Omaha streetcorner selling papers. He picked up other work when he could in the nearby theater district. Like many shy children, he yearned to perform. He ushered for the privilege of watching the shows, performed on amateur nights, and learned how to post bills, sell tickets, and sweep out.

At thirteen, he was allowed to join a traveling medicine show. For a couple of years, on the road and in Omaha, he did comedy routines, sang, danced and played various instruments, and later joined a circus, where he tumbled and clowned and worked the trapeze. In 1903, when he was nineteen, he married an aspiring actress and wrote a comedy skit for the two of them called Johnny's New Car. For the next twenty years they did this same skit (and one or two others) over and over in vaudeville.

Eventually Langdon's sure-fire act was seen in Los Angeles. Harold Lloyd praised him to Hal Roach, who made an offer which Langdon turned down. Sol Lesser met his demands, then sold his contract to Mack Sennett, who was fresh out of a leading comic in 1923. The "new car" episode was soon on film. It was a lot like the Sennett tradition: the car stalls, then starts, then steams, and once the radiator is fixed the fenders fall apart and the door comes off.

This was a recognizable American theme, making fun of every man's love affair with machinery. But what could they do for an encore? And another and another? Movies don't run for twenty years. Sennett took the Langdon persona, still undeveloped but obviously on the sagging side of inaction, and put it seventeen times through familiar Sennett situations — bathing girls, danger, slapstick, and chaos. It was mostly a mismatch. A character pattern like Chaplin's was needed.

Enter Frank Capra and Arthur Ripley, writers. Capra was running in place at the Sennett factory, with no inkling of his future fame as a comedy director, but determined to get ahead somehow in the movie business he had happened into. Having won a degree at Caltech, he had flunked out badly during the depression after World War I. He wanted no more near-starvation, no more selling door to door. This Langdon character could be his meal ticket for the foreseeable future.

Capra saw him as "the little elf," in contrast to Chaplin's little tramp. Unlike Chaplin, who might be beset by hopeless odds but could often take arms against a sea of troubles, Langdon was funny because of inability to take action. He would have things happen to him, and these surprises would be entertaining. But he would never save himself. He would be saved only by a benevolent Providence.

This Capra prescription, applied, seemed to work. After five short subjects written by the Capra-Ripley team, Sennett's new star was becoming popular. By 1925 he was conceded a salary of $7500 a week. Then Langdon chose to leave the Sennett factory. He joined First National Pictures (where Chaplin had moved eight years before) demanding full creative control as star and producer. He took his two writers with him. His first feature was directed by Harry Edwards.

In *Tramp, Tramp, Tramp* (1926) Langdon is the son of a poor cobbler. The town's wealthy shoe manufacturer puts on a coast-to-coast walkathon. Harry determines to win the $25,000 after being overwhelmed by the tycoon's beautiful daughter (Joan Crawford). He has various adventures on the trip, including a brief tour of duty with a chain gang and an encounter with a cyclone, in which he bests the frightened world champion walker by throwing stones at the cyclone and chasing it away.

The solid success of this hour-long feature fed the confidence and the ego of both Capra and Langdon. Edwards got the blame for some cost overruns and dropped out, commending Capra to Langdon as ready to be a director. Langdon was already nursing a desire to direct himself (like Chaplin) but felt it was not the right time. His conflict with Capra began with the beginning of his second feature film.

In *The Strong Man* (also 1926) Langdon is a Belgian world war veteran who comes to America as assistant to "the great Zandow." He also hopes to find the girl who corresponded with him through the Red Cross. He finally finds her in Cloverdale and discovers she is blind, but this seems somehow to suggest that she and the "little elf" belong together because they are equally handicapped. Now he has the strength to go on stage in place of the intoxicated Zandow, fires a prop cannon over the threatening crowd, and together with Mary's pastor father cleans up the town. Thus, after many discouragements, with the help of a spunky girl and the challenge of a mob, the worm turns and triumphs.

Film historians, with hindsight, can see here the future Capra hero. He is more assertive than the pattern of behavior Capra first theorized for Langdon, and required more control over the star himself. For Arthur Ripley, who wrote the story but saw it adapted by Tim Whelan, Tay Garnett, James Langdon, Hal Conklin, and of course in all practical details by Frank Capra, the plot must have seemed excessively simple and optimistic. The break between Capra and Ripley was now beginning.

The Strong Man was a very big hit and prompted *Photoplay* magazine and other sources to place Harry Langdon in the select company of the top money-making comedians, Chaplin and Lloyd. Yet instead of binding the principals together to work out differences and build on success, the situation got worse. The third feature, this time dominated by Ripley as story writer, was supposed to be more "sophisticated."

In *Long Pants* (1927) Langdon is a compulsive reader of romantic fiction who fancies himself as a Don Juan. Once he does get, with his father's help, a set of trousers of the appropriate length, he is smitten with desire for a world-weary woman whose car has a flat tire in front of Harry's house. He performs for her on his own very unsophisticated vehicle, a bicycle, and gets her attention, but she goes away. Later he determines that he must save her from the clutches of the law (having read in the paper that she has been arrested) and since it is his wedding day, he must get rid of his unsophisticated bride in the only way that seems final — by killing her. This turns out to be a heavy, self-conscious farce: in a scene in the woods, he fumbles every attempt to use a pistol. Finally, having tracked down the big city vamp, he is forced to witness two murders in a backstage dressing room and gets arrested. He returns home, having learned that life is ugly and cruel.

"Ugly and cruel" is no way of describing a Capra movie's view of life, at least up until *Meet John Doe* (1941), with its chilling intimations of wartime fascism. No, this was some kind of early film noir — a Ripley film, not a Capra film. And in fact, during production when Ripley and Capra had disagreements on the script or the performance, Langdon evidently sided with Ripley. He wanted "more pathos," more art, more tragedy. As producer, he could have his way.

Frank Capra, in his autobiography, claims that he laid down the law to Langdon after shooting was over, berating him as "an impossible, opinionated, conceited, strutting little jerk," and warning him not to try to direct himself. "Sure, Chaplin writes his own stuff and directs himself. But he created his own character. He understands it, better than anyone else. But you didn't create your character. And you don't understand it."[7]

What Capra expected to accomplish by this outburst is hard to say, but he got what he says he expected: his closing check. The long-term result was that each of them spread the word around Hollywood that the other one was impossible to work with. Capra was unemployable for months. He managed to direct an independent film in New York, then rejoined Mack Sennett at his old salary as a gag man, until Harry Cohn plucked him out of a list of directors to come to Columbia Pictures.

Langdon went on to direct himself in *Three's a Crowd* (1927) and *The Chaser* (1928). The reviews were generally poor, partly because of noticeable technical inadequacies, partly because the stories provided little of the variety needed for entertainment. *The Chaser* largely depended on the peculiar presupposition that Langdon had some sort of hypnotic power over women.

7 Capra, *The Name Above the Title* (1971) p. 77.

Three's a Crowd aspired to the pathos and family feeling in *The Kid*, but unlike the Chaplin story, which provided a lively youngster and a conflict with social uplifters for pleasure and drama, Ripley gave his performer only a passive role.

A pregnant woman lies unconscious at the foot of his stairway when Harry comes from work. He takes her in, and neighbors help when the baby comes. After an elaborate nightmare (quite unlike the dream of angels in *The Kid*) he wakes up to find the father of the child returned to reclaim his family. About all Harry can do through all of this is to look woebegone, hanging around in the background. At the end, he is alone again.

In a letter to William Schelly, the great mime Marcel Marceau pointed out that Chaplin offered both the "joy and tragedy" of human life, and this made him "a universal artist," whereas "in Harry Langdon we see only one side of human fragility: a terrible loneliness and melancholy of a poor soul lost in a dark and wild world."[8] This was the legacy of Arthur Ripley, supported of course by Langdon himself, who wanted to be thought of as an artist.

But a hazy, lonely, melancholy character was not one that most Americans wanted to watch, much less identify with. Schelly points out that Chaplin's tramp is in the end a jaunty survivor, a wiry individualist. He may well be alone by choice, or quite often win the girl, whereas the Langdon of the Ripley stories is tragically ostracized or rejected, his pathos enforced by fate.

Joyce Rheuban, in her book-length study of the cinematic aspects of Langdon's comedies, discovers not only a lack of variety but very nearly a kind of monotony. Trying to justify his characterization by examining his style, she says that, like Chaplin, he relates himself primarily to *mise en scene*, placing

8 Schelly, *Harry Langdon* (1982) p. 109. On p. 23 Schelly describes Ripley as "an essentially pessimistic graduate of the New York film and theater world . . . a brooding intellectual with sunken eyes, a moustache, and stooped shoulders." Rheuban adds a whole last chapter on "Arthur Ripley and the Dark Side of Langdon's Comedies." She finds a "perverse undertone . . . bizarre eroticism . . . amorphous sexual identity" in the Ripley/Langdon pictures, followed by comparable content and style in later films noir and other B-pictures directed by Ripley.

himself against a background and showing himself off, rather than providing for us the vigor of cutting from shot to reverse shot. There is almost no action, since the Langdon character is incapable of "such qualities as initiative, ambition, motivation."[9] We merely view his slowness in reacting to whatever is going on, and the camera holds on that slowness in each scene to the bitter end. Thus did the actor give instructions to himself, the director.

The American people during the late 1920s were fascinated by the continuing euphoria of individual success stories in American business life and in the talent world of Hollywood itself. This meant they had little time to give attention to unrelieved melancholy. In reverse order, later on, Americans enmeshed in the depression of the 1930s would not want the outsize cheerfulness of Harold Lloyd.

Langdon's three memorable films were not enough to make him rich, but after the failure of the next three, he continued to be in fairly comfortable circumstances through the 1930s and early 40s, starring in short subjects for Hal Roach, for Educational Pictures, for Paramount, and for Jules White at Columbia. He took jobs as gag man and writer, as supporting actor, and occasional cameos. He worked with Al Jolson in *Hallelujah! I'm a Bum* (1933) and teamed with Oliver Hardy (with the blessing of his old friend Stan Laurel) in *Zenobia* (1939). He had the comfort at last of a happy third marriage before he died in 1944.[10]

"I am convinced," Langdon wrote in 1927 at the brief height of his fame, "that comedy is much harder to achieve than drama." His short piece in *Theater* magazine in December may have been a collaboration with Arthur Ripley: the word "tragedy" occurred eleven times. There is the behind-scenes danger of tragedy in trying to offer the audience scenes of peril and thrills, "an essential element of successful comedy." More important, the comedian's duty is to "make all people laugh — the rich, the poor, the bereaved, the sick." There is "genuine heartbreak" for the star, the crew, the producer, and the audience when they find "their most cherished material is not funny."

9 Rheuban, p. 128.
10 Much of my biographical material and description of films is drawn from the very helpful Schelly book.

HAROLD LLOYD
Magic Glasses

This is the story of a stage-struck lad with a strong practical sense of business, and how he began to make his way to the top. Chance played a part at least three times. John Lane Connor met him in downtown Omaha and later gave him a job in San Diego. That move was made possible by a traffic accident in Omaha. A toss of a coin determined where he would go. In Los Angeles the young actor found employment as an extra at the Edison company.

Universal was more of a challenge, but he learned how to infiltrate the ranks under cover of some artful greasepaint. Hal Roach was one of the extra players he got to know. Before long a fortunate inheritance set Roach up in a production office in "the Bradbury mansion" in downtown L.A. which harbored various film enterprises. Harold was his star. Eventually, as the "glasses character," he became the most popular and prosperous comedian of the 1920s.

In 1928 Lloyd wrote his autobiography, An American Comedy *(with Wesley Stout, a prominent magazine writer). From this engaging and rather modest book, published by Longmans Green & Co., we have chosen pages 56-58, 75-77, 78-79, 82, 84, 92, 101-107.*

. . . It was a saloon convention that when the drivers had shot a loaded keg down the skid into the cellar and wrestled up an empty, the bartender would, without prompting, draw two large steins for the refreshment of the men after their labors, the same being on the house. A generous custom, but resulting sometimes in the truck crew driving breweryward in a beery mist. Such a crew in such a haze ran down dad and his buggy.

After a siege in the hospital and a lawsuit, a jury brought in a judgment of six thousand dollars against the brewery — divided evenly later between the lawyer and father. Such a sum as three thousand dollars suggested a move. Dad was divided between New York, where he never had been, and Nashville, Tennessee, where a relative published a religious journal. New York tempted me, for it meant Broadway; but Connor had moved to San Diego, where he was playing in stock and running a dramatic school, and I sensed that as between the chances of a green boy of eighteen on Broadway and under the wing of such a guide and friend in San Diego, there could be no question of choice. Dad never had seen the Pacific Coast, either, and was open to reason. "We'll toss a coin," he said at last. "Heads is New York or Nashville or where I decide, tails is San Diego."

The coin went up, hit the ceiling, dropped and rolled under a bed. It was a pre-buffalo nickel and it stopped wreath side up.

Had it fallen heads, this story would not have been written. The possibilities are infinite; the probabilities are that we would have gone to New York and I would have become a Broadway actor — I hope a good one. Had we turned Eastward rather than West, certainly the odds are long that it wouldn't have been pictures, for I went into pictures only because they were on hand in California when nothing else offered.

In San Diego dad bought a pool hall and lunch counter with his three thousand dollars. Why a pool hall and lunch counter is one of those California mysteries; he knew nothing of either. A passing attack of pool fever in my freshman year in Omaha had left me a good shot, qualified to take a cue for the house any time a house man was called for, but dad had to learn even how to rack the balls. He had neglected, too, to take a tip from chain-store practice and count the pedestrians before he bought. To a stranger in San Diego the location on Grant Park appeared to be ideally central; actually, it was fifty feet off the main traveled path, and only merchants know what a vast distance fifty feet can be.

These are some of the things I did in San Diego: Finished high school; relieved my father in the pool hall and lunch counter; played leads in high school shows and aided Connor in staging them; acted as assistant in fencing, dancing and elocution in Connor's dramatic school; played in and helped Connor stage lodge and club entertainments; played characters in four local stock companies and was assistant stage manager of one; gave Shakespearean readings before high school English and elocution classes; worked as stage hand at the Spreckels, the road-show theater. Many, if not most, of these activities were concurrent.

High-school vogues vary with the schools; in San Diego amateur dramatics were a major activity, nearly on a par in student esteem with football. My first choice naturally would be dramatics, and formal school athletics demanded more time than could be squeezed out of my routine. I had so enormous an advantage over schoolboy amateurs, moreover, that the leading parts fell to me without question; and I came nearer losing my head here than ever before or after. I have many reasons to be grateful to Connor, but the greatest service he did me was to reduce this swelling at the psychological moment. . . .

Four companies were working on the Universal lot. For extras there was a casting window and a bull pen with benches where you sat all day unless you could get through the gates and dog the heels of an assistant director. If you want a perfect picture of it I refer you to *Merton of the Movies*. That is a story I read and a play and picture I saw with more emotions than the author. It will be a great surprise to Harry Leon Wilson, no doubt, but I was Merton — or one of many Mertons.

The gatekeeper was a crabby old soul who let me understand that it would be a pleasure to keep me out. As I lurked about I noticed that at noon a crowd of actors and extras drifted out in make-up to eat at a lunch counter across the way, passing the gatekeeper without question each way. The next morning I brought a make-up box. At noon I dodged behind a billboard, made up, mingled with the lunch-counter press and returned with them through the gate without challenge. Once inside, I was assumed to be an extra on the job. I got no work — hardly expected to get it — but I did learn useful things about studio routine, meet older heads among the extras, learn the names of directors and assistant directors and after a time begin to register on their memories as a regular. On the way out I made a point to speak to the gateman, and on future entrances, if he looked the least suspicious I would say, carelessly, "With Smalley" — Philip Smalley being one of the directors.

Other than the leads there were four grades of picture actors. The highest made up the stock company — that is, supporting players regularly employed. Next below ranked the guaranty people — extras at the regular three dollars a day, but assured of a minimum of four or five days' work a week and given group dressing rooms. Just extras, my own classification, formed the third group, cooling their heels from eight until mid-afternoon in the bull pen. No casting window ever admitted until late in the day that no work was in prospect — a device that cost the studio nothing and assured a supply of extras if a director suddenly called for them. At two or three o'clock, when it was too late to try other studios, the word was passed from the window:

"Nothing to-day, folks; but be sure to be here in the morning."

Below us were only the mob extras, recruited when needed by want ads and paid one dollar a day, luncheon and car fare. They were almost exclusively hobos and an unfragrant lot, pictures not yet having attracted the curiosity seekers.

The ruse of slipping through the gates in make-up with the returning lunchers had the disadvantage of not being workable until midday, by which time all parts would have been given out. Once acquainted with the guaranty actors, however, they let me in through a window of their dressing room before the cameras started the morning grind, and I began to get work. . . .

Six months or so of this, and Universal opened a large new studio across the street, turning the old lot over to small comedy companies. By this time I was more or less attached to J. Farrell Macdonald, who was directing J. Warren Kerrigan; extras who got on regularly usually were identified with one director. Kerrigan recently had come to Universal from the Flying A at Santa Barbara at the published salary of $300 a week, a figure which they could tell to the Marines as far as we extras were concerned. There wasn't that much money anywhere outside a press agent's mind, or so we thought. In Macdonald's unit I worked up from three dollars a day occasionally to five dollars and five days' work guaranteed, and picked up a character bit now and then.

Among the guaranty group was an extra who seemed to have first call on such bits. He was a good type, but a bad actor. Macdonald and his staff would struggle with him patiently while the rest of us stood by and bit our nails, half in envy, half in agony at the man's awkwardness. Just to convince myself that the bit was child's play, I would slip behind a set and rehearse it with myself, then come back and grit my teeth.

Another teeth-gritting extra was a young fellow named Hal Roach. Born in Elmira, New York, Roach had gone to the Pacific Northwest and Alaska, then drifted down the coast and got on at the Universal ranch in the San Fernando Valley as a cowboy in Kerrigan Westerns by virtue of being able to stick on a horse. Kerrigan liked him, and when the star returned to the studio he brought Roach along. . . .

Roach surprised me — though "surprise" is a faint word for it — one day by announcing that he had got hold of several thousand dollars with which he intended making pictures on his own. He would be the director and I could be the first brick in his company at the usual three dollars a day. A few days later he rented a corner in the Bradbury mansion as an office, with the use of a stage in the back yard, and Hal Roach was a producer. . . .

I experimented with dress and make-up and about the fifth picture settled on a character we christened Willie Work. The name wrongly suggests a tramp; it was, instead, a hash of different low-comedy get-ups, with a much-padded coat, a battered silk hat and a cat's-whisker mustache as its distinguishing marks . . . .

I told Roach that I had something that was an improvement on Willie Work, at least. When he saw it he approved. Later it was tagged with the name of Lonesome Luke. . . .

. . . We began making Lonesome Luke in two reels in answer to exhibitor demand, giving two weeks instead of one to each.

Roach is a born leader, an excellent business man and an original comedy director, but he was not so happy at the new two-reel length. When he had worked a week on one he had a way of asking, "How much footage have we now?" The answer would be 1400 feet or thereabout, whereupon Hal would call "Well, boys, let's finish her up," and shoot the remainder as if he had a train to catch. No matter what went before, the slighted final 400 feet would let the picture down with a soggy thud. It brought my discontent with Lonesome Luke to a head.

I was convinced both that the character had gone as far as we could take him and that I had a better. The hazy idea in the back of my head was crystallizing. I had been feeling around for youth, possibly a boy who could be carried through a college series, a comedy Frank Merriwell, for a long time, when I saw a dramatic picture at a downtown theater while we still were at Norbig. The central character was a fighting parson, tolerant and peaceful until riled, then a tartar. Glasses emphasized his placidity. The heavy had stolen the girl, carrying her away on horseback. The parson leaped on another horse, pursued, overtook the villain, dragged him from his horse and the two were lost in a cloud of dust. When the dust cleared, the heavy lay prone and still, while the parson dusted his clothes with careless flecks of his handkerchief, replaced his glasses and resumed his ministerial calm.

I did not feel cut out for a fighting parson, but the basic idea was there. A picture actor named Mortenson, who lived in the same apartment house on Fourth Street just off Hill, and I talked over its comedy possibilities night after night. The glasses would serve as my trade-mark and at the same time suggest the character — quiet, normal, boyish, clean, sympathetic, not impossible to romance. I would need no eccentric make-up, "mo" or funny clothes. I would be an average recognizable American youth and let the situations take care of the comedy. The comedy should be better for not depending upon a putty nose or its equivalent and the situations should be better for not being tied to low-comedy coat tails; funnier things happen in life to an ordinary boy than to a Lonesome Luke. Exaggeration is the breath of picture comedies, and obviously they cannot be true to life, but they can be recognizably related to life.

Probably the vision was not so clear in my mind at the time as all this; what I write now benefits by hindsight, yet I saw it clearly enough. How about Pathé, though? They could not be expected willingly to trade Lonesome Luke for a pig in a poke. By advertising, promotion and good distribution they had done their part to create a market for him and make him a comedy staple, the demand growing healthily. This new idea of mine might be anything or nothing — probably nothing; but whichever, it called for scrapping a going commodity at nothing on the dollar and starting from scratch with an unknown quantity. Had I been in New York I doubt that I could have transmitted my enthusiasm convincingly, and I was a long way from New York.

So discouraging was the prospect that I decided to give up comedy pictures and make a fresh beginning myself. After long, hard work, I was getting $100 a week, a fortune relative to my past earnings, but not so much alongside Chaplin's reputed $1000 a week. I told Roach that I was fed up on Luke, convinced that Pathé never would agree to a change and resolved to go into dramatic pictures, where I was certain I could do something. Roach was going to New York anyway. On a previous trip he had seen a clown at the Hippodrome and become enthusiastic about his picture possibilities. Now he was returning to bring him to the coast and star him in two-reel pictures.

The situation was a strain on Roach's optimism, but it was equal to it.

"It won't do any harm to put it up to Pathé anyway," he argued. "As I see it, they are going to lose Luke whichever way the bird jumps. Unless they think you are bluffing, they are likely to take a chance on a change, and I think I can show them that you mean it."

Privately I believed that Pathé would conclude to hire another comedian and carry on with Lonesome Luke. Audiences would detect the substitution, but the picture was Luke, not Lloyd. Roach, however, argued my case better than I could have done, and won. He wired back that Pathé consented. Did I wish to make one- or two-reel pictures in the new character?

One, I decided. One-reel subjects still were popular with exhibitors as program fillers. We could make and release a picture a week; a new character needed the constant hammering of fifty-two releases a year to familiarize it. And if we made a bad one, worse luck, it would be forgotten quickly.

There is more magic in a pair of horn-rimmed glasses than the opticians dream of, nor did I guess the half of it when I put them on in 1917.

With them, I am Harold Lloyd; without them, a private citizen. I can stroll unrecognized down any street in the land at any time without the glasses, a boon granted no other picture actor and one which some of them would pay well for. At a cost of seventy-five cents they provide a trademark recognized instantly wherever pictures are shown. They make low-comedy clothes unnecessary, permit enough romantic appeal to catch the feminine eye, usually averted from comedies, and they hold me down to no particular type or range of story.

It was chance that they are horn-rimmed. The parson's glasses in the dramatic picture that inspired them were not tortoise shells, but when I came to choose a pair of my own the vogue of horn rims was new and it was youth, principally, that was adopting them. The novelty was a picture asset and the suggestion of youth fitted perfectly with the character I had in mind.

We took out the lenses immediately, knowing that the reflection of light on the glass would be troublesome, and thought we were doing a new thing. As usual, however, the Chinese did it first. Give a historian time and he will prove that Mack Sennett did not invent the Keystone cop and the bathing beauty, but that both were popular comedy pictures in Cathay in the Ming dynasty and are mentioned by Marco Polo. A correspondent wrote me from Peking recently that not only were tortoise-shell glasses worn in China as a mark of rank in the time of the Middle Kingdom, more than a thousand years ago, but that it was not uncommon to wear them without lenses. "Damned clever, these Chinese," as Bobbie Clark said.

The first pair, bought out of stock, were too heavy; the second pair had so large a diameter that the rims covered my eyebrows and killed a great deal of expression. A third pair that just suited was found in a little optical shop in Spring Street, after scouring Los Angeles. I remember hunting through a tray containing probably thirty pairs before coming on the right one. I wore them for a year and a half, guarding them with my life. When the frame broke from wear and tear I went on patching it with everything, from paste to spirit gum for three months, until progressive dissolution forced us to send them East to an optical-goods manufacturer for duplication.

The manufacturers shipped us back twenty pairs tailored to the measure of the old faithfuls and returned our check. The advertising we had given tortoise-shell rims, they wrote, still left them in our debt. Since then all our rims have been tailor-made by this firm.

ROBERT E. SHERWOOD
Grandma's Boy

Sherwood, one of a greatly talented series of playwrights who flourished on Broadway in the 1920s, was also a film critic for "the old Life, " then a weekly humor magazine. Like Gilbert Seldes, he had no fear of expressing enthusiasm about movies, and he found Harold Lloyd, like Douglas Fairbanks, to be gifted, enjoyable, and symptomatic of the times. This extended review appeared on pages 9-12 of a collection called The Best Moving Pictures of 1922-23, *published by Small, Maynard & Co. in 1923.*

Directed by: Fred Newmeyer
Written by: Harold Lloyd, Sam Taylor and Jean Havez
Produced by: Hal Roach
Distributed by: Pathé
Released: September 3, 1922.

Principal characters:

The Boy	Harold Lloyd
The Girl	Mildred Davis
Grandma	Anna Townsend
The Rolling Stone	Dick Sutherland
The Sheriff	Noah Young

The success of Harold Lloyd during the past two years has been phenomenal, but not incomprehensible. This buoyant, bespectacled young comedian is an apostle of the American faith: he represents the personification of pep, spontaneity and determination. He is a natural-born world beater. He delights in building apparently insurmountable obstacles and then, with a sunny smile, surmounting them.

Moreover, Lloyd's humor is as native to these United States as George Ade's. Charlie Chaplin is distinctly continental in style, and Buster Keaton's comedy smacks of the London 'alls; but Lloyd, clad in a pinch-back suit, a straw hat and a pair of horn-rimmed spectacles, is at least one hundred per cent American. He is clean and wholesome, but not to an offensive degree (like Chaplin, he knows the most vulnerable and laughable portion of a policeman's anatomy, and is not afraid to exploit it); he is as fresh as an Oregon breeze and he is willing to play the goat as long as it is profitable. Indeed, his shyness, and his excessive timidity, serve to heighten the effect of his ultimate triumph.

Harold Lloyd has rushed forward lately at an increasing rate of speed. Always popular, since the days when he appeared as "Lonesome Luke," he has now established himself ahead of all the other stars as a box-office attraction. Within two years he has produced five pictures, *A Sailor Made Man, Grandma's Boy, Dr. Jack, Safety Last,* and *Why Worry?* all of which have achieved astounding success. No actor or producer in movie history has ever made such a record — or so much money; no star at the present time is so much in demand as Harold Lloyd. Douglas Fairbanks, Mary Pickford, D.W. Griffith and Charlie Chaplin may absorb all the prestige, but it is Harold Lloyd who ranks at the top in the vital statistics.

Although the remarkably high standard that he has maintained throughout all his recent comedies makes it difficult for me to indicate any decided preference, I place *Grandma's Boy* in this book because it happened to be his most original effort of the year, and also the greatest departure from his usual form. It was his first five-reel venture and his first attempt at anything approaching serious drama.

Lloyd started out to make a two-reel comedy of *Grandma's Boy,* but his first idea grew as the production progressed, and he worked over the picture for six months before he was satisfied that it was ready for release. He had a theme in mind — that cowardice is a complex which can be cured by psychoanalytical treatment — and this presented so many possibilities that Lloyd simply could not restrain himself. He ran wild.

His hero was a hesitant youth ("the boldest thing he ever did was to sing out loud in church," to quote a subtitle). Whenever this boy scented danger he would seek refuge behind the frail person of his aged grandmother, who, for all her years, knew something of the teachings of the ultra-modern Dr. Freud.

The boy loved a girl — as boys frequently do — but his painful timidity restrained his amorous impulses and prevented him from pressing his suit with any degree of success. The situation seemed hopeless.

Then, one dark night, a ferocious tramp visited the quiet community in which the boy lived, and terrorized the local citizenry. The sheriff decided that a state of military law must be declared, and appointed his fellow townsmen deputies to find and apprehend the unwelcome guest. Among the motley mob thus armed with authority was the boy, and it was he of course who first encountered the tramp. As usual, he fled for protection to his mild little grandmother. She seized a broom and chased the tramp away.

At this point the sweet old lady realized that violent curative measures were essential, and she decided to subject her grandson to the power of suggestion. Removing the small ivory figure from the head of her umbrella, she told the boy that it was a charm, given to his grandfather during the Civil War by a witch. Grandpa, she explained, had been timorous himself — until he came into possession of this talisman; then he stepped out and, single-handed, subdued a large portion of the Federal Army.

This fantastic tale was visualized on the screen, and formed one of the most hilariously funny episodes in the picture. Harold Lloyd, wearing square-lensed spectacles, whiskers and a Confederate uniform, impersonated his grandfather.

When the boy had absorbed this story from his grandmother, he grasped the confidence-giving charm and started after the tramp. After a chase as thrilling and as broadly comic as any in the literature of slapstick, Lloyd captured the brute and dragged him home by the heels. His final conquest, of course, was the girl.

Lloyd constructed each scene of *Grandma's Boy* as carefully as though it were the mainspring of a watch. He is always a conscientious craftsman, and his work is a subject of tremendously serious importance to him. There is nothing haphazard about his methods; he puzzles over every episode and situation, working it out first in his mind and then in the action itself. He has a remarkably clear vision and an acute sense of risibility; he knows instinctively what will be naturally funny, and what will merely be forced.

Together with his principal gag-men, Jean Havez and Sam Taylor, his producer, Hal Roach, and his director, Fred Newmeyer, Lloyd practically resolved *Grandma's Boy* to blue-prints. Although the foremost quality of the finished product was its spontaneity, it was actually a well-calculated, studied piece of work.

Long after the picture had been completed and shown to audiences at various theatres in and about Los Angeles, Lloyd continued to pore over it — cutting, editing, revising, polishing and retaking scenes that didn't obtain sufficiently stentorian laughs. I accompanied Lloyd on one of his preview expeditions (it was at Hoyt's Theatre, in Long Beach, California), and I had an opportunity to observe how keenly and intelligently he can criticize his own work. *Grandma's Boy* was run for the assembled audience with no previous announcement, and without musical accompaniment. "I want it to be cold turkey," said Lloyd to Mr. Hoyt, the exhibitor. "If they like it this way, I'll know it's pretty near right."

Needless to say, they liked it, but Lloyd himself found a few flaws, which he proceeded to remedy when he took the film back to his studio.

The girl in *Grandma's Boy* was played by Mildred Davis, who has since become Mrs. Harold Lloyd. Dick Sutherland was sufficiently formidable as the burly tramp, and Mrs. Anna Townsend made a charming, appealing figure of the grandmother. Mrs. Townsend lived for seventy-nine years before she made her debut on the screen; a year later she died. But she will be remembered by everyone who was privileged to see her in *Grandma's Boy*.

HAROLD LLOYD
The Serious Business of Being Funny

Here are some illuminating remarks by Harold Lloyd on (1) previews (2) his four favorite film works (3) whether it is better for a gag to be a surprise or known ahead of time (a reference to The Kid Brother*) (4) the contrast between appearance and character in "the boy with glasses" (5) the variety of types the boy played (6) his own role as director (7) the dangers of shooting before writing.*

Hubert Cohen (then an assistant professor of English in the college of engineering at the University of Michigan) invited Lloyd to share his ideas on comedy production with an audience of film buffs and students in November of 1966. An audio transcript of the occasion was published in Film Comment *(volume 5, number 3, fall 1969). These extracts are from pages 47, 49, 51, and 54.*

Look, all the comedians of my day had to be *students* of comedy. You *studied comedy*, it just didn't happen, believe me.

You finally got to know, by trial and error — you began to find out pretty well what you know is funny and what is not funny. But that's a long way from being a sure method. I was one of the first ones — I have been given credit for starting what they call "previews." Even back in the one-reel days, I would take a picture out to a theater when I knew the picture wasn't right. I wanted to get John and Mary's opinion of it. And the manager used to always have to come out and explain what was going on. When we were doing two-reelers, he came out in white tie and tails to do it, and it was quite an event for him and the audience would listen attentively. The audience didn't know what "previews" were, but there's nothing like an audience to tell you where you go wrong.

So "previews" were one of the best methods we had and, I think, it saved us a great deal of — not that we didn't go off the track many times in spite of it — but it saved us many times because we would find out that certain sequences were splendid and others weren't. So we would come back in and go to work, and we would work for a month afterwards to remedy it, and if we found a scene wasn't as we wanted it, why, we would pull it out and try something else, then take it all out and "preview" it again. Of course, you can't always tell by that method, because all audiences are not the same.

Of all my films, four I like best — *Safety Last* (1923), *Grandma's Boy* (1922), *The Freshman* (1925), and *The Kid Brother* (1927). They are character comedies except for *Safety Last*, which is a gag comedy. I would say that the majority of the features that I made were gag comedies and *all* the two-reelers were gag comedies. I don't think we made a character comedy in two reels — the two-reelers were all dependent on the gag business.

We had difficulty lots of times deciding whether we wanted the gag to be a surprise or whether we should let the audience in on it. You'd be surprised how important that is. Sometimes the surprise is much funnier, but sometimes when the audience realizes what's going to happen and anticipates it, it's more fun. So you really have to *judge*.

We had one piece of business that was always what we called "sure-fire" — a piece of comedy business that anybody can do and get big laughs. This particular one was down in the hold of a ship. This big fellow — we were having a fight — he was trying to kill me and nearing that objective. He threw me up against the side of the hold and came over and picked up a big iron belaying-pin and took ahold of me and hit me over the head with this big iron — which should have crushed my skull. All I did was blink my eyes, and, of course, he was amazed and so naturally he struck me again, but with the same result. The third time he hit me, he even bent the bar. Then he was so flabbergasted he let go of me, and as I ran away, you see that when I was thrown against the wall, there was a bracket, an iron bracket that fitted over my head. He was hitting the iron bracket, of course, and his weapon wasn't touching me at all, but you can't see that in the picture until we're ready to let you see it. That's very "sure-fire." Now, we shot the scene two ways. We thought it would be good to let the audience know that the iron bracket was there. And the funny thing is, they laughed both ways. We had a hard time figuring which was the better. We finally left it a surprise. I think surprise has a *sharper* laugh to it.

This character of the boy with glasses, you see, started off with an inner character that belied his outward appearance. He looked like he was a milk-and-toast character and anybody could push him around. But when you pushed him too far, he bounced back. So we had *that* to start with. And also, because he was not a grotesque, that character allowed us to do more *situation* than I had done before. But I never lost the idea of the gag or the carry-on. If you would look at my one-reelers and at two-reelers, you would see a gradual transition.

Whereas my character was always the boy with the glasses, and whereas he was always fighting odds, fighting the big fellows, nevertheless his attitude of thinking was entirely different from one character role to another. Not that we didn't occasionally repeat the same type. Sometimes he was a brash character, sort of a go-getter like we have in *Safety Last*. Another time, like in *Grandma's Boy*, he was a bashful shy type of character. Sometimes he was rich, sometimes he was poor, sometimes he was a sophisticate, sometimes he was a dreamer, and each quality would motivate a lot of gags we'd do.

At that time, practically all the top comedians had control of their pictures. Up to a certain point Roach had control of my early films, but afterwards Roach had other pictures and so I took over and I was completely responsible — even though Hal and I remained partners. That's the reason we finally split up — it was his idea. He came to me — this was near the time that we separated — and he said "I'm contributing very little to your offers and I've got so many of my own, I think it's no more than fair that you should carry on on your own and have the whole thing." At that time, I was getting 75 percent of it and Hal was getting 25 percent.

There wasn't a picture in which I wasn't in on the direction. Some of them I directed entirely on my own because most of the directors I had then were boys who had been gag men for me. I brought them in to direct a picture and made directors of them. Sam Taylor — who was one of the best I had and who afterwards went out and directed John Barrymore, Mary Pickford, Douglas Fairbanks and Beatrice Lilly — well, he was a gag man and I brought him in to direct. He was probably the best I had. I never took credit, and I never have to this day, on the *direction* of a picture. On the production — producing it, yes. Even in pictures where I directed practically the whole thing, I didn't take the directing credit.

About using scripts. In *Safety Last*, probably one of our most popular films, we did the final scenes of that clock climb *first*. We didn't know what we were going to have for the beginning of the film. We hadn't made up the opening. After we found that we had, in our opinion, a very, very good thrill sequence, something that was going to be popular and bring in a few shekels, we went back and figured out what we would do for a beginning and worked on up. We tried the same thing in *The Freshman*.

In *The Freshman* we tried to shoot the football sequence first — it's the best sequence, naturally — and we tried to do it first just as we had done the clock climb first in *Safety Last*. We went out to the Rose Bowl where we did a great deal of the picture, and we worked for about a week and a half, but it didn't come off. It *didn't* come off because we didn't know the character at that time — we didn't understand him well enough, and we were off with the wrong kind of material. So we went back and did that story from the beginning, and the football game was shot *at the last*. By the way, we were granted permission to do something that I don't think anyone was able to do at that time — we shot between halves during the California-Stanford game. They gave us permission, and in their card maneuvers on the side of the field they had — of course, we couldn't use that in the picture — but, nevertheless, they had LLOYD spelled out and GREETINGS and WELCOME, too. We felt very much at home and we had a nice audience of about 90,000 to witness half a dozen of the scenes, but we had to work pretty doggone fast there.

SCOTT O'DELL
Safety Last

Here is a description of Lloyd's most famous film, one he describes as primarily gag-oriented. The Palmer Institute of Authorship was a school for scenario writers located in Hollywood. Among its services was a volume called Representative Photoplays Analysed, *which provided quite detailed synopses plus advisory material calling attention to structural aspects of the story. This one was on pages 77-81 in 1924.*

(*Hal Roach production; starring* Harold Lloyd; story by Hal Roach, Sam Taylor and Tim Whelan; directed by Fred Newmeyer and Sam Taylor)

SYNOPSIS

Tearfully saying goodbye to his mother and sweetheart, Mildred, Harold leaves his small town home to make his way in the city. The set is so arranged as to make it appear that Harold is going to his execution. Iron bars separate them and back of Harold we see a priest and a uniformed guard. In the background a noose is swinging. A subtitle states that Harold is " going on the long journey." Then the scene is turned to surprise as the gate is opened and the mother and sweetheart hurry through; the priest (only a traveler) picks up his bag and departs. The uniformed guard announces the train. A messenger hangs a dispatch on the noose.

Harold starts for the train, picking up a wicker baby-carry-all containing a weeping pickaninny, thinking it is his suitcase. The baby's mammy quickly retrieves it and Harold swings onto an ice wagon instead of the coach. At last, however, he is off for the city.

The boy's golden dreams of a swiftly made fortune are not so quickly realized. In the city he and his pal live the life of poor "hall room boys." Their landlady is mercenary and insistent. When she calls they hang themselves to pegs on the wall concealed under their overcoats, awaiting the bang of the door in signal of her departure. The pal bothers Harold while he is trying to write to his sweetheart, so Harold goes out and imitates the landlady's approach. The pal hangs himself upon a hook in the customary concealment, while Harold complacently finishes his letter. The pal is indignant, especially because Harold is sending his sweetheart a lavalliere while the rent is in arrears.

The pal, somewhat of a braggart, is a structural iron worker. He runs about on girders high up in the sky without a quiver. He can crawl any place that affords a hand-hold.

Harold's own chief virtue is punctuality. He is not only on time for his work, but ahead of time. He is sitting on the doorman's box writing to Mildred, when the doorman arrives and claims the seat. Harold, still intent upon his letter, jumps into a towel service truck which is standing near. Suddenly the driver hops into his seat, closes the door by an automatic device, and Harold is whirled away. The driver is deaf and Harold is borne across the city before the truck stops to make another delivery.

Once out of the truck, Harold begins a mad dash through the traffic to be on time at the store. The street cars are packed. Harold jumps on to the shoulders of a man only to find that the man has stepped off the car just as it starts. He cranks a Ford that is stalled, only to find that the driver is turning at the next corner. Next he sees an ambulance at the curb. The man for whom the ambulance has been called has gotten up, brushed himself off and refuses to be taken away. Harold sees that the ambulance is headed for the store. He lies down and simulates illness; whereupon he is placed in the ambulance. He remains there, apparently unconscious; until his surreptitious glance through a window shows him he is near his destination. He now orders the ambulance stopped and escapes from the surprised attendants. Despite his frantic attempts, he is, nevertheless, late for work.

He gets through the door concealed under a style dummy carried by a burly negro. He sets back the time clock and punches himself in on time. Hiding between a janitor's cart and the counters, he hops along in ridiculous posture until the cart turns down another aisle and his hopping is in plain view. He dashes behind a counter, appropriates another clerk's customer so that the floorwalker cannot immediately reprimand him. So in one way or another Harold gets through the day.

Leaving the store in the evening he meets a policeman whom he formerly knew in his home town. They laugh and joke, and Harold is very familiar, thumping the officer on the back and tilting his hat. Later, Harold meets his old pal just as the policeman is phoning at the end of his beat. Harold boasts about his stand-in with the police and tells his pal that if he wishes he may knock the policeman down with impunity because Harold can "square" it. With some misgivings the pal agrees to do this. In the meantime friend policeman has been relieved by another officer. So the pal's encounter is most unfortunate. He flees up the side of a building, while Harold, seeing the mistake, goes into concealment. The policeman attempts to climb after the pal, but falls flat after ascending a few feet. This makes him very bitter.

Meeting again, Harold compliments his pal's climbing, and the pal boasts that he could go up the side of a sixteen-story building with his eyes shut.

The next day is bargain day. Ill-mannered women fight for a place at the counter. Harold's coat is pulled off. He is reprimanded by a floor-walker because of his appearance, and is summoned to the manager's office. He first combs his hair, using a customer's bald head as a mirror.

Mildred unexpectedly arrives on a visit. She appears in the store. Harold sees her first and immediately begins his bluff of being general manager. She insists upon seeing his office. He is obliged to take her into the manager's office, just then unoccupied. The girl is interested in the call buttons. She presses one. An office boy appears and is astonished to find Harold. Harold, however, is equal to the occasion and dropping a dollar bill into the waste basket, tells the boy he has called him to empty the paper. Before the boy's departure, however, he recovers the dollar bill. Then Harold unfortunately sits upon the whole row of call buttons, with the result that a number of employees appear. The girl is seated behind the desk. As the employees line up, Harold steps into line with them, pretending that he knows no more than they do of the summons. They depart and Harold remains, explaining to the girl that this was a fire drill. The next caller is the floor-walker in charge of Harold's department and the boy, concealed behind a newspaper and pretending to be general manager, tells him that he wants no more complaints about clerks' personal appearance.

So they get out of the office, but Mildred forgets her purse. Harold must go back after it. The real manager is now in his office and Harold, hesitating at the door, overhears a conversation in which the manager offers the publicity man $1000.00 for an advertising idea. Immediately he thinks of this pal's ability and proposes a spectacular climb up the outside of the department store as a means of attracting attention to the store. The manager and the publicity man are somewhat dubious but are finally won over and arrangements are made for the novel climb. The pal tells Harold that it is a cinch and both boys feel that the thousand dollars is already theirs.

The crowd is assembled for the exhibition when the pal is discovered by the policeman whom he had upset. The latter promptly pursues him. The pal tells Harold that he must climb to the second story while the policeman is outwitted. After a series of mishaps Harold reaches the second story, only to be signaled by his pal that the policeman is still on the trail and that he must climb one more floor.

This continues from story to story and Harold goes up and up. A paper bag of candy is dropped from the window above and scatters upon his head and shoulders. Pigeons flock around him, and in fighting them off he almost loses his footing and handhold. Harold looks down. Automobiles and streetcars below look like toys. A tennis net, being demonstrated above in the sporting department, falls from a window and Harold becomes entangled. A board is shoved out of a window by some painters. Harold seizes it, swings out and nearly falls.

Meanwhile the pal is still pursued by the policeman.

Another floor up a photographer is making pictures of a western gunman. The "gunman" fires. Harold is frightened.

Further up Harold actually falls and lands in a cornice clock. He is entangled in wheels, springs — and everything. The face of the clock pulls out. The pal has reached the window above and lets down a rope, intending to tie one end to a desk leg. The policeman appears and the pal is forced to flee. Harold seizes the unfastened rope and falls at a sickening speed — but the pal and policeman catch the rope end just as it is slipping over the window sill.

So Harold reaches another window ledge — and the policeman continues pursuit of the pal.

As Harold reaches the window ledge of the top floor and feels that victory is won he is menaced by a bulldog which threatens him from the window, and he seeks safety by hanging suspended from an outstanding flagpole. At last he reaches the roof and is met by his sweetheart. They embrace while the crowd applauds from below. This leads to an immediate happy ending for Harold and his sweetheart — but the pal is still pursued by the policeman.

ANALYSIS

Safety Last is more of a test of audience psychology than the spectator might think. It runs into an extravagance of thrills probably beyond anything previously produced; wherein there is also excellent work in characterization and coherence of action. To preserve the unity of impression (in this case, the effect of comedy) is no easy task when the action tends so strongly to horror due to the apparent imminence of Harold's death.

In considering the successful manner in which the comedic impression was preserved, there must be a careful study of the preparatory sequences which develop Harold as impellingly humorous even in every sharp test of circumstances and also develop the character of the pal somewhat as a braggart. This last brings into full effect his ludicrous plight during the long pursuit through the building.

The incident of Harold's meeting his old friend the policeman which leads to the encounter between the pal and the strange policeman, starts this element of comedy with a punch which keeps it in strong contrasting effect all through the ensuing action. If this incident and the characterization of the pal had been slightly treated, there would have been danger of throwing the effect of the picture to a succession of terrorizing thrills without adequate comedy relief. As it is, the balance of sympathy and effects is well preserved. This matter of preserving perfect balance of emotional effects lies at the heart of successful comedy making.

Of equal importance is the perfect sequence of incidents. In *Safety Last* each sequence dove-tails into its logical successor. The absence of cutbacks and parallel action is noticeable. In the beginning interest is focused upon the leading character and the other characters are developed through their relations with him.

Harold Lloyd in *For Heaven's Sake*

ANTHONY SLIDE
The Kid Brother

One of those stories in which Lloyd was "not impossible to romance," The Kid Brother is at once a traditional fairy tale of the bright youngest son who overcomes great odds and a tale of the poor American boy who gets ahead with pluck and luck. The Lloyd interview (reprinted above) described his "surprise gag" on the abandoned ship. Anthony Slide, one of the best informed scholars of the silent era, wrote this review for Magill's Survey of Cinema: Silent Films, *1982, pp. 625-627.*

Released: 1927
Production: Harold Lloyd for Paramount
Direction: Ted Wilde
Screenplay: John Grey, Lex Neal, and Howard J. Green; based on a
   story by John Grey, Tom Crizer, and Ted Wilde
Cinematography: Walter Lundin
Length: 8 reels/7,654 feet

Principal characters:
Harold Hickory	Harold Lloyd
Mary Powers	Jobyna Ralston
Jim Hickory	Walter James
Leo Hickory	Leo Willis
Olin Hickory	Olin Francis
Sandoni	Constantine Romanoff
"Flash" Farrell	Eddie Boland
Sam Hooper	Frank Lanning
Hank Hooper	Ralph Yearsley

The amazing thing about the films of Harold Lloyd is not their quality or the years that they span — 1913 to 1946 — but rather that one is continually surprised by the excellence of a newly re-discovered feature. Such is the case with *The Kid Brother,* long unseen until fairly recent years, but a Lloyd vehicle which must be considered one of the comedian's finest works, possibly superior even to *Safety Last* (1923) or *The Freshman* (1925).

When it was first released, there was little question as to its popularity. Mordaunt Hall of *The New York Times* saw it when it opened at New York's Rialto Theater on January 23, 1927, and reported in the following day's issue of his newspaper, "Mr. Lloyd displays no little ingenuity, none of his gags being inspired by any other comedian." He goes on to comment that audiences of all ages "simply let themselves roar to their heart's content."

Laurence Reid in *Motion Picture News* (February 4, 1927) called it simply, "A Great Picture"; "Lloyd never mixed a pleasanter blend of laughter and pathos," reported *Photoplay* (March, 1927).

Laughter and pathos were the two elements present in many of Lloyd's best films, such as *Grandma's Boy* (1922), *The Freshman*, *For Heaven's Sake* (1926), and *Girl Shy* (1924), but not *Safety Last*. Lloyd seemed to have a way with pathos that few of his contemporaries could match. Buster Keaton, of course, seldom used pathos. Harry Langdon usually did, but not always with perfect results. Charlie Chaplin is generally conceded to be the master when it came to mixing pathos and comedy, but in too many cases there is a forced artificiality to the Chaplin pathos. This is not true with Lloyd, to whom pathos is genuine and a necessary part of plot construction. As with Lloyd's best films, the pathos in *The Kid Brother* is provided by the thwarted love affair between the comedian and his greatest leading lady, Jobyna Ralston, here making her final appearance with Lloyd.

The Kid Brother is set in a small mountain community, where Harold is the youngest, much maligned son of the county sheriff, Jim Hickory (Walter James). While Hickory and his two older boys, Olin (Olin Francis) and Leo (Leo Willis), handle the traditionally male chores, Harold takes care of the household tasks. He does the laundry: washing the clothes in the milk churn, feeding them through a wringer, and finally hanging them out on a line attached to a pack. He washes the dishes inside a fishing net, and when the plates are ready to dry, places them on a shelf over the stove. Harold Hickory is very much a comic version of the Richard Barthelmess character in *Tol'able David* (1921).

While his father and brothers are attending a town meeting, at which the father persuades the townspeople to hand over to him the money that they have collected for a new dam, Harold puts on his father's badge and gun just at the precise moment that a medicine show happens to be passing by. The show is operated by Mary (Jobyna Ralston), aided by two villainous characters. Mary easily persuades Harold, whom she assumes to be the sheriff, to give her a permit to play the town, although neither really sees the other. After the show is set up, Mary goes for a walk in the woods, pursued by one of her associates, the terrifying Sandoni (Constantine Romanoff). Mary and Harold meet, but just as they are getting acquainted Sandoni appears on the scene. Harold grabs a stick and, in horror, Sandoni runs off — the stick has a snake attached to it.

Mary has to leave Harold and return to her medicine show and there follows one of the most hauntingly beautiful farewell scenes ever filmed for a comedy or a drama. As Mary leaves, Harold climbs higher and higher up a tree so that he can still see her, calling out, asking for her name and where she lives. When he reaches the top of the tree, he shouts good-bye and from Mary, now only a speck in the distance, comes a tiny good-bye on the title card. In his happiness, Harold begins to sway backward and forward in the tree and, of course, eventually comes crashing down to the ground.

When his father learns of the permit for the medicine show, he sends Harold into town to close the show down. At the show, Harold is humiliated. At one point, he is even suspended in air from a trapeze. When the show catches on fire, Harold saves Mary and takes her back home with him. Comical complications ensue when the brothers mistake Harold for Mary, who has promptly been removed to a neighbor's home. As the plot thickens, the money for the dam is stolen and, naturally, the sheriff is suspected. When Harold is accidentally set adrift in a small boat on the river, he floats down to an abandoned ship called *The Black Ghost*, on which he sees the monkey from the medicine show with the stolen money, taken by the two showmen. Harold witnesses a fight between the two men, during which one is killed; and then he must try to escape from the maniacal Sandoni. The sense of comic timing and the use of sight gags is perfectly coordinated as, for example, Harold places his boots on the monkey's feet to lead Sandoni astray. Just as the townspeople are about to lynch the sheriff for the crime he did not commit, Harold returns with the money, and his father greets him as "a real Hickory."

Obviously Lloyd's gag men deserve much of the credit for the film's comedic success, in particular writer-turned-director Ted Wilde, who, according to Adam Reilly in his book, *Harold Lloyd: The King of Daredevil Comedy*, took over from the original director, Lewis Milestone. As a result of his success with *The Kid Brother*, Wilde was asked to direct Lloyd's next film, *Speedy* (1928). Many of the critics were rather amused by the number of writers credited on the film. Louella Parsons commented, "I never saw so many names. Mr. Lloyd certainly believes in safety in numbers, for there are at least three men to every job."

It would be grossly unfair, however, to assume that the film's success lies solely on its sight gags. Without question, *The Kid Brother* appeals and delights thanks to Lloyd's acting. Here he demonstrates his ability not only to play comedy, but also to hold his own with a basically melancholy role. If one were to take away the comedy and play *The Kid Brother* as a straight, dramatic feature it would still have tremendous impact.

WILLIAM SCHELLY
Harry Langdon

Schelly's was the first book about Langdon, published in 1982 by Scarecrow Press. It is well researched and at the same time benefits from the author's critical judgments. We have chosen passages about Langdon's beginnings in both show business and film plus descriptions of his costume and comic image (pp. 2-3, 6-7, 14, 37-40).

Harry Langdon was born on June 15, 1884, in Council Bluffs, Iowa, the son of Salvation Army workers. He grew up across the Missouri River in Omaha, where his parents were able to eke out only the barest of livings. Langdon himself repeated stories of his early near-poverty, and Salvation Army records indicate that his parents were simply humble workers in the Army. By the time Harry was ten years old, he found himself hawking the *Omaha Bee* on the street corners of the teeming midwestern metropolis.

Omaha in the late 1880's was booming. With increasing commerce on the Missouri, and with the railroad through the Platte Valley having been completed just a decade earlier, the population grew tenfold between 1870 and 1890. Although Omaha could in no sense be considered cosmopolitan, Langdon was a city boy.

One of young Langdon's street corners where he sold papers was located in the theatrical district of town, a mishmash of burlesque joints, "legit" theaters, and penny arcades. Always on the lookout for extra money, the enterprising youth began doing odd jobs for the theater owners. The shy, near-sighted boy (who wore specs) was irresistibly drawn to the glamour of live theater and wanted to be part of it. He found acceptance among the worldly show business folk who befriended him.

Langdon didn't often get friendship from his peers. He spent all his spare money on theatrical make-up, phoney moustaches and nose putty, hoping to impress them. The ploy backfired. His play-acting only set him apart from the less imaginative kids.

He even played truant from Sunday school (surely a risky matter, given his parents' strict religious beliefs) to help the bill-posters plaster barns and fences with colorful announcements of the latest coming attractions.

One of Harry's first jobs inside a theater was prop boy at a local Opry House. He had a lot to learn. He infuriated the manager when the centurions of Caesar (in a cornfed version of *Quo Vadis*) marched on stage carrying Revolutionary muskets. Fortunately, he was agile enough to avoid trouble by climbing into the rigging above the stage, safely out of reach.

Langdon would take any job to be near the theatrical world. He sold tickets, worked as a concessionaire and even assisted a theater janitor. "My parents couldn't afford to give me money for theater tickets but I always managed in some way to see most of the shows," he later recalled. "When I was twelve years old I got my job as an usher. The only pay I got was the privilege of watching the show when I wasn't seating customers, but I was satisfied." Langdon was an usher at the Doheney Theater in Council Bluffs.

Soon Harry yearned to perform more than anything else. All the time he was working backstage, he would make anyone available laugh with routines both borrowed and original. When a local outlet inaugurated a series of amateur nights, Harry was ready. His planned ineptitude reportedly brought the house down that evening in 1896. He continued appearing on amateur nights sporadically for nearly a year.

Then Langdon had his first "solid" job offer. Shortly after celebrating his thirteenth birthday, Harry asked his parents if he could leave home to take a job with Dr. Belcher's Kickapoo Indian Medicine Show. Surprisingly, his mother accepted his decision. She even packed his trunk and gave him her blessing. . . .

In 1899, at fifteen, Langdon teamed up with another young man and went on the road in vaudeville. Actually, he tried most of the formats then available: burlesque, musical comedy, minstrel shows. He performed a chair-balancing specialty during his period with the well-known Gus Sun Minstrels.

The year 1903 was an important one for Harry. At the age of nineteen, he met and eloped with Rose Frances Mensolf. They formed a team (she had been a musical comedy actress when they met) and Langdon wrote the comedy act that became their bread and butter for the next twenty years: "Johnny's New Car."

This well-known act began with Harry and Rose "driving" onstage in a wooden breakaway car, with the nickname "Baby" on the license plate. The balky flivver would then stall in front of a hospital set (a cloth drop). Rose played the shrewish wife to Harry's meek, helpless little husband.

As the engine "exploded" and steam shot skyward, Harry's every effort would systematically worsen his predicament. Just when he thought he had the radiator fixed, the car wouldn't start. Then the fenders would fall off, the door would come off in his hands and his wife's temper would explode again. With the automobile a newfangled, slightly ridiculous phenomenon, audiences loved it.

The Langdons performed "Johnny's New Car" thousands of times, with mounting success, on the Orpheum and Keith vaudeville circuits. . . .

By the time Harry Langdon came to films, the standard comedy format was the two-reeler, about twenty minutes in length. Even though dramatic films had long since expanded to a seventy-minute average, the shorter running time remained the most popular for comedy. Literally thousands of two-reelers were produced between 1912 and 1955.

Just because they were briefer than features didn't mean short comedies were looked down upon. Two-reelers provided the proving ground for all the great silent clowns, even though a select few were graduating to longer formats. Often the comedy featurette was the most popular item on the bill. Every theater program had to include a comedy. . . .

The year 1924 had been one of charting a direction for Harry's screen character. The early months of the following year represented a period of consolidation. Not until *Plain Clothes*, released in the spring of 1925, was Langdon closer to the finished image of his later feature films than to the ordinary comic of the first two-reelers.

Remember When? (1925) provides one of the most satisfying narratives of his first period in "full bloom." Harry Hudson's childhood is economically established in the opening segment. Six-year-old Harry must say goodbye to a fellow orphan, young Rosemary Lee. (A rather woeful looking boy stood in for Harry as a child, adding sincerity and realism to the story.) Rosemary's new mother gives Harry a locket with the girl's picture.

Grown-up Harry becomes a tramp as he wanders through the countrysides and hobo-habitats, hoping to find his childhood love. He wears a long, ankle-length coat and carries a bindle stick. In the woods, he discovers a picnic table laden with food. He is so overeager to eat that he can't make up his mind where to start. Before he can bite into one sandwich, he is distracted to another, then another. His indecision gives the picnickers time to catch Harry hovering over their food.

Harry resorts to stealing chickens. He opens his coat, tosses a handful of feed inside, and the chicken obligingly jumps after the food. The Elf smiles, pleased with his ingenuity, until he comes face-to-face with the irate farmer. Harry's coat bulges ridiculously. When a chicken's head pops into view, the game is up, and Harry is quickly divested of his loot.

Seeking a quick escape, Harry joins "Mack's Circus Caravan," not suspecting that his childhood sweetheart (Natalie Kingston) is also aboard. When the circus sets up, Harry first unloads some heavy trunks (using Minerva the elephant as a chiropracter for his bent-over back), then helps pound some tent stakes. Suddenly, the Elf notices an incredible coincidence: the circus is setting up nearby the Hillcrest Orphanage, where he got his start in life. He smiles as the happy memories flood back. He pulls out the locket and kisses it. A quick kick in the pants from a co-worker brings Harry out of his daze.

Soon Harry meets Rosemary, but doesn't recognize her in her guise as the Bearded Lady. He is not sure how to act. At first he starts to tip his hat, then (taking notice of the beard) he offers her a cigar. After he agrees to deliver a note for her to the orphanage, Harry meekly touches her beard. He rubs his own bare chin, trying to comprehend the gender confusion. Scratching his forehead, a befuddled Harry leaves to run his errand.

Rosemary has also been looking for Harry. A note from the orphanage reveals his identity, and the lost lovers happily embrace. At that moment, the phoney beard falls off. Harry gently touches her face, then his own. With their search at an end, the film closes.

One of the last elements of Harry's comedy arsenal that jelled was his costume, his "official duds." In his first efforts, he dressed for whatever role he assumed: doughboy, football player, street cleaner. Just as his role varied, the image he presented shifted from film to film.

By the time Langdon became the Little Elf, and no one else, the Langdon Unit saw the need to give him one identifiable costume which, with a few variations, would remain constant. The Little Tramp had proven the commercial advantage of wearing essentially the same outfit in successive films. Furthermore, the outfit was perfectly suited to his tramp-clown image. Langdon, too, needed a costume that would compliment his babyish nature.

He took to wearing a felt hat with the brim turned up all the way around. It had a big dent on top, possibly a symbol of his mental deficiencies. He wore a tight double-breasted coat with two rows of dollar-sized buttons. It was snug around his narrow shoulders and tended to flair out wide at his waist.

He wore baggy pants and a pair of trusty slapshoes (of comparatively normal size). The coat in particular had a Little Lord Fauntleroy look that enhanced his boyish appearance. On several occasions, as in *Remember When?*, he also donned a floor-length overcoat that dwarfed his diminutive frame still further.

The formulation of the "Langdon Look" coincided with the precipitation of the Little Elf's persona. The Langdon team had swept away most of the chaff, leaving only the elements that contributed to his portrait of a full-grown man with the mind of a child. As his screen dimensions took shape, audiences grew to enjoy and anticipate Harry's understated comedy style. The Little Elf became a viable, recognizable presence.

Confronted with the unknown, the Elf would invariably blink slowly several times and try to make the best of things. If good times came, he'd flip a little wave of welcome — tentatively, though, since he'd been wrong before. Down on his luck, he'd grow wistful beyond words, and rest a puffy cheek on a stubby fist.

In a three-quarters shot (almost always from the left), one cheek would puff way out if he set his jaw a certain way. The cheek would grow and grow, as if someone was inflating it with a bicycle pump. It made the bottom of his face look soft and doughy. On an adult, those cheeks would come from years of chewing tobacco. On Langdon, they helped form his babyish pout.

Forever bewildered and confused, Harry stumbled through life, constantly trying to make good. Critics have observed that Harry was always imitating his betters, forever rehearsing for adulthood. Fortunately, dim-witted Harry never had to pass an I.Q. test. If he had the mind of a child, it was a child who flunked kindergarten. Who else would try to hide while running across an open lawn by simply ducking his head?

In *His Marriage Wow* (1925), he is late for his wedding. When he finally arrives, the church entrance is too crowded to permit him passage. He starts running along the sidewalk to the backdoor. Midway he stops. He has noticed something — a window he might jump through. Too bad it is at least ten feet over his head, made of stained-glass and therefore welded shut. He jumps. His feet clear the sidewalk by all of six inches. It is a pathetic attempt, but Harry was always hopeful, even when the odds were stacked against him.

To add to his perpetual confusion, Harry was constantly stunned by various sleep-inducers. Often, a clunk on the head (with a brick in *Feet of Mud*) would do the trick. His eyes would mist over, his smile would flicker momentarily and his legs would grow rubbery. Sometimes he would curl up on the floor in the fetal position. He never seemed very far from the womb.

In *Plain Clothes*, detective Harry opens a gas jet in a wall to "gas out" the villains, but stands too close. Gradually his eyelids grow heavier until he sinks senseless to the floor. The advent of slumber by many means was a Langdon specialty.

Although his face and hands are generally considered his best points. Langdon's footwork was astonishingly nimble and completely individual. Encountering an unusual object in his path, he used a little sideskip to avoid trouble. If an enemy chased him around a table, and he couldn't decide to break left or right, Harry would dance back and forth (his arms and legs stiff), looking as if he was being pulled both ways by unseen forces.

When angered (or pushed too far) he would pull his hand up to his face, point an index finger and squint at the enemy as if to say: "Now you better look out, buster!" If the foe yelled "BOO!" Harry's eyes would pop in shock, his hands would fly to his hat-brim, and he'd run for cover. His coordination always evoked the awkwardness of a youth getting used to his body.

HARRY LANGDON
The Serious Side of Comedy Making

When a Hollywood star, or a publicity writer standing in for him, is asked for a statement on his "art" by a magazine editor, the problem often is to find an "angle." Here Langdon (or possibly Arthur Ripley, his screenwriter) chose to take a consciously contrary view on the challenge of achieving audience laughter. He called it a "tragic business" and then suggested how it could be interpreted as such: the stress and danger of thrill scenes, the everpresent possibility that all efforts to achieve audience amusement will fail, and the sadistic side of slapstick.

Langdon's list of basic sources for laughter differ widely from those suggested by Chaplin and Sennett. They closely correlate with the comic image he had to offer. "Systematic absentmindedness" is the most comical, then rigidity, automatism, and unsociability. His article appeared in Theatre *magazine (New York) in December 1927.*

There are few more tragic businesses in the world than the making of funny pictures.

There is the tragedy, for example, of working for weeks, sometimes months, on a sequence which the producer expects to be extremely funny, only to find that it fails to evolve even a ripple from the audience. In the producing of any big feature comedy this situation is certain to arise at least once. The producer and the star often find that their most cherished material is not funny when transmitted to the screen and the result is a tragedy not only for the audience, but for the makers of the picture.

I am convinced that comedy is much harder to achieve than drama. There is more worry, more disappointment, more genuine heartbreak. A comedian must realize that it is his duty to make all people laugh — the rich, the poor, the bereaved, the sick. He must attempt to reach all of these with a message which will make them forget their woes, and cause them to laugh. There is a great deal of tragedy for the producer in facing this realization every time he starts to make a picture.

Comedy is the satire of tragedy. Serious matters repeatedly turn to comic as they pass through a morbidly active conscience. Most deliciously comic moments on the outside, are full of sad significance for those who realize the sinister characterization of the situation.

A man walks into a ballroom and forgets to put his suspenders on. To him it is a tragedy, to an audience it is comical. A despondent man goes up to leap to death from a high building; his coat catches on an awning and he dangles in midair. It is tragic to him, but the audience screams. A man is in love, the girl rejects him for another. That is tragedy, but the things the comedian does are funny. A man buys a new hat, it blows off and a horse steps on it. It is a calamity to him, but a howl to an audience.

Have you ever analyzed why you laugh at these things? It is the concentration on the physical, as opposed to the spiritual.

Any individual is comic who automatically goes his own way without troubling himself about getting in touch with the rest of his fellow beings. It is the trifling faults of our fellow men that make us laugh. A comic can make us laugh, providing care be taken not to arouse our emotions. To view comedy is delightful, but to partake of its ingredients, might leave a bitter taste.

Systematic absentmindedness, like Don Quixote, is the most comical thing imaginable. The four greatest stimuli to laughter are rigidity, automatism, absentmindedness and unsociability.

John Bunyan said: "Some things are of that nature as to make his fancy chuckle while his heart doth ache."

One cannot give himself up to tears, yet there are few comedies in which tragedy does not play its newly developed role. Comedy at its best, has always pointed a moral. It has not set out to do so, but instead, has assumed seriousness as the foundation of laughter.

Tragedy frequently stalks behind the scenes during the making of feature comedies, more so, perhaps, then during the making of dramas, for an essential element of successful comedy is thrill, and thrills are seldom obtained without some actual physical danger. During such moments there is no hilarity in the producing company. There seldom is for that matter. I have often thought a comedy "lot" is the saddest place on earth and comedy constructionists are, as a rule, the saddest people. You will find them, without exception, a serious-minded group of men, seldom smiling and not at all given to outbursts of mirth. This, however, is beside the point.

Every man in a comedy company dreads to make thrill scenes. So often a man's life hangs on a bit of invisible wire, or his ability to conquer the instinctive fear of danger. A slip of the foot may mean actual peril to a comedian during such moments — but it is always good for a gale of glee from an audience.

During the filming of *Tramp, Tramp, Tramp*, nobody in the company wanted me to hang on a fence at the edge of a steep cliff. There was no one else to do it, so I had no alternative. You can be quite sure there was not a laugh in the crowd back of the camera while this stunt was being done. The cliff dropped precipitately for several hundred yards with nothing to break the fall. When it was finished I was greatly worried about it, because there hadn't been a titter from the crew. Usually, you know you can judge whether your stuff is funny by the reaction it gets from your impromptu audience. When I got off the fence I met nothing but blanched faces and silence. On the screen, as you know, the stunt proved tremendously successful. Audiences laughed.

During the filming of *The Strong Man*, a trick cannon exploded as I pulled the lanyard to fire the final shot of the scene. In the noise, the smoke and confusion, I didn't even know there had been an accident. When the smoke cleared away, we found that one piece of the metal cannon had grazed the back of my head, struck a musician a glancing blow in the cheek and buried itself in the wall of the stage. On the screen this scene was a scream.

The enjoyment of comedy, just like the enjoyment of tragedy, is the result of the feeling of remoteness from the situation caricatured.

Appendices

Appendix A

Some Possible Mechanisms and Motivations for Comedy

For my meditations on comedy in the introduction to this book I have made no attempt at any comprehensive matching of films with comic structures or ideas. I hope the ideas are suggestive enough for future students to do so.

In my last semester before retirement, however, I did offer to my class in American film comedy—from Charlie Chaplin to Woody Allen—the following "ten kinds of comic mechanisms or motivations," which they might find useful in their observation of the weekly double bills of films shown for the course.

These are of course not adequately described, not equal in importance, not in any special order, and not intended to put a damper on the pleasures of watching funny movies.

1. Superiority. Looking down on "lower types." Aristotle.
2. Danger. Not serious, we know, but enough for nervous laughs. Harold Lloyd/Buster Keaton.
3. Misogyny/romance. Escaping from or rushing toward a member of the opposite sex. John Bunny, Mack Sennett, Laurel & Hardy.
4. Slapstick. Pain and embarrassment in various degrees, providing sadistic "pleasures." Stressed by Freudians.
5. Absentminded people acting like machines. Henri Bergson's notion.
6. Childlike tricks/adolescent overcoming. Charlie Chaplin, Keaton, Mary Pickford, Douglas Fairbanks.
7. Simple spirit of play. Max Eastman's idea.
8. Character foibles and what they lead to. Molière, Shakespeare.
9. Parody, with exaggeration. Sennett.
10. Examinations of public characters with intent to improve them and us. Ben Jonson. Frank Capra and other American directors.

—R.D.M.

Appendix B

Silent Feature Films by Four Comedians

Starring Charlie Chaplin

Released by Mack Sennett
1914   Tillie's Punctured Romance

Released through United Artists
1920   The Kid
1923   A Woman of Paris
1925   The Gold Rush
1928   The Circus
1931   City Lights

Starring Buster Keaton

Released through Metro and M-G-M
1920   The Saphead
1923   The Three Ages
        Our Hospitality
1924   Sherlock Jr.
        The Navigator
1925   Seven Chances
        Go West
1926   Battling Butler

Released through United Artists
1926   The General
1927   College
        Steamboat Bill Jr.

Released through M-G-M
1928   The Cameraman
        Spite Marriage

Starring Harold Lloyd

Released through Pathé
1921   A Sailor-Made Man
1922   Grandma's Boy
        Doctor Jack

1923   Safety Last
        Why Worry?
1924   Girl Shy
        Hot Water
1925   The Freshman

Released through Paramount
1926   For Heaven's Sake
1927   The Kid Brother
1928   Speedy

Starring Harry Langdon

Released through First National
1926   Tramp, Tramp, Tramp
        The Strong Man
1927   Long Pants
        Three's a Crowd
1928   The Chaser
        Heart Trouble
[In 1927, Mack Sennett released His First Flame, a feature starring Langdon he had produced in 1925]

Appendix C

Comedy Performers in Silent Films

Arbuckle, Roscoe "Fatty" (1887-1933). Born Roscoe Conkling Arbuckle in Smith Center, Kansas, he was a plumber's assistant when attracted by the life of carnival performer. He was in films as early as 1908 for the Selig company, but turned up on Keystone's doorstep in 1913, where his 285 pounds failed at first to impress Sennett but carried some kind of weight with Mabel Normand, who persuaded Mack to hire him. Often his face would fill the screen with a slowly changing expression from frown to smile or vice versa and his dexterity as dancer and pie-thrower became legendary. He wrote and directed many of his own films and worked with top people like Chester Conklin, Mabel, and Chaplin. In 1917 he set up his own company, and in one of his first films Buster Keaton was introduced to the screen. In film history, Arbuckle is unfortunately remembered because of a 1921 trip to San Francisco between productions, when a drinking party met disaster. A starlet named Virginia Rappe claimed to be sexually assaulted and died a few days afterward. Arbuckle's trial for manslaughter, heavily promoted by the state's attorney and the newspapers, resulted in a hung jury twice and a final acquittal. His career as an actor was effectively ended, although he was later given directing jobs (as "William Goodrich") and acted in a few sound comedies.

Bevan, Billy (1887-1957). Born William Bevan Harris in Australia, he worked in opera, did small roles in comedy shorts starting in 1917, and between 1920 and 1929 starred in two-reelers for Mack Sennett. His brush mustache turned up in many sound pictures till he retired in 1952.

Bunny, John (1863-1915). Born and raised in Brooklyn, he ran away to join a minstrel show, later worked as actor and director for stock companies. At Vitagraph in 1910, he weighed in at 300 pounds, became the first comic star of the U.S. screen, making 200 shorts in five years, usually with skinny Flora Finch as co-star....See Chapter 1.

Chaplin, Charlie (1889-1977). Born Charles Spencer Chaplin, in London, he was the son of music hall entertainers who separated when he was a year old. After his father died and his mother was committed to an asylum, eight-year-old Charlie worked at odd jobs, in time was given theater and dance roles, and with his brother Sydney, joined the music hall troupe of Fred Karno. A second U.S. tour in 1912 brought him a contract with Mack Sennett, for whom he made 35 films (and began to direct himself on the 12th). Essanay signed him in 1915, Mutual in 1916, First National in 1918 for a million dollars plus. In 1919 he joined Mary Pickford, Douglas Fairbanks, and D.W. Griffith in founding United Artists....See Chapter 2.

Chase, Charlie (1893-1940). Born Charles Parrott in Baltimore, he was in vaudeville before working at Keystone in 1914, sometimes with Chaplin. At other studios he worked as comic and as director for himself, for Arbuckle, Sterling, Pollard, and others, his best period being with Hal Roach as writer-director from 1921 and comedian from 1924. As a slender persecuted character, with a dominant wife or other kinds of trouble, he won considerable popularity, and could be judged one of the top stars of the two-reel era. His long list of credits continued with supporting roles (sometimes singing) in sound features and as director of the Three Stooges and others at Columbia after 1937. Last picture 1940.

Clyde, Andy (1892-1967). Born in Scotland, he started in films as support for Sennett two-reeler stars like Billy Bevan in the 1920s, then played character roles in sound pictures, including William Boyd's Hopalong Cassidy series. Last picture 1955.

Conklin, Chester (1888-1971). Born in Oskaloosa, Iowa, he was working in the circus when he decided that movies might be more of a steady business. Sennett hired him as a Keystone Kop and in time he became a regular, offering behind an oversize mustache a characterization of overwhelming bewilderment and puzzled innocence when extraordinary things happened to him. Later he joined with Mack Swain in more unpleasant villainies. Conklin left Sennett in 1920 and continued doing comic parts at various studios through the 1940s.

Durfee, Minta (1897-1975). A chorus girl at 17, she married Fatty Arbuckle in 1908 and they went together to Keystone in 1913. She worked in his films and with Chaplin but left Arbuckle in 1918, retiring from the screen except for a few appearances through 1964. She and Arbuckle separated legally in 1921 (the time of his trials) and were divorced in 1925.

Fazenda, Louise (1895-1962). Born in Lafayette, Indiana, she learned the ways of an eccentric comedienne at Universal, but joined Keystone in 1915, where she became popular as a rural type in pigtails, often put upon but capable in a pinch of holding her own. Wife of producer Hal Wallis. Active in films through 1939.

Griffith, Raymond (1890-1957). Born in Boston to a show business family, he entered films in 1914, but didn't hit his stride as an arch bumbler (Peter Sellers style) till the 20s. *Hands Up!* was a spoof of Civil War westerns and *You'd Be Surprised* a spoof of drawing room whodunits: both these 1926 features have survived. He could not speak above a whisper: when sound came in he was given important associate producer jobs at Warners and Fox (1933-40) by Darryl Zanuck.

Keaton, Buster (1895-1966). Born Joseph Francis Keaton in Piqua, Kansas, the son of medicine show barkers, he fell down stairs at the age of six months and was admiringly dubbed "Buster" by the family friend and professional magician, Harry Houdini. Onstage almost as soon as he could walk, he was soon taking countless falls and was billed above his parents as "the human mop." When the act broke up in 1917 Buster chose to try movies with Roscoe Arbuckle instead of joining a top Broadway revue. By 1919 he had a contract with Joseph Schenck to make comedy shorts on his own, and in 1923 he began a two-a-year feature schedule — the heart of his movie achievement. In 1928 Schenck advised him to sign with M-G-M and give up his own studio. This bad advice led downhill to loss of control and the rest of his life was a series of unhappy stabs at acting, writing, and assisting other comics....See Chapter 3.

Kennedy, Edgar (1890-1948). Born in Monterey, California, he worked in vaudeville as singer and comedian before finding

Keystone in 1914. After freelancing and directing features, he joined Hal Roach, in 1928, acting and directing for Laurel and Hardy shorts. His special "slow burn" response to provocations went with him into a 17-year series under his own name and into innumerable sound features. Last picture 1949.

Langdon, Harry (1884-1944). Born in Council Bluffs, Iowa, he was the son of Salvation Army employees and was allowed to join a medicine show. For 20 years a traveling performer, using over and over an act called "Johnny's New Car," he came in 1923 to Mack Sennett, who needed a new face. It was a baby face, often actually in white makeup, a character incapable of judgment or action. Frank Capra took charge of it for a while, even after Langdon went independent, but in spite of three feature-length successes, he was dropped as writer in favor of Arthur Ripley's more somber plots. Langdon's popularity was short-lived, and he went on to failed projects and supporting roles. Last film 1945.

Lloyd, Harold (1893-1971). Born in Nebraska, the son of an unsuccessful photographer and pool-hall owner (who moved with him to San Diego after breaking up with his mother), Lloyd won roles in stock companies and also did extra parts in movies. He met Hal Roach, another extra, who inherited $3000 in 1914 and hired him to act in comedy shorts. "Lonesome Luke" lasted for some 100 outings but Lloyd asked Roach to sell Pathé on a new "glasses character" who would be a recognizable young American facing challenges and winning. This new concept and the decision to turn to feature length in 1921-22 made him the highest paid actor in Hollywood. He did do a few sound features successfully, but never had the same steady popularity he had up to 1928. Last film, a compilation of old movies, 1963.

Mace, Fred (1872-1917). Giving up dentistry in Erie, Pennsylvania, he acted in stock and met Mack Sennett there. He was a round-faced, hefty mainstay of the earliest films directed by Sennett at Biograph in 1911. Briefly with IMP and Ince, he joined up with Keystone in California when it was founded in 1912. Playing restrained roles as a bumbling police chief or a boxer named "One-Round" O'Brien, he became overconfident about his ability to go it alone and left Keystone after eight months. He gave up as producer-director in 1915, was taken back by Sennett, but wasn't used much in the new Keystone/Triangle regime. While planning another independent effort, he was found dead in a New York City hotel.

Murray, Charlie (1872-1941). Born in Indiana, he was a child circus performer. In vaudeville he became half of the famous Murray and Mack stage team. At Biograph in 1911, he went west to Keystone in 1915, doing a regular stint as a character named

Hogan. Popular as the Irish side of the "Cohens and Kellys" film series in 1930s. Last picture 1938.

Pollard, Snub (1886-1962). Born Harold Frazer in Australia, he came to America with a musical comedy touring company and decided to stop off with Hal Roach in 1915. There he worked with Harold Lloyd in one-reelers for four years, when he started his own series directed by Charlie Chase. Starting his own company in 1926 didn't pan out, and he took all sorts of roles in sound features through the 30s. Last picture 1961.

St. John, Al (1893-1963). Born in Santa Ana, California, a nephew of Roscoe Arbuckle, he found roles in Keystone comedies in 1913 as a country boy. He followed his uncle into independent production and later had his own series at Paramount, Fox, and Educational. His long career included many supporting roles in cowboy pictures, the last in 1949.

Semon, Larry (1889-1928). Born in Mississippi, the son of a professional magician, he became a New York newspaper cartoonist, then went to Vitagraph as comedy writer-director. He developed a white-faced dumb character for himself and became extremely popular here and abroad. After 1922, he attempted feature films on his own (doing the Scarecrow in *The Wizard of Oz* in 1925) but overspent and went into bankruptcy in 1928.

Sterling, Ford (1883-1939). Born George Ford Stitch, in La-Crosse, Wisconsin, he ran away from home as a teenager to join Robinson's circus, where he played a "boy clown." After a stint in vaudeville, he tried movies at Biograph, where he worked with Sennett and went with him to Keystone. He often played, in heavy pantomime, a square-bearded comic heavy, and was the mainstay of the studio in 1913. He was offered more money and his own Sterling Comedies at Universal, but fell out with Henry Lehrman, who had gone along with him as director. He was taken back at Keystone then and later, after other tries at independence. Despite a leg lost in an accident, he was still working in films in 1935.

Swain, Mack (1876-1935). Born in Salt Lake City, he had been in minstrel shows and vaudeville before joining Keystone late in 1913. At six feet two and 280 pounds, he was massive beyond villainy, a gloomy presence in many of the early Chaplin shorts. With a grand mustache and a yen for the ladies, he was greatly popular as "Ambrose" in other Keystone shorts up to 1917. Chaplin used his intimidating bulk in longer films in the early 1920s, culminating in *The Gold Rush* (1925). He continued to work in features through 1932.

Turpin, Ben (1874-1940). Born in New Orleans and raised in New York, his crossed eyes worked for him in burlesque. He went with Essanay in 1907, working hard and often but not gain-ing much fame. After another turn at burlesque, he was back at Essanay in 1914, where he worked opposite Chaplin but found that Charlie considered him too much of a competitor for press notices. He then made 31 pictures for Vogue Comedies before Mack Sennett signed him for the last few months of the Triangle contract in 1917. After that, the new Paramount releases depended a great deal on Turpin and he found himself Sennett's top star in the early 1920s, often doing crazy take-offs on well known figures like Stroheim and Valentino. He worked occasionally in sound films until his death in 1940.

[Much of the information above comes from Ephraim Katz, *The Film Encyclopedia* (1979).]

Appendix D

Bibliography

Basic books for students of American silent films are:

Kevin Brownlow, *The Parade's Gone By* (1968), interviews with survivors;
Richard Griffith, Arthur Mayer, Eileen Bowser, *The Movies* (1957/1984), a valuable picture history;
Lewis Jacobs, *The Rise of the American Film* (1939);
William Everson, *American Silent Film* (1978);
Magill's *Survey of Cinema: Silent Films* (1982, 3 vols), film reviews that emphasize story content and historical background.

High quality biographical studies are now in reasonably good supply for the first thirty years (see bibliographies in earlier volumes) and the major comedy figures are fairly well covered.

From Chaplin (*My Autobiography*, 1964), Keaton (*My Wonderful World of Slapstick*, 1960), and Lloyd (*An American Comedy*, 1928) we have useful, serious, and rather revealing autobiographies. Mack Sennett's (*King of Comedy*, 1954) is more mythic, swinging, and undependable, and Gene Fowler's treatment (*Father Goose*, 1934) is more so.

On Chaplin, David Robinson, who was given access to the family papers, has given us in turn as complete a life story (*Chaplin: His Life and Art*, 1985) as we are ever likely to get. Charles Maland has given us a new approach (*Chaplin and American Culture: The Evolution of a Star Image*, 1989) and Theodore Huff (*Charlie Chaplin*, 1951) is still valuable.

For Keaton, we have from Daniel Moews an analysis of the features (*Keaton: The Silent Features Close Up*, 1977) which is as meticulous as anyone could wish. J.P. Lebel (*Buster Keaton*, 1967) has given us a different view. Rudi Blesh (*Keaton*, 1966) and Tom Dardis (*Keaton: The Man Who Wouldn't Lie Down*, 1979) have added important interpretations to the biographical record.

For Lloyd, Adam Reilly has created an illustrated book (*Harold Lloyd: The King of Daredevil Comedy*, 1977) that is truly remarkable for coverage of the films and the ideas in them. Richard Schickel has given us a meditation on the man and his films (*Harold Lloyd: The Shape of Laughter*, 1974) and Tom Dardis, again, has summarized the life (*Harold Lloyd: The Man on the Clock*, 1983).

On Langdon, we have at last a well researched and useful life story by William Schelly (*Harry Langdon*, 1982) plus a cinematic and critical analysis by Joyce Rheuban (*Harry Langdon: The Comedian as Metteur-en-Scene*, 1983).

And there are the important books by Donald McCaffrey (*Four Great Comedians*, 1968), Raymond Durgnat (*The Crazy Mirror: Hollywood Comedy and the American Image*, 1970), Walter Kerr (*The Silent Clowns*, 1975), and Gerald Mast (*The Comic Mind*, 1973) which attempt to deal with early film comedy in a more comprehensive way.

The following lists can only be a start for the devoted scholar. They do make some effort to discriminate in favor of both quality and the unusual. Readers may find here surprising and tempting items. They are advised to look further at the bibliographies in the *International Dictionary of Films and Filmmakers*, Vol.III, Actors and Actresses (1986).

Books from which extracts are printed in this volume

Agee, James. *Agee on Film*. N.Y., McDowell-Obolensky, 1958.

Chaplin, Charles. *My Autobiography*. N.Y., Simon & Schuster, 1964.

Franklin, Joe. *Classics of the Silent Screen*. N.Y., Citadel, 1959.

Huff, Theodore. *Charlie Chaplin*. N.Y., Henry Schuman, 1951. Copyright not renewed. Reprints by Pyramid Books 1964 and Arno Press, 1972.

Keaton, Buster (with Charles Samuels). *My Wonderful World of Slapstick*. Garden City, N.Y., Doubleday, 1960. Reprint by Da-Capo 1982.

Lahue, Kalton and Samuel Gill. *Clown Princes and Court Jesters* Cranbury, N.J., A.S. Barnes & Co., 1970.

Lahue, Kalton. *Mack Sennett's Keystone: The Man, the Myth, and the Comedies*. Cranbury, N.J., A.S. Barnes & Co., 1971.

Lathrop, William Addison. *Little Stories From the Screen.* Britton Publishing Co., 1917.

Lebel, J.P. *Buster Keaton.* Cranbury, N.J., A.S. Barnes & Co., 1967.

Lloyd, Harold (with Wesley Stout). *An American Comedy.* N.Y., Longmans Green & Co., 1928. Copyright not renewed.

Magill, Frank. *Magill's Survey of Cinema: Silent Films.* Pasadena, CA, Salem Press, 1982.

Maland, Charles J. *Chaplin and American Culture: The Evolution of a Star Image.* Princeton, N.J., Princeton University Press, 1989.

McCaffrey, Donald W. *Four Great Comedians: Chaplin, Lloyd, Keaton, Langdon.* N.Y., A.S.Barnes & Co., 1968.

Moews, Daniel. *Keaton: The Silent Features Close Up.* Berkeley, University of California Press. 1977

O'Dell, Scott. *Representative Photoplays Analyzed.* Hollywood, Palmer Institute of Authorship, 1924.

Robinson, David. *Buster Keaton.* Bloomington, Indiana University Press, 1969.

Schelly, William. *Harry Langdon.* Metuchen, N.J., Scarecrow Press, 1982.

Articles reprinted in this volume

Chaplin, Charlie. "What People Laugh At," *American Magazine,* November 1918.

Houston, Penelope. "The Great Blank Page," *Sight & Sound,* Winter 1965-66. Keaton's films.

Johnson, Timothy. "Sherlock, Jr." In Frank Magill, *Magill's Survey of Cinema: Silent Films* (see above).

Keaton, Buster. "Keaton at Venice." Interview by John Gillett and James Blue. *Sight & Sound,* Spring 1968.

Langdon, Harry. "The Serious Side of Comedy Making." *Theatre Magazine,* December 1927.

Lloyd, Harold. "The Serious Business of Being Funny," *Film Comment,* Fall 1969. Interview by Hubert Cohen.

Lorenz, Janet. "The Gold Rush." In Frank Magill, *Magill's Survey of Cinema: Silent Films* (see above).

Petrie, Graham. "So Much and Yet so Little: A Survey of Books on Chaplin," *Quarterly Review of Film Studies,* November 1977.

Roemer, Michael. "Chaplin: Charles and Charlie," *Yale Review,* December 1974.

Sennett, Mack. "The Psychology of Film Comedy," *Motion Picture Classic,* November 1918.

Sherwood, Robert E. "Grandma's Boy." In The Best Moving Pictures of 1922-23. N.Y., *Small, Maynard & Co.,* 1923.

Slide, Anthony. "The Kid Brother." In Frank Magill, *Magill's Survey of Cinema: Silent Films* (see above).

Bibliography related to Introduction and comedy in general

Brownlow, Kevin. *The Parade's Gone By.* N.Y., Alfred Knopf, 1968. Interview with Eddie Sutherland on Chaplin as director. Chapters also on Lloyd and Keaton.

Capra, Frank. *The Name Above the Title.* N.Y., Macmillan, 1971. Autobiography, including material on Sennett and Langdon.

Cooper, Lane. *An Aristotelian Theory of Comedy.* N.Y., Harcourt Brace, 1922.

Durgnat, Raymond. *The Crazy Mirror: Hollywood Comedy and the American Image.* N.Y., Horizon Press, 1970.

Enck, John J., Elizabeth T. Forter, and Alvin Whitley. *The Comic In Theory and Practice.* Englewood Cliffs, N.J., Prentice-Hall, 1960.

Jacobs, Lewis. *The Rise of the American Film.* N.Y., Harcourt Brace, 1939.

Jagendorf, Zvi. *The Happy End of Comedy.* Newark, University of Delaware Press, 1984.

Janko, Richard. *Aristotle on Comedy: Towards a Reconstruction of the Poetics.* London, Duckworth, 1984.

Jenkins III, Henry. *What Made Pistachio Nuts? - Early Sound Comedy and the Vaudeville Aesthetic.* N.Y., Columbia University Press, 1992.

Kerr, Walter. *The Silent Clowns.* N.Y., Alfred Knopf, 1975.

Lauter, Paul. *Theories of Comedy.* Garden City, N.Y., Doubleday & Co./Anchor Books, 1964.

Maltin, Leonard. *The Great Movie Comedians.* N.Y.,Crown, 1978.

Mast, Gerald. *The Comic Mind: Comedy and the Movies.* Indianapolis, Bobbs-Merrill, 1973.

———. *A Short History of the Movies.* Indianapolis, Bobbs-Merrill, 1971. Chapter on *The Gold Rush* and *The General.*

National Society of Film Critics on Movie Comedy. N.Y.,Viking Grossman, 1977. Penelope Gilliatt on Langdon and Keaton, Richard Schickel on Harold Lloyd.

Robinson, David. *The Great Funnies: A History of Film Comedy.* N.Y. Dutton Vista, 1969.

Seidman, Steve. *Comedian Comedy: A Tradition in American Cinema.* Ann Arbor, UMI Research Press, 1981. From 1979 UCLA thesis.

Seldes, Gilbert. *The Seven Lively Arts.* N.Y., Harpers, 1924. Reprinted with his comments, Sagamore Press 1957.

Sypher, Wylie. *Comedy.* Garden City, N.Y., Doubleday Anchor, 1956. Includes essays by Henri Bergson and George Meredith.

Callenbach, Ernest. "The Comic Ecstasy," *Films in Review*, January 1954.

Christie, Al. "What Makes You Laugh?" *Photoplay*, September 1925.

Drew, Sidney. "Comedy Picture Production." *Moving Picture World*, July 21, 1917.

McCaffrey, Donald W. "The Evolution of the Chase in Silent Screen Comedy." *Journal of Society of Cinematologists*, 1964.

Additional bibliography related to Chapter 1
[Sennett and Others]

Capra, Frank. *The Name Above the Title*. N.Y., Macmillan, 1971. Autobiography, including material on Sennett.

Durgnat, Raymond. *The Crazy Mirror: Hollywood Comedy and the American Image*. N.Y., Horizon Press, 1970. Chapter on Sennett.

Fowler, Gene. *Father Goose: The Story of Mack Sennett*. N.Y., Covici Friede, 1934.

Fussell, Betty Harper. *Mabel: Hollywood's First I Don't Care Girl*. N.Y., Ticknor & Fields, 1982.

Jacobs, Lewis. *The Rise of the American Film*. N.Y., Harcourt Brace, 1939.

Kerr, Walter. *The Silent Clowns*. N.Y., Alfred Knopf, 1975.

Lahue, Kalton. *World of Laughter: The Motion Picture Comedy Short, 1910-1930*. Norman, OK, 1966.

———. *Kops and Custards*. Norman, OK, 1967.

St. Johns, Adela Rogers. *Love, Laughter, and Tears: My Hollywood Story*. Garden City, N.Y., Doubleday, 1978.

Seldes, Gilbert. *The Seven Lively Arts*. N.Y., Harpers, 1924. Reprinted with his comments, Sagamore Press 1957.

Sennett, Mack (as told to Cameron Shipp). *King of Comedy*. Garden City, N.Y., Doubleday, 1954; Pinnacle Books, 1975.

Yallop, David A. *The Day the Laughter Stopped: The True Story of Fatty Arbuckle*. N.Y., St. Martin's Press, 1976.

[Anon.] "It's No Laughing Matter." *Photoplay*, May 1922. About Comedian Larry Semon.

Badger, Clarence G. "Early Days of Movie Comedies." *Image*, May 1957. Reminiscences by Sennett director; details on 1904 Biograph movie called *Personal*, model for *Seven Chances*.

Christie, Al. "What Makes You Laugh?" *Photoplay*, September 1925.

Drew, Sidney. "Comedy Picture Production." *Moving Picture World*, July 21, 1917.

Giroux, Robert. "Mack Sennett," *Films in Review*, December 1968 and January 1969.

Howe, Herbert. "The Life Tragedy of a Sennett Beauty," *Photoplay*, November 1928. Ben Turpin.

LeFanu, Mark. "Pordenone: Vitagraph and the Great Arbuckle." *Sight & Sound*,Winter 1987-88. Italian festival of silent films.

McCaffrey, Donald W. "The Evolution of the Chase in Silent Screen Comedy." *Journal of Society of Cinematologists*, 1964.

Pryor, Thomas. "Then and Now," *New York Times Magazine*, February 1953. Mack Sennett at 68.

Roach, Hal. "The Gag's the Thing." *Popular Mechanics*, May 1935.

———. Interview by David Robinson. *Sight and Sound*, Winter 1986-87, p. 3. "Children have made all the great comedians."

Stempel, Tom. "The Sennett Screenplays." *Sight & Sound*, Winter 1985-86. Hampton Del Ruth, head of story department in Triangle period 1916: scripts at Motion Picture Academy.

Additional bibliography related to Chapter 2
[Chaplin]

Bowman, William Dodgson. *Charlie Chaplin: His Life and Art.* N.Y., John Day, 1931; London, Routledge, 1931; reprinted N.Y., Haskell, 1974. With character sketch as introduction by Douglas Fairbanks Jr.

Brownlow, Kevin. *The Parade's Gone By.* N.Y., Alfred Knopf, 1968. Interview with Eddie Sutherland on Chaplin as director.

Chaplin, Charles. *My Life in Pictures.* N.Y., Grosset & Dunlap, 1976.

Chaplin, Charles/edited by Harry M. Geduld. *Charlie Chaplin's Own Story.* Bloomington, Indiana University Press, 1985. Reprint of same title published by Bobbs-Merrill, 1916.

Chaplin, Jr., Charles (with N. and M. Rau). *My Father, Charlie Chaplin.* N.Y., Random House, 1960.

Chaplin, Lita Grey (with Morton Cooper). *My Life With Chaplin.* N.Y., Bernard Geis, 1966.

Cooke, Alistair. *Six Men.* N.Y., Alfred Knopf, 1977. Chapter on Chaplin.

Durgnat, Raymond. *The Crazy Mirror: Hollywood Comedy and the American Image.* N.Y., Horizon Press, 1970. Chaplin chapter.

Gehring, Wes D. *Charlie Chaplin: A Bio-Bibliography.* Westport, Connecticut, Greenwood Press, 1983.

Jacobs, Lewis. *The Rise of the American Film.* N.Y., Harcourt Brace, 1939.

Kamin, Dan. *Charlie Chaplin's One-Man Show.* Metuchen, N.J., Scarecrow Press, 1986. As mime.

Lyons, Timothy J. *Charles Chaplin: A Guide to References and Resources.* Boston, G.K. Hall, 1979.

Maland, Charles J. *American Visions: The Films of Chaplin, Ford, Capra, and Welles,* 1936-41. N.Y., Arno Press, 1977.

Mast, Gerald. *A Short History of the Movies.* Indianapolis, Bobbs-Merrill, 1971. Chapter on *The Gold Rush* and *The General.*

McCaffrey, Donald W. *Focus on Chaplin.* Englewood Cliffs, N.J., Prentice-Hall, 1971.

Negri, Pola (with Alfred Allan Lewis). *Memoirs of a Star.* N.Y., Doubleday, 1970. Her romance with Chaplin, pp. 214-224.

Parrish, Robert. *Growing Up in Hollywood.* N.Y., Harcourt Brace, 1976. As a child, he was directed by Chaplin in *City Lights.*

Robinson, David. *Chaplin: The Mirror of Opinion.* London, Secker Warburg, 1983.

———. *Chaplin: His Life and Art.* N.Y., McGraw-Hill, 1985.

Bentley, Eric. "Charlie Chaplin and Peggy Hopkins Joyce," *Moviegoer,* Summer 1966. On *A Woman of Paris.*

Brooks, Louise. "Charlie Chaplin Remembered," *Film Culture,* Spring 1966.

Brownlow, Kevin. "The Early Days of Charlie Chaplin," *Film,* Summer 1964.

Capp, Al. "The Comedy of Charlie Chaplin," *Atlantic,* February 1950.

Chaplin, Charles. "Give Us More Bombs Over Berlin." From Anthony Slide, *The Best of Rob Wagner's Script* (a Hollywood publication). Dated August 1, 1942, vol. 27, no. 634.

Churchill, Winston. "Everybody's Language," *Collier's,* October 26, 1935. Chaplin, pantomime, and silent movies.

Cooke, Alistair. "Charlie Chaplin at 50," *Atlantic,* August 1939.

Eisenstein, S.M. "Charlie the Kid," *Sight & Sound,* Spring 1946.

———. "Charlie the Grown Up," *Sight & Sound,* Summer 1946.

Frye, Northrop. "The Great Charlie," *Canadian Forum,* August 1941.

———. "The Eternal Tramp," *Here and Now,* December 1947.

Grace, Harry A. "Charlie Chaplin's Films and American Culture Patterns," *Journal of Aesthetics and Art Criticism,* June 1952.

MacCann, Richard Dyer. "Theater Chain Bans Chaplin's 'Limelight,'" *Christian Science Monitor,* January 27, 1953.

Madden, David. "Harlequin's Stick, Charlie's Cane," *Film Quarterly,* Fall 1968.

Meyerhold, V. "Chaplin and Chaplinism," *Tulane Drama Review,* Fall 1966.

Micha, Rene. "Chaplin as Don Juan," *Sight and Sound,* January 1953.

Pritchett, V.S. "Charlie," *New Statesman,* October 2, 1964.

Renoir, Jean. "Chaplin Among the Immortals," *Screen Writer,* July 1947. Chaplin and Molière.

Rosen, Philip G. "The Chaplin World-View," *Cinema Journal*, Fall 1969.

St. Johns, Ivan. "Everything's Rosy at Chaplin's," *Photoplay*, February 1926. Charlie and Lita have made up.

Silver, Charles (et al.) "Charlie Chaplin: Faces and Facets, Twelve Essays," *Film Comment*, September 1972.

Spears, Jack. "Chaplin's Collaborators," *Films in Review*, January 1962. Henry Lehrman, Mabel Normand: unacknowledged teachers.

Young, Stark. "The Circus," *New Republic*, February 8, 1928.

Additional bibliography relating to Chapter 3
[Keaton]

Blesh, Rudi. *Keaton*. N.Y., Macmillan, 1966.

Brownlow, Kevin. *The Parade's Gone By*. N.Y., Alfred Knopf, 1968. Chapter on Keaton.

Dardis, Tom. *Keaton: The Man Who Wouldn't Lie Down*. N.Y., Scribners, 1979.

Kerr, Walter. *The Silent Clowns*. N.Y., Alfred Knopf, 1975.

Mast, Gerald. *The Comic Mind: Comedy and the Movies*. Indianapolis, Bobbs-Merrill, 1973.

———. *A Short History of the Movies*. Indianapolis, Bobbs-Merrill, 1971. Chapter on *The Gold Rush* and *The General*.

National Society of Film Critics on Movie Comedy. N.Y.,Viking Grossman, 1977. Penelope Gilliatt on Keaton.

Badger, Clarence G. "Early Days of Movie Comedies." *Image*, May 1957. Reminiscences by Sennett director; details on 1904 Biograph movie called *Personal*, model for *Seven Chances*.

Bishop, Christopher. "The Great Stone Face," *Film Quarterly*, Fall 1958. Interview. Reprinted in Andrew Sarris, *Interviews with Film Directors* (Bobbs-Merrill, 1967).

Brownlow, Kevin. "Buster Keaton," *Film*, Winter 1964. Interview.

Friedman, Arthur B. "Buster Keaton: An Interview," *Film Quarterly*, Summer 1966.

Gilliatt, Penelope. "Buster Keaton." *New Yorker*, September 26, 1970.

Huie Jr., William O. "Buster Keaton and the Near-Miss Gag," unpublished paper.

Kauffmann, Stanley. "Buster Keaton Festival." *New Republic*, October 24, 1970. Comparisons with Chaplin life and career; credit to Raymond Rohauer for saving rare prints of features.

Keaton, Buster. "Why I Never Smile." *Ladies Home Journal*, June 1926.

McCaffrey, Donald W. "The Evolution of the Chase in Silent Screen Comedy." *Journal of Society of Cinematologists*, 1964.

McCaffrey, Donald W. "The Mutual Approval of Keaton and Lloyd," *Cinema Journal* (1966-67).

Reed, Rex. "Buster Keaton, October 1965." *Do You Sleep in the Nude?* N.Y., New American Library, 1968. The last interview.

Additional bibliography related to Chapter 4
[Lloyd and Langdon]

Brownlow, Kevin. *The Parade's Gone By.* N.Y., Alfred Knopf, 1968. Chapter on Lloyd.

Capra, Frank. *The Name Above the Title.* N.Y., Macmillan, 1971. Autobiography, including material on Langdon.

Dardis, Tom. *Harold Lloyd: The Man on the Clock.* N.Y., Viking Press, 1983.

Durgnat, Raymond. *The Crazy Mirror: Hollywood Comedy and the American Image.* N.Y., Horizon Press, 1970. Langdon chapter.

Kerr, Walter. *The Silent Clowns.* N.Y., Alfred Knopf, 1975.

McCaffrey, Donald. *Three Classic Silent Screen Comedies Starring Harold Lloyd.* East Brunswick, N.J., Associated University Presses, 1976. His dissertation at University of Iowa, 1965.

National Society of Film Critics on Movie Comedy. N.Y.,Viking Grossman, 1977. Penelope Gilliatt on Langdon. Richard Schickel on Harold Lloyd.

Reilly, Adam. *Harold Lloyd: The King of Daredevil Comedy.* N.Y., Macmillan, 1977. Includes contributions by Andrew Sarris, William Everson, Leonard Maltin, Len Borger, and John Belton. Also credits, descriptions, and critical responses to each of the features. Lavishly illustrated.

Rheuban, Joyce. *Harry Langdon: The Comedian as Metteur-en-Scene.* East Brunswick, N.J., Associated University Presses, 1983.

Schickel, Richard. *Harold Lloyd: The Shape of Laughter.* Boston, New York Graphic Society, 1974.

Albert, Katherine. "What Happened to Harry Langdon," *Photoplay*, February 1932. His side of the story, Capra not named.

[Anon.] "Harold Lloyd Heads List of Huge Earnings of Stars and Directors." *New York Times*, May 16, 1926, reprinted in *N.Y. Times Encyclopedia of Film.*

[Fred.] "For Heaven's Sake," *Variety*, April 7, 1926. Review.

Friedman, Arthur B. "Interview with Harold Lloyd," *Film Quarterly*, Summer 1962.

Lloyd, Harold. "The Autobiography of Harold Lloyd." *Photoplay*, May 1924, first installment of material later used in his book, *An American Comedy.*

McCaffrey, Donald W. "The Mutual Approval of Keaton and Lloyd," *Cinema Journal* (1966-67).

Roach, Hal. "The Gag's the Thing." *Popular Mechanics*, May 1935.

——. Interview by David Robinson. *Sight and Sound*, Winter 1986-87, p. 3. "Children have made all the great comedians."

St. Johns, Adela Rogers. "What About Harold Lloyd?" *Photoplay*, September 1922.

Schonert, Vernon. "Harry Langdon," *Films in Review*, October 1967.

Sherwood, Robert. "The Perennial Freshman," *New Yorker*, January 30, 1926. Profile of Harold Lloyd.

Truscott, Harold. "Harry Langdon," *Silent Picture* #13, Winter/Spring 1972.

Index

[This index does not cover footnotes, cast lists, filmographies, lists of names or titles, picture captions, the preface, the contents page, or the appendices.]

About the Author

Richard Dyer MacCann (A.B., University of Kansas; M.A., Stanford University; Ph.D., Harvard University) is Emeritus Professor of Motion Picture History at the University of Iowa, where he taught from 1970 to 1986 and part time in 1987 and 1988. His degrees were all in political science, but he spent most of his career as a professor of film studies. His dissertation on U.S. government documentary films (published by Hastings House in 1973 as *The People's Films*) led him to a position as staff correspondent for the *Christian Science Monitor* in Hollywood and Los Angeles from 1951 to 1957. He has taught film writing, documentary film, and American motion picture history at the University of Southern California and the University of Kansas.

Dr. MacCann was founding editor of *Cinema Journal* for the Society for Cinema Studies (1967 to 1976) and is Distinguished Life Member of the University Film and Video Association. He was State Department film adviser to the Republic of Korea in 1963 and was awarded the first Senior Fellowship in film by the National Endowment for the Humanities for study in London in 1973. He is the author of 40 published articles and 12 books, including *Hollywood in Transition* (Houghton Mifflin, 1962), *Film and Society* (Scribners, 1964), *Film: A Montage of Theories* (Dutton, 1966), *The New Film Index* (Dutton, 1975). He has produced five film works and two video series, including 12 illustrated lectures coordinate with the titles of the books — notably *The First Film Makers* (1989) and *The Stars Appear* (1992) — in this Scarecrow Press series. His most recent book is *A New Vice Presidency for a New Century* (Image & Idea, 1991).